The other Side of Desire

SUNY series in

Psychoanalysis and Culture

Henry Sussman, editor

The other Side of Desire

Lacan's Theory of the Registers

Tamise Van Pelt

State University of New York Press

Published by
State University of New York Press, Albany

© 2000 State University of New York

All rights reserved

Printed in the United States of America

For information, address State University of New York Press,
State University Plaza, Albany, NY 12246

Production, Laurie Searl
Marketing, Fran Keneston

A portion of Chapter 5, "The Discourse of Desire and the Registers in *Hamlet*" was originally published as "Hamlet's Desire and the Rules for Lacanian Reading." *Proceedings of the Twelfth International Conference on Literature and Psychology*. Lisbon: Instituto Superior de Psicologia Aplicada, 1996.

Chapter 6, "Symptomatic Perfectionism in the *Journals* of Sylvia Plath," was published in an earlier version, "Perfect: Ideal Ego and Ego Ideal in the *Journals* of Sylvia Plath." *Literature and Psychology* 43 (1997).

A portion of Chapter 7, "Being and Otherness," originally appeared as "Dys-seminating Lacan." *Proceedings of the Thirteenth International Conference on Literature and Psychology*. Lisbon: Instituto Superior de Psicologia Aplicada, 1997.

A version of Chapter 7, "Being and Otherness," has been published as "Otherness," *Postmodern Culture* 10.2 (January, 2000).

Écrits: A Selection by Jacques Lacan, translated by Alan Sheridan. Copyright © 1966 by Les Editions du Seuil. English translation copyright © 1977 by Tavistock Publications. Reprinted by permission of Routledge, London.

The Seminar of Jacques Lacan: Book I: Freud's Papers on Technique, 1953–1954 by Jacques Lacan, translated by John Forrester. Copyright © 1975 by Les Editions du Seuil. English translation © 1988 by Cambridge University Press. Reprinted by permission of W. W. Norton & Company, Inc.

The Seminar of Jacques Lacan: Book II: The Ego in Freud's Theory and in the Technique of Psychoanalysis, 1954–1955 by Jacques Lacan, translated by Sylvana Tomaselli. Copyright © 1978 by Les Editions du Seuil. English translation copyright © 1988 by Cambridge University Press. Reprinted by permission of W. W. Norton & Company, Inc.

The Seminar of Jacques Lacan: Book III: The Psychoses, 1955–1956 by Jacques Lacan, translated by Russell Grigg. Copyright © 1981 by Les Editions de Seuil. English translation copyright © 1993 by W. W. Norton & Company, Inc. Reprinted by permission of W. W. Norton & Company, Inc.

Library of Congress Cataloging-in-Publication Data

Van Pelt, Tamise.
    The other side of desire : Lacan's theory of the registers /
Tamise Van Pelt.
        p.   cm. — (SUNY series in psychoanalysis and culture)
    ISBN 0-7914-4475-9 (hardcover : alk. paper). — ISBN 0-7914-4476-7
(pbk. : alk. paper)
    1. Psychoanalysis. 2. Lacan, Jacques, 1901–   . I. Title.
II. Series.
BF173.V248 2000
150.19′5—dc21   99-43545
                                                                                              CIP

10 9 8 7 6 5 4 3 2 1

In memory of my mother,

Gayle Bozeman Van Pelt

Page vi blank.

Contents

Page viii blank.

Illustrations

Page x blank.

Acknowledgments

This book would never have been written without the unfailing support of my mother Gayle Bozeman Van Pelt. It was Nancy Blake who introduced me to Lacan and to the Institute for Psychological Study of the Arts, the group who first showed me Lacan in an international context. My respect and gratitude extends to the many scholars who have shared ideas with me at the conferences of IPSA and of the Association for the Psychoanalysis of Culture and Society.

To the people who read parts of the manuscript along the way and offered suggestions and encouragement, my gratitude: Nancy Blake, Peter Garrett, Michael Shapiro, Richard Wheeler, Maire Jaanus, Jonathan Westphal, Sharon Sieber, Kassie Fleisher, Kathy Davis, Shuli Barzilai, and Virginia Blum. Hélène Varsamidou, ma maîtresse, corrected my fractured French with more patience than I deserved. My gratitude as well to the readers (known to me only by their letters), and to my editors James Peltz and Henry Sussman for their insights.

To the philosophers at Idaho State University and to the participants in philosophy paper exchange, my appreciation for creating an intellectually sustaining environment.

Finally, to those friends without whose affection this whole academic experiment would have been meaningless—thanks for going the distance with me. To Robert Johnson, to Jackie Gerard and "the Girls," to Sheryl Landrum, Glenda Allen, Linda Mehrens, Robert McRuer, Tom Murray, Shuli Barzilai, Virginia Blum, Dacia Soulliere and the "Idaho survivors," my love.

Page xii blank.

Introduction

In the summer of 1993, I attended a conference on Shakespeare and the Sexual Relation at the University of West Virginia. The featured speaker was Catherine Belsey whose work at the time was a distinctive blend of new historicism, deconstruction, and Lacanian psychoanalysis. Over lunch, a graduate student attendee remarked to me that she'd love to read Lacan, but she found him too difficult. In subsequent years, the echo of her comment has returned to me from other academics who believe that Lacan is just "too hard." I've wondered what it is that makes Lacan "too difficult" for highly motivated graduate students who genuinely want to read him, and why it is that professionals reject Lacan as incomprehensible while readily embracing writers of equivalent difficulty—Heidegger, Derrida, Butler come immediately to mind. Looking back, I see the *answer* to Lacan's "difficulty" in the very seminar that constellated the *question* of his difficulty in the first place. The student who wanted to learn Lacan sought out Belsey's elegant theoretical synthesis in a seminar that emphasized Lacan's essays on the mirror stage and the signifying phallus. Neither the synthesis nor those brief essays gave the student the one thing she needed to enter into the Lacanian conversation: the paradigm of the registers.

The registers (the symbolic, the imaginary, and the real) define the conceptual model informing Lacan's early Seminars and *Écrits*; thus, Lacan's theory of the registers provides a paradigm of reading as analytic listening. "Commenting on a text is like doing an analysis," he writes, depicting analytic reading as a distinguishing of textual levels.[1] Lacan's textual levels reiterate Freud's comparison of analysis to archaeology, a comparison that pervades Freud's writings.[2] Lacan's central metaphor is not an archaeological but a musical metaphor, however, so he distinguishes several "registers," and occasionally "keys," of textual signification.[3] A musical metaphor seems particularly apt for Lacan since he compares speech itself to a musical staff, seeing discourse as a rich orchestration of registers rather than a monotone. Just as a vocal instructor remarks upon the quality of a singer's upper or lower registers, Lacan distinguishes the registers of a text, noting the qualitative difference between the subject's symbolic discourse of desire and the ego's imaginary demands.[4] Though Lacan occasionally uses the term "register" in the narrowly linguistic sense of a specialized vocabulary, as when he talks about the "register of psychoanalysis," he chooses the more evocative musical metaphor whenever he refers to his own theoretical paradigm.[5]

Lacan uses the paradigm of disjunct registers to reiterate the crucial Freudian hypothesis of the unconscious. Thus, he expresses his vision of the Freudian unconscious as a decentering of the speaking subject from its ego. Because subjectivity is a process sustained by speech in the symbolic register while the ego is an image maintained by the imaginary, the gap between the subject and the ego reiterates the gap between the registers—and vice versa. These gaps, like Freud's anti-Cartesian insight, inform Lacan's psychoanalytic legacy. Therefore, Lacanian analysis constitutes one among many contemporary theories critical of the vision of human beings as rational thinkers in conscious control of their actions. Consequently, Lacanian ideas have been assimilated into a variety of recent social and historical critiques: Marxism, feminism, postmodernism, new historicism, postcolonialism, critical legal studies. All have adopted Lacanian terms into their own vocabularies and adapted Lacanian insights to their own issues. Not surprisingly, with so many varieties of Lacan in print, the introduction to Lacanian concepts via secondary uses of them has become the norm rather than the exception. I believe that these extra-analytic introductions to Lacan account in part for the difficulty of subsequent direct encounters with Lacan's own writings. Too often, Lacan himself doesn't say what the reader of secondary adaptations of him expects him to say![6]

Since Lacan's key terms and ideas entered the American theoretical mainstream through a variety of secondary works long before his own texts saw translation, the loss of Lacan's central paradigm is not as odd as it might at first seem. Althusser's "Freud and Lacan," first translated into English in 1969, presented a materialist, ideological "Lacan" a full eight years before Lacan's *Écrits* spoke English. Lacan had barely had his own say in English when his work was overshadowed by Fredric Jameson's enormously influential adaptation of it in *The Political Unconscious*.[7] No sooner had Jameson laid claim to a politicized version of Freud's greatest discovery than American Marxism found its Lacanian colony—indeed its own territory—coopted by semiotic critics who saw both materialism and psychoanalysis as assimilable to a broadly defined concept of linguistic code. Thus, Kaja Silverman made bold to wrest Lacan away from the Marxists with the claim that "both Freud and Jacques Lacan have demonstrated that psychoanalysis is in effect a branch of semiotics."[8] As a result, readers of Silverman might understand a semiotic symbolic, and readers of Jameson might conceive a Marxist imaginary *without* grasping the Lacanian metaphor of the registers themselves, seeing neither their musical connotations nor their linguistic affiliation.

In previous decades, readers who took the direct approach to Lacan via Lacan's own texts weren't much closer to his paradigm of the registers than readers of Lacan in application. This is because register theory *as a theory* got lost in the international shuffle of translation. For instance, translation of Lacan's *Écrits*, a book whose essays summarize both Lacan's early work and his first Seminars on the registers, preceded translation of the Seminars themselves. As a result, his developmental mirror stage theory leapt to the critical forefront while its more complex reincarnation in the structural theory of the registers was largely ignored. Similarly, translation of Seminar XI on the fundamental concepts of psychoanalysis—a Seminar in which the theme of desire predominates—preceded translation of the first three Seminars on the registers of the imaginary and the symbolic and their specific implications for the reading of literary texts. Consequently, the gaze took on a theoretical life of its own quite apart from its structural and philosophical roots.[9] Between *Écrits* 1977 translation and Michael Clark's 1988 bibliography of Lacan, there were no less than five books and fifty-seven essays on mirror stage theory alone. An additional six essays on the imaginary register plus dozens of related essays on film theory made the dominance of the imaginary register in critical studies absolute.[10] Though critics eventually turned their attention from the imaginary to the symbolic and from the symbolic to the real, and though critiques of Lacan's theory of desire abound, readers still find themselves bereft of the Lacanian paradigm of the registers since single-register explorations stop short of the paradigm while sophisticated Lacanian critiques assume it.

So, Lacanian terms have floated free of their informing paradigm, and because they have, myths about Lacanian ideas now pervade the intellectual community. As a theory generalist, I hear these myths repeated both by students and by professionals, in the classroom, at conferences, and in everyday conversation. The myths frequently accompany questions (from the theory-unenthused) about why I do theory, or (from the theory-literate) about why I do Lacan. This book constitutes my response. Thus, I take up the mythic view of the "mirror stage" as Lacan's great discovery, the myth of Lacan as a binary thinker, the categorical opposition of the symbolic to the imaginary, and the "entification" of the subject and the Other as if these constructs referred to persons. Together, the demythifications in the first four chapters constitute my response to the problem of binary thinking in the reading of Lacanian analysis (and in the reading of theory in general). The last three chapters foreground a different theoretical problem, examining ways in which humanistic assumptions about the individual insinuate themselves back into discourses ostensibly committed to the decentering of subjectivity.

My method throughout this book is to offer a Lacanian reading of Lacan in reply to some common misunderstandings about Lacan, misunderstandings occasioned by the diffusion of Lacanian significations bereft of their overarching paradigm. How important is a paradigm? Annette Kolodny suggests that paradigms are foundational, pointing out that "insofar as we are taught how to read, what we engage are not texts but paradigms" (280). I would rearrange Kolodny's observation slightly: insofar as we engage texts but not paradigms, we risk accumulating signifiers without insight—sans paradigmatic insight, we only parrot the words. The loss of Lacan's paradigmatic insight is rendered all the more ironic by the fact that among those theorists who have influenced twentieth-century thought, he arguably takes the greatest pains to spell out specifically the relationships between his central theoretical constructs. His readers need not guess how the imaginary relates to the symbolic or how the ego relates to the subject; nor need they hypothesize how key Lacanian terms relate to analytic practice. Readers only need to consult Lacan's "Classified Index of the Major Concepts" appended to his *Écrits* (EE 326–31). Moreover, Lacan is so concerned about his paradigms that he frequently illustrates them, literally drawing his readers a picture of the conceptual connections he wants them to make. Lacan's pictures frame the paradigmatic re-readings of his major essays in this volume: "Aggressivity in psychoanalysis," "The mirror stage . . . ," "The Seminar on 'The Purloined Letter,'" "The subversion of the subject . . . ," and "The signification of the phallus." In these paradigmatic rereadings, I make explicit the implicit conceptual connections Lacan assumes his readers—familiar with his models—will themselves supply.

To illustrate the consequences of meeting Lacan through arguments about him, I put the reader of this book in the place of the uninitiated, starting out with some close secondary encounters of the Lacanian kind. Chapter 1, therefore, begins with a sequence of disputed constructions— of sexuality in Plato's *Symposium*, of gender disguise in *Tootsie*, of code in Althusser's "Freud and Lacan" and Barthes's *S/Z*—all of which invoke Lacan but fall prey to the powerful categorical impulse to oppose the Subject to the Other and the imaginary to the symbolic. These oppositions, in turn, lead to contradictory readings, readings that illustrate the improbability of learning Lacan via applications of him or disputes over him—no matter how insightful those applications or critiques may be. In fact, the participants in chapter 1's experiment in Lacanian confusion are all respected scholars, well known for their theoretical work. Their readers' confusion doesn't arise from exposure to misreadings of Lacan, nor does confusion necessarily arise from Lacan's theoretical diffusion per se. The deployment of Lacanian constructs in so many diverse areas of textual study and practice indicates the vitality of Lacan's ideas. The appropriation of analytic ideas acknowledges their value. Lacan himself uses Saussure to read Freud, after all. However, risks do arise with intellectual pluralism, risks Rachel Bowlby acknowledges in her caution that theoretical assimilations always threaten to turn "helpful contacts" into "sterile fusion."[11] Thus, my central aim in this chapter is to illustrate the loss of Lacan's paradigm of the registers as one such helpful contact, a loss that has led to the domestication of Lacan's more radical implications in theoretical studies generally.

In my second chapter, I address the myth that the "mirror stage" is central to Lacanian theory. Unfortunately, Lacan's translation history obscures his rejection of the mirror stage as a sufficient explanation for the decentering of the subject. So that the reader can experience Lacan's significant shift away from his mirror stage model, chapters 2 and 3 delineate the disjunction between Lacan's early hypothesis of a mirror stage and his subsequent paradigm of the imaginary, the symbolic, and the real. Lacan's mirror stage essay and its companion essay on aggressivity rely on

Hegel's myth of master and servant to provide a phenomenal paradigm for his analytic observations. Though this *Ur*-theory suggests a distinction between the imaginary and the symbolic registers, the implications of this distinction are subordinated to the idea of maturation in Lacan's early work. Seeing the imaginary and the symbolic as sequential developmental stages leads to the unfortunate conclusion that the imaginary can and should be left behind if maturity is to be achieved. Because of its shortcomings, Lacan exchanges his phenomenal model of interpersonal mirroring and aggressive, rivalrous interaction for an intrapsychic model structuring the subject's relation to language as an in-mixing of Otherness.

It isn't uncommon for readers of theory to look for oppositions in the theories they read since there is a powerful reductive tendency in the very process of abstraction that seeks to rest on the comfortable foundation of opposed ideas. Thus, my third chapter addresses the popular myth that Lacan is a binary thinker and that the symbolic and the imaginary are opposed categories. Lacanian analysis is not the only theory to have suffered this reduction, though it has arguably suffered from it more than most. Though Lacan characterizes reading as a "differentiation of levels" and a "critique of concepts . . . with the aim of avoiding confusions" (Sem I 57), this differentiation should not be taken as a search for opposites. The imaginary discourse of the ego and the symbolic discourse of desire suffuse the text, which is why the registers of a text (like the registers of an analysand's speech) resemble the staves of a musical composition. Because each register composing the music of signification denotes a range of analytic phenomena, the musical paradigm operates with great sophistication and explanatory subtlety in Lacan. Not only is each register qualitatively distinct from every other register in nonoppositional ways, an individual register is internally complex. In order to convey this complexity, Lacan literally enumerates each register's attributes in his early Seminars and *Écrits*, leaving his readers an explicit map of the structural complexity of the registers and an exemplary reading of Poe.

The micromyth of foundational theoretical binaries is paralleled by the macromyth of the one "right" theory. Because theories are hypothetical rather than factual, they are never right or wrong, however. Theories are, instead, useful (to a greater or lesser degree) or appropriate (to the issue at hand). Since theories shape conjecture, they tell people how to go about asking questions in relevant circumstances. In other words, theories don't provide answers; they inform methods of inquiry.

Theories are measured by their explanatory power, by their ability, if employed, to provoke the phenomena at hand to yield up interpretable patterns. So that my readers can get a sense of the explanatory power of Lacan's theory of the registers, I next place chapter 1's critical positions on Lacan's paradigm within Lacan's paradigm. Chapter 4's Lacanian epistemology offers an analytic alternative to the impoverishment that comes from settling theoretical disputes by deciding who's right and who's wrong. This analysis also illustrates the way in which attributions of right and wrong to positions in texts can be the product of oppositional assumptions about texts. By contrast, Lacanian theory looks for truth in the error that opposition generates.

Though the content of a theory cannot profitably be carved up into right or wrong, the practice of theorizing—of analyzing—is amenable to critique. Therefore, in chapter 5, I reconstruct Lacan's dispute with Ernest Jones over analytic methodology. Specifically, Lacan believes that Jones's technique humanizes analysis in unacceptable ways. Lacan seems to be saying to Jones, "Though you embrace the decentered subject of the unconscious as a Freudian premise, your methods fail to keep that decentering in play." Thus, Lacan offers his *Hamlet* as a genuinely anti-Cartesian alternative to Jones's traditional Freudian reading in *Hamlet and Oedipus*. Chapter 5's debate over humanism and analysis allows me to address two points at which critiques of Lacan insert humanistic meanings into his decentering of the subject. The first humanizing impulse reads the symbolic mother, the mOther, as if "she" were a person, an entity. The second insists that the phallus is a body part rather than a signifier, a myth that stems from a residual humanist view of the body. Chapter 5 ends with some rules for Lacanian reading drawn from the Seminars and *Écrits*. In this methodological "how to," I make explicit the reading methods Lacan himself employs.

I conclude my discussion of the decentered subject in chapter 6's exploration of Sylvia Plath's subjectivity, offering an alternative practice to the "application" of theory to text as if it were paint to a chair. In this chapter, I contrast Lacanian analysis with the interpretation of Plath's writing by Ted Hughes, whose assumptions about a "real self" buried beneath layers of artifice provide a humanistic counterpoint to Lacanian reading. Reading Plath's subjectivity in contrast to Hughes's search for her Self, I explore the symptomatic perfectionism manifest in her *Journals* where the changing registers of Plath's voice reveal moments when either the imaginary or the symbolic dominates her prose. As Sylvia

Plath confronts and struggles with her perfectionism, the grandiose voice of her imaginary ideal ego can be heard to give way, under crisis, to the pensive voice of her ego ideal. Throughout, Plath's repetition of the signifier "perfect" marks a path through her *Journals* indicating her struggles with the symptom. In this case study, I follow Lacan's advice and allow Plath's text to pose its own questions and to struggle to find its own answers. Reading the registers does not, in the end, permit me to project my concerns into Plath's *Journals*. Lacanian analysis simply tells me with which ear to listen. This is its genius.

To this point, I have explored Lacan's discovery of the decentering of the speaking subject, but his decentering of the object has equally profound implications. I conclude with an examination of the mythic Other-as-individual, noting the humanism that oppositional theories of identity return to theoretical studies generally, and proposing Lacan's theory of the decentered Other as a more powerful paradigm for examining political difference. The decentered object—indicated in Lacanian analysis by a distinction between the imaginary other and the symbolic Other—may be Lacan's most radical and theoretically helpful discovery. Otherness has great currency as a theoretical construction, and Lacan's explication of the dynamics of paranoid identity, impure recognition, and domination addresses issues central to current debates over race, gender, colonialism, and nationalism. Since contemporary theories of identity frequently invoke ideas of Otherness that have little to do with either the Lacanian otherness of aggressive alienation or the Otherness of the linguistic unconscious per se, I survey some current constructions of Otherness for the sake of contrast. Next, I examine essays by Abdul R. JanMohamed (who employs Lacan's theory of the registers in a reading of the colonial novel) and by Judith Butler (who argues that there is, in fact, no genuine distinction between the imaginary and the symbolic registers). Since Butler's *Bodies That Matter* links her critique of register theory to Lacan's essay on the signifying phallus, I conclude with a reexamination both of the phallic signifier and it's role within the symbolic register. This leads to some last thoughts on the implications of analytic reading for antifoundational approaches to identity. These final encounters suggest, as well, that all paradigms have their limits, Lacan's among them.

There is a powerful, though not seamless, overlap between Lacan's discourse on the registers and his discourse on desire. It is my intention, throughout, to foreground the former, since the discourse on the registers seems more frequently to have gone awry in contemporary adaptations of Lacanian theory. Since my purpose here is to sort through and clarify some of Lacan's most important constructs, I have made distinctions between theoretical terms as clear-cut as possible. If Lacanian terms are more subtle and overlapping in practice than I make them out to be in this discussion, I can only say that it is easier for the reader to complicate a clear idea than to clarify a nebulous one. Wherever I felt that familiarity with Lacan's discourse on the registers was a prerequisite for engaging difficult terms—especially those terms that by a sort of double meaning render the distinction between the intrapsychic and the intersubjective ambiguous—I erred on the side of clarity. I preferred to omit Lacan's most polyvalent constructs rather than to exceed the scope of this inquiry focused on the imaginary and the symbolic registers, especially since a number of sophisticated and insightful discussions of desire, the real, and Lacan's late work have recently appeared. Throughout this book, I draw upon Lacan's first three Seminars and his *Écrits*, allowing Lacan's own commentary to correct misunderstandings about Lacan's own theory. My emphasis on these texts stems both from their expression of an important phase of Lacan's thought and from their ready availability to English-speaking readers of theory. Trusting in Lacan's advice that real psychoanalysis (if it is done well) ought to be funny, I have selected whenever possible those moments that reveal Lacan's attraction to the bizarre, his eye for a good story, and his humor.

Page xxii blank.

Abbreviations

The following frequently cited works will be abbreviated for ease of reference:

EE   *Écrits: A Selection* by Jacques Lacan. Trans. Alan Sheridan. New York: W.W. Norton & Company, 1982.

Sem I   *The Seminar of Jacques Lacan: Book I: Freud's Papers on Technique 1953–1954* by Jacques Lacan. Trans. John Forrester. New York: W.W. Norton & Company, 1988.

Sem II   *The Seminar of Jacques Lacan: Book II: The Ego in Freud's Theory and in the Technique of Psychoanalysis 1954–1955* by Jacques Lacan. Trans. Sylvana Tomaselli. New York: W.W. Norton & Company, 1988.

Sem III *The Seminar of Jacques Lacan: Book III: The Psychoses 1955–1956* by Jacques Lacan. Trans. Russell Grigg. New York: W.W. Norton & Company, 1993.

Page xxiv blank.

1

A Funny Thing Happened
on the Way to the *Symposium*

How to begin to discuss the decentered subject of psychoanalysis?

Perhaps it is best to yield the stage to Jacques Lacan who emphasizes Freud's most radical insight, saying that the "Freudian notion of the ego is so upsetting as to warrant the expression Copernican revolution" (Sem II 3). In the introduction to his second seminar on the ego in Freud's theory and the technique of psychoanalysis, Lacan highlights Freud's central idea: "the I is not the ego, the subject is not the individual" (3). Lacan frequently compares Freud's discovery to that of Copernicus, often using the comparison as a jumping-off point for the discussion of analytic technique. Thus, Freud's discovery that "the very centre of the human being [is] no longer to be found at the place assigned to it by a whole humanist tradition" frames Lacan's discussion of "the Freudian thing" in which he articulates the meaning of his own "return to Freud" (EE 114). This revolutionary decentering allows Freud to ask the question preliminary to any possible treatment of psychosis, a question that distances the psychic faculties of the subject from the certainties of positivist science (179). In the English *Écrits's* concluding essay, Lacan's Copernican Freud-as-revolutionary succeeds Darwin-as-evolutionary in a genealogical chain leaping from the decentering of the earth, to the decentering of humankind, to the decentering of the subject (295).

This Freudian decentering of the subject provides the material for Lacan's oral teachings, and in the early 1950s Lacan discusses Freudian texts in order to come to terms with Freud's discovery and its implications for analytic practice. In "Overture to the Seminar," a brief introduction to Lacan's public teachings, Lacan remarks on the "ambiguity that is to be found throughout [Freud's] corpus" (Sem I 3). "Is a dream desire?" Lacan asks, or "the recognition of desire?" (3). Is the ego "like an empty egg, differentiated at its surface" or is it that "which says *no* or *me* . . . which expresses itself in different registers" (3). Here, in unraveling Freud's ambiguity, Lacan introduces an ambiguity of his own. On the one hand, Freud's revolutionary discovery raises questions about desire and its interpretation. On the other hand, Freud's discovery raises questions about the decentering of the speaking subject from the ego, about the gap between the symbolic register and the imaginary register. (The musical metaphor "register" allows Lacan to designate a range with an emphasis on its qualities rather than its boundaries.) Neither the motive force of desire nor the structural patterning of the registers alone exhausts the Freudian field, yet, paradoxically, either can organize it.

Because they engage Freud's double discourse, Lacan's Seminars and writings frequently cover the same conceptual territory twice using two distinct maps—the diachronics of desire and the synchronics of the registers. Jacques-Alain Miller observes that at the time of his earliest seminars, "Lacan seems to be asking himself whether there are in fact two different directions implicit in Freud's work and thus in psychoanalysis as a whole"(19).[1] A glance at the index of major concepts Miller has appended to *Écrits* reveals the overlapping of the schema of the Lacanian registers with the conceptual apparatus of desire.[2] The registers have pride of place, and among them, the symbolic order dominates. However, the language of desire is embedded in the discussion of the symbolic order, and desire's first cousin, "the demand for love," appears under the heading of the imaginary register's "primary identification." In a second set of concepts outlining the registers of the imaginary ego and the symbolic subject, critiques of the ego's illusion of autonomy and of the subject's division, splitting, and fading are cross-referenced: "see: *Desire and phantasy*" (328; 329). When the classic Freudian idea of the unconscious is at issue, register theory's famous aphorism "the unconscious is the discourse of the Other" is cross-referenced: "see: 'Man's desire is the desire of the Other'" (329).

Just as the discourse of desire can be found embedded in the conceptual structure of the registers, the registers appear in the section of the index devoted to "Desire and its Interpretation." Here, the analysis of empty speech invokes "the discourse of the imaginary"; here, the analysis of demand and suppression adds "see: The locus of the Other" (330). Given Lacan's two theoretical discourses, it isn't surprising that Anika Lemaire's systematic articulation of Lacanian concepts ends up covering the same conceptual territory twice.[3] After devoting half her volume to a discussion of structural linguistics, the signifier, and the registers of the symbolic and the imaginary, Lemaire turns to the topic of desire. In differentiating the terms "need," "demand," and "desire" from one another, she finds herself repeating register theory's concepts of *Spaltung* (entry into the symbolic order) and Splitting (alienation in the imaginary) "in different terms" (161). "Lacan seems to have provided two different perspectives on these themes" Lemaire remarks (161), and she concludes that the force of desire sets the apparatus of the registers in motion.

Twin discourses/three registers. A pair and a set of three relations. This seems simple enough. But when twos meet threes, complications abound as we shall see in the following psychoanalytic readings of Plato's *Symposium*. These readings—by astute and insightful readers— try to resist dualism, try to get beyond the bedrock of foundational difference, try to set aside limited, categorical thinking. In fact, on the surface, Plato's text with its originary *trio* of sexes would seem inherently resistant to dualism. Yet Plato's man, woman, and androgyne are no more immune to category than Lacan's imaginary, symbolic, and real registers. Both the Lacanian and the Platonic discourses show the enormous difficulty of keeping the psychoanalytic decentering of the subject in play while discussing a text that treats of paired relations. Thus, the following critiques stitch together disparate elements of the source text into satisfyingly centered interpretive realities. Each reduces Plato's tale of sexual plurality to a foundational either/or. Cast into Plato's multiple possibilities, binaries offer a fundamental resting place. Foundational binaries ground positions from which to read, to speak, and even to argue because they present two alternatives, both of which revolve around a single interpretive axis. When readers for whom the decentering of the subject is a given reduce Plato's *Symposium* to binary interpretations, they demonstrate the problem of the linguistic unconscious and illustrate the pull toward binaries inherent in language itself.

A Symposium on the Subject

Plato's dialogue the *Symposium* boasts an honored cast of characters including Socrates, Phaedrus, and Aristophanes. Though each speaker offers his thoughts on love, it is Aristophanes' comic theory of the origin of sexual desire that echoes through the psychoanalytic writings of Freud and Lacan and echoes through psychoanalytic literary theory as well. Aristophanes emerges as a recurrent signifier in a long chain of signification because of the structural properties of his discourse, structural properties that combine two-termed and three-termed constructions in various unstable ways. In fact, if Lacan had sought an allegory to fuse his early mirror stage theory with his later structural theory of the three registers, he might easily have used Aristophanes' tale since the story's three human conditions parallel an original naïve symbolic (three sexes are formed), followed by a powerful narcissistic fusion with an ideal mate (two severed parts are coupled), finally resolved by an appropriate intersubjectivity (three forms of sexual relation are practiced). I paraphrase here the tale that Plato gives to Aristophanes:[4]

> Lamenting humankind's lack of appreciation and understanding of the healing and helping qualities of love, Aristophanes offers a parable of love's power: The original human sexes were not two but three, a man, a woman, and a double-natured union of the two whose name has been lost and is merely suggested by the pejorative "androgyne." Each round being had four hands and feet, two faces looking opposite directions, and two "privy members." The sexes were three because the man was child of the sun, the woman of the earth, and the man-woman of the moon, and all creatures were as round as their parents.
>
> Insolent and powerful, these creatures threatened the gods even as they provided them with necessary adoration. So Zeus discovered a way to diminish these roundlings' strength while increasing their numerical potential for devotion: he cut them in two. After the severing, however, each part experienced such longing for its other that when reunited in couples they nearly starved through refusing again to be parted—even long enough to eat. Compassionately, Zeus turned their organs of generation to the front so that the male/female couple could breed and so the male/male couple could "be satisfied, and rest, and go their ways to the business of life."
>
> It is thus that three kinds of relationship have formed. Men originally androgynous have become the lovers of women. [And presumably, vice versa, though Aristophanes does not explicitly say so. What he does say explicitly is that the males and females descended from the androgyne are "adulterous" (561).] Women originally of the woman have "female attachments" and become "female companions." Men

sprung from the ur-male "have the most manly nature" and are thus youths who "hang about men and embrace them" and who upon maturity become "statesmen" not inclined to marry or father children.

Plato's pointed genealogy of the human sexual condition could not fail to attract the attention of later theorists of desire. Thus, Freud turns to the Aristophanes story not once but twice. Lacan, too, mentions the *Symposium.* Aptly, the Aristophanes story reappears in Malcolm Bowie's *Freud, Proust and Lacan: Theory as Fiction,* and the tale of sexual origins figures yet again in Rachel Bowlby's review of Bowie's book. However, rereadings of Aristophanes' tale of the two become three—this clearly structured tale encompassing the transition from narcissism to intersubjectivity—so frequently run awry in the retelling that it seems imperative to ask why. What is it about these apparently straightforward relations between a two and a three that throws interpretation into disarray?

Freud first cites the *Symposium* in his *Three Essays on the Theory of Sexuality* [1905], where he writes that "the popular view of the sexual instinct is beautifully reflected in the poetic myth which tells how the original human beings were cut up into two halves—man and woman—and how these are always striving to unite again in love."[5] Freud's relentlessly binary foreshortening of the story stresses the opposites man/woman and parts/whole. His excisions of both the originary three sexes and the resultant three sexual orientations, allow him to conclude with mock astonishment: "It comes as a great surprise therefore to learn that there are men whose sexual object is a man and not a woman, and women whose sexual object is a woman and not a man" (136). Freud appears to have corrected himself when, in *Beyond the Pleasure Principle* [1920], he cites Aristophanes' story again, this time as an exemplary myth of the origin of instinct:

> [S]cience has so little to tell us about the origin of sexuality that we can liken the problem to a darkness into which not so much as a ray of a hypothesis has penetrated. In quite a different region, it is true, we *do* meet with such a hypothesis; but it is of so fantastic a kind—a myth rather than a scientific explanation—that I should not venture to produce it here, were it not that it fulfills precisely the one condition whose fulfillment we desire. For it traces the origin of an instinct to *a need to restore an earlier state of things.* What I have in mind is, of course, the theory which Plato put into the mouth of Aristophanes in the *Symposium,* and which deals not only with the *origin* of the sexual instinct but with the most important of its variations in relation to its object.

> "The original human nature was not like the present, but different. In the first place, the sexes were originally three in number, not two. . . ." Everything about these primeval men was double: they had four hands and four feet, two faces, two privy parts, and so on. Eventually Zeus decided to cut these men in two, "like a sorb-apple which is halved for pickling." After the division had been made, "the two parts of man, each desiring his other half, came together, and threw their arms about one another eager to grow into one."[6]

Freud halts Aristophanes' account at a line replete with dualities: "division"/ "two parts"/ "other half"/ "together"/ "one another"/ "grow into one," and even his nod in the direction of Aristophanes' concluding trio of adulterers, companions, and statesmen reduces itself to *the* sexual instinct versus its "variants." Freud makes this norming of heterosexuality explicit in a footnote in which he thanks Professor Heinrich Gomperz for pointing out what is "essentially the same theory" in the Upanishads:

> [T]he origin of the world from the Atman (the Self or Ego) is described: "But he felt no delight. Therefore a man who is lonely feels no delight. He wished for a second. He was so large as man and wife together. He then made this his Self to fall in two, and then arose husband and wife. Therefore Yagnavalkya said: We two are thus (each of us) like half a shell. Therefore the void which was there is filled by the wife."[7]

Freud's "same theory" leaves little doubt that the theory in question is fundamentally binary. Rhetorically distanced from its potential androgyny, any hint of sexual plurality seems further precluded by the Upanishad variant's initial emphasis on the comparative size of the original one Self, the Atman, rather than its composition. Freud's "same theory" asserts that so long as the theory gets to the husband and wife, it doesn't really matter whether the heterosexed opposites emerge from a splitting of the one or from an eliding of a third. For the father of the Oedipal triangle, this omission of variant modes of coupling seems an uncharacteristic lapse of distinction indeed.

While Freud's readings of Aristophanes privilege the male and the female, Malcolm Bowie's readings of Freud invert Freud's emphasis. Bowie introduces the Aristophanes quotation from *Beyond the Pleasure Principle* with the observation that "Plato's fabulous hermaphrodites . . . may perhaps suggest one way in which science, destitute of illuminating hypotheses about the origin of sexuality, could proceed"

(*Freud* 79). Bowie continues, noting that "[Freud's] own text returns upon the anterior textual world of Plato just as Plato's returned upon the fabled 'initial hermaphroditism' of the human species" (80). Lest Bowie's reader conclude that he means hermaphroditism in some purely structural sense that would include the dualities of the originary male/male and female/female creatures, Bowie again emphasizes that both Freud and Proust offer "fantasticated accounts of the yearnings felt by unisexual human creatures for their bisexual pre-existence" (81). In a review of Bowie's text, Rachel Bowlby points out that Freud and Bowie both read the Aristophanes narrative in ways that create "oversights [which] invert each other." Thus, "Where Freud sees in the *Symposium* only the origins of heterosexuality, to which homosexuality must be added on, Bowie sees only the buried bisexuality concealed beneath the surface mask of unisexual uniformity. In both instances, Aristophanes' trio of sexes is forgotten in favour of a coupling of heterosexuality and homosexuality" (94).

The three sexes of Aristophanes' theory are man, woman, and androgyne (the union of the two), Bowlby reiterates, stressing plurality over duality. Symbolically, she emphasizes the multiplicity of possible relations resulting from Zeus's cut and its creation of a universal desire among half-creatures. Desire, as a signifier, emerges in various ways when the resulting split-sexes, each seeking its object, define three forms of sexual relation: the male/male creature reunites in a male homosexual relation, the female/female creature reunites as lesbian companions, and the female/male hermaphrodite reunites in a heterosexual coupling of woman with man. The irony that Bowie's critique misses and Bowlby points out is that, "far from being bisexual or homosexual, the hermaphrodite is the paragon of heterosexuality" (93).

Bowlby sees the irony in the inverted critical readings because she reads the larger symbolic context rather than the critical arguments alone. Bowlby strives, in the language of Lacanian analysis, to *read* the registers, to decide how the text functions rather than to decide what the content "really" says. The problem posed here in this symposium on the decentered subject is endemic to critical reading; the challenge posed by Aristophanes' tale is posed by other texts as well. Consequently, I want to expand this decentering of Plato's text to include wider circles of reading, beginning with some issues in the reading of the film *Tootsie* which bear a close family resemblance to the issues raised by the *Symposium*.

Marjorie Garber's *Vested Interests: Cross-Dressing and Cultural Anxiety* replicates the critical problematic at issue in the *Symposium* readings and suggests the Lacanian registers as a theoretical solution.[8] A parallel inversion of critical perspectives—invited by a parallel problem of one-sexed versus androgynous characters—emerges when Garber discusses critical responses to transvestite disguise in the contemporary film *Tootsie*. The analytic problem posed by the out-of-work male actor Michael Dorsey, competing against actresses for a plum soap opera role while disguised as Dorothy Michaels, echoes the analytic problem posed by Aristophanes' tale of the sexes. Similarly, critical responses to the film echo the binary impulses of Freud's and Bowie's responses to Plato.

Some feminist critics read *Tootsie*'s transvestite disguiser Michael Dorsey/Dorothy Michaels as "affirming" feminist discourse by presenting a strong, subversive feminist image.[9] Others see the disguiser as "containing" feminist discourse by showing feminism's apparent subversiveness to rely on masculine power in female dress.[10] Garber, however, insists that "in *Tootsie* transvestitism is an enabling fantasy, not merely a joke or a parody, whether the laugh is thought to be on men or on women" (6). She points out that this "tendency to . . . appropriate the cross-dresser 'as' one of the two sexes, is emblematic of a fairly consistent critical desire to look away from the transvestite as transvestite, not to see cross-dressing except as male or female manqué" (10). Here, Garber's analysis of the critical pursuit of binary positions yielding inverted interpretations parallels Bowlby's. Moreover, Garber's concentration on a third possibility, "the transvestite as transvestite," parallels Bowlby's emphasis on the three sexes and the three unions as well.

Not only do Garber and Bowlby define parallel critical problems, they also invoke Lacanian psychoanalytic reading as a critical alternative. Their estimations of what Lacanian reading entails, however, differ. Garber, unlike Bowlby, locates power in the "blurred" gender disguise itself and insists that it has an ability to initiate "category crisis" which Garber defines as "a failure of definitional distinction, a borderline that becomes permeable, that permits of border crossings from one (apparently distinct) category to another" (16). Thus, for Garber, categorical distinctions such as male/female, black/white, Jew/Christian, noble/bourgeois, master/servant, this/that, him/me are put "under erasure" by figures such as the transvestite (16). Here, Garber's privileging of the function of the transvestite replicates Bowie's privileging of the bisexual in The *Symposium*. In fact, "category crisis" with its disruptive transvestitism pitted against the categorical sexes evokes the binary homosexual/heterosexual rather than displacing it.

This return to binary categories can be seen most clearly in Garber's use of the Lacanian registers to explain the relation between the transvestite and the more conventionally gendered others. The transvestite, Garber claims, is typical of all "third terms" which expose the fictional basis of distinction, not as a third one that could easily align itself with either of the elements of difference but rather as "something that challenges the possibility of harmonious and stable binary symmetry" (12). Third terms, in turn, imply the Lacanian symbolic register, she argues.[11] Thus Garber ultimately parallels the difference between the undisguised and the transvestite with the difference between the imaginary and the symbolic registers.

For Garber, the symbolic represents a force that disrupts the imaginary, an imaginary that constitutes "a dimension in which the human subject's relation to himself, and to other people, is structured like, and by, his relation to his mirror image: a dyadic, symmetrical complementarity . . . based on the fiction of a stable identity" (12). Consequently, Garber describes the symbolic as the source of contextualization for the binaries of the imaginary. "What once stood as an exclusive dual relation becomes an element in a larger chain" (12), the signifying chain. To this sophisticated and insightful description of the registers, Garber adds additional meanings. In Garber's interpretation of the Lacanian registers, "the Symbolic order . . . is the register of language, hierarchy, law, and power . . . to which the human subject must come to relate not only through one-to-one or face-to-face dyads (though these remain inescapable) but through immersion in the codes and constraints of culture" (12).

After its brief theoretical introduction, the bulk of *Vested Interests* devotes itself to the elaboration of the contents of specific codes and their various subversions. The binary political trope of subversion and containment thus reinforces the binary Lacanian registers of symbolic transvestite versus imaginary male or female, and Garber's celebration of the transgressive ultimately amounts to a critical reduction that treats the imaginary and the symbolic registers as just one more set of opposed categories. In fact, the sophisticated structural sensitivity that Garber's definitions of the imaginary and the symbolic reveal is not borne out in her critical application. Garber's reductive move occurs when she equates the symbolic register with the "codes and constraints of culture," and Garber is not alone in equating code with the symbolic register. However, as the following set of readings will show, it is always possible to read the registers otherwise.

The Problem of Encoding

The idea of code has had enormous critical appeal, and Garber writes in the established theoretical tradition that merges the construct of code with culture and then merges both with Lacan's symbolic register. Because the code has been a dominant idea in cultural studies and in semiotics, and because these two branches of interpretive theory routinely assimilate Lacanian concepts, it was probably inevitable that the concepts of "code" and the registers would converge. Though the concepts of "encoding" and "decoding" were available to Lacan's founding influence Saussure, these concepts were strictly metaphors to the linguists of Saussure's day, alternative expressions of the idea of translation (Hill 205). Saussure does not associate codes with language or with semiology and, in fact, sees the systematic fixing of the arbitrary meaning of the sign within a society as "belong[ing] to a different order of questions altogether" than questions of the signifier, the signified, and language (219). It is not from Saussure but from Barthes, and most specifically from Barthes's extensive elaboration of codes in *S/Z*, that the popular idea of code springs.[12]

Recall that in Roland Barthes's *S/Z*, the *symbolic* code is only one of five master codes, each of which has its own semiotic domain (18–21). The symbolic code, which is the place for "multivalence" and "reversibility," differs from the four remaining codes, the hermeneutic code which allows an enigma to be distinguished, formulated, and disclosed; the semic code which expresses the "Voice of the Person" (21) through "flickers of meaning" (19); the proairetic code which relates to action and empiricism and unfolds through sequence as naming; and the cultural code which includes the reference codes that "afford the discourse a basis in scientific or moral authority" (18). When the whole of *S/Z* unravels Balzac's *Sarrasine* into its constituent codes, it is clear that the idea of cultural code predominates; in fact, Barthes specifically notes that "all codes are cultural" (18). Thus, Barthes essentially subordinates the idea of the symbolic to distinctly un-Lacanian concepts of code and culture, even though his use of the musical metaphor—"the (readerly) text is comparable at every point to a (classical) musical score"—clearly parallels Lacan (28).

Where Barthes disagrees with Garber over the relation of the idea of culture to the symbolic and to code, Kaja Silverman disagrees with Garber over the symbolic register's relation to the binary. In her psychoanalytic study of the subject of semiotics, Silverman concludes not with Lacan or with Freud but with Barthes, and she offers the following expanded definition of the function of symbolic codes: "The symbolic code inscribes into literary and cinematic texts antitheses which are central to the organization of the cultural order to which they belong. Indeed, it could be said that the symbolic code is entrusted with the maintenance of that order's dominant binary oppositions. Its failure to do so thus has ramifications far beyond the boundaries of any individual text" (270). The link here between the symbolic, the code, and culture seems profound. Surprisingly, however, this description of the function of symbolic cultural code insists that code organizes and maintains binaries. Silverman, citing *S/Z* specifically, elaborates on symbolic binary codes at some length: "Barthes consistently links the symbolic code to the formulation of antitheses, especially that variety which admits of no mediation between its terms. In other words, he associates it with the articulation of binary oppositions, with the setting of certain elements 'ritually face to face like two fully armed warriors' ([*S/Z*] 27). These oppositions are represented as eternal and 'inexpiable.' Any attempt to reconcile them is seen as 'transgressive'" (270). Finally, Silverman gives the difference between male and female as the "most dominant and sacrosanct of all binary oppositions" supported by the *symbolic* cultural codes (270). Silverman's heterosexual symbolic binary seems definitively at odds with Garber's transvestite symbolic third term.

Together, Silverman and Garber have given theorists a *Symposium* on the symbolic. Where Silverman, using Barthes, links the symbolic with culture, code, and binary opposition, Garber, citing Lacan, links the symbolic with culture and code against an imaginary host of binaries. Moreover, Silverman locates male/female in the symbolic register while Garber sees male/female as imaginary. Finally, for Silverman, the symbolic defines irreconcilable oppositions whose violation would be transgressive; for Garber, the symbolic defines the transgressive itself. Given the two registers of the symbolic and the imaginary, Silverman and Garber produce a series of inverted critical positions and concepts evocative of the inverted readings of the *Symposium*.

What Silverman and Garber have done for the symbolic register, film theorists have done for the imaginary. Silverman's penultimate chapter on the symbolic, suture, and subjectivity in film complicates register theory still further. In her discussion of suture and ideology, Silverman notes that ideological studies of suture in film hark back to the writings of Althusser on the apparatus and draw heavily on his use of the term "imaginary." She points out that "when Althusser uses the term 'imaginary' he means identifications which have been culturally initiated" (216) in contrast to the spontaneous identifications Lacan describes in his mirror stage essay. Because Althusser associates the imaginary with culture, he concerns himself with "the operation whereby individuals are compelled to identify with the representations which their culture supplies" (218), an operation he terms "interpellation." Silverman notes that Althusser's imaginary is the locus of identificatory activities Lacan attributes to the symbolic.

Following Althusser, the Israeli film critic Daniel Dayan complicates the theoretical imaginary even further.[13] Dayan writes in the film tradition that brings together semiology and Marxism and indicates that he sees Althusserian Marxism and Lacanian psychoanalysis as two theories having "a structural conception of causality" (23). Consequently, he links a series of critical concepts including semiotics, ideology, history, and code to the registers. Drawing on Jean-Pierre Oudart's previous discussion of these concepts,[14] Dayan uses Oudart's example of the discourse of classical figurative painting to advance the idea of code as produced by ideology, subject to historical change, and masked by "the imaginary" (26). The classical cinema masks its filmic message by "account[ing] *within itself*" for its own code and by providing "imaginary answers" to the viewer's questions (28). Where Althusser inverts both Garber's and Barthes's link between culture and the symbolic, Dayan goes even further to invert the register of code itself, associating code with imaginary meaning effects rather than with symbolic laws.

Consequently, the registers of the imaginary and the symbolic, so distinct in Lacanian theory have, in this chain of applications, become virtually indistinguishable. Both the symbolic and the imaginary have been read as the locus of code, of culture, or of binary, the distinction between the registers reflecting the critical assimilation of Lacanian theory rather than Lacanian theory itself. This critical impasse arises first and foremost because the imaginary and the symbolic have been treated as opposed functions. Once opposed, the registers are reduced to categories, functioning not as analytic dynamics but as baskets into which concepts like code or culture or even binary itself can be stashed. What begins as exploration of the psychoanalytic paradigm ends as argument about classification—the implications of the decentering of the subject getting lost along the way, (lost from the content, though certainly not from the process, of the disagreements). Together, these inversions suggest that the reading of critical texts is as vulnerable to reduction as the reading of literature. The same problems arise in the interpretation of the psychoanalytic writings of Jacques Lacan as in the interpretation of Plato's *Symposium*. In response, I will search Lacan's Plato for evidence of another kind of reading—a reading that employs the registers to trace the path of the decentered subject. First, however, I will review Lacan's visual counter to the categorical opposition of the registers in his illustrations of the position of the unconscious.

Coming to Terms with the Subject of Psychoanalysis

The old joke about ambiguity aptly captures Lacan's theory of the registers: Q. Is Lacan a structuralist or a post-structuralist? A. Yes. In a sense, the inverted readings of the Lacanian registers just surveyed have their genesis in this ambiguity. For heuristic purposes, the problems presented by the inverted critical readings and by the assimilation of Lacanian theory into other critical schools of thought can be positioned in the generic structural model, the semiotic rectangle defined by two terms A and B, their negations, and their combinations. If the imaginary and the symbolic registers occupy the first two terms of the basic structural relation, then the real must be the double negation, or negative complex term since the real is the register which is neither the imaginary nor the symbolic. The real is not the symbolic but rather "what resists symbolisation absolutely" (Sem I 66). Nor is the real the imaginary, for imaginary objects and real things "are not in the habit of co-existing for the subject" (Sem I 175). In fact, Lacan so frequently writes of the real as the "ineffable" or the "impossible" that his sense of the real as a double negative seems evident.

The structural model falters when we come to the "third term" or double positive, that which is both A and B. Though Lacan frequently refers to the symbolic as the "third term," this seems not to be a general structural reference. Lacan calls the symbolic the third term only in connection with the idea of the Oedipus complex and with the addition of the symbolic father to the imaginary mirroring interaction between mother and child. The missing double positive fits Lacan's sense that positivism is the problem, the problem of everyday "reality," the problem of empty speech in which the imaginary confirms itself in the symbolic, the problem of self-certainty. Consequently, Lacan reserves the "between" of positivism for constructs such as the symptom or the "suture" which imply psychopathology or, at the very least, error. Lacan repeatedly shows that the symptom links the registers. The suture, too, is quite clearly a positive complex term since Lacan's only use of the word "suture" is in his discussion of the "frozen attitude" or the "anti-movement" of the *fascinum* as "a suture, a conjunction of the imaginary and the symbolic" (Sem XI 118). Suffice it to say, at this point, that when Lacan uses the phrase "third term" he does not mean what structuralists mean by it, and when Lacan employs the structuralist double positive, he does so reproachfully.

This generic structural heuristic invites the kinds of dualism and categorical thinking that dead end theoretical discussions of Lacan, however. Thus, for heuristic purposes of his own, Lacan employs a number of drawings and diagrams that resemble the basic semiotic rectangle in design but differ from it in dynamics. Two such diagrams, Schema L and Schema R, use the Lacanian registers to express the decentering of the subject. Lacan discusses his Schema L repeatedly both in his Seminars and in his *Écrits*. Schema L offers a "schema of the intersubjective dialectic" (EE 332), while Schema R weds the more basic Schema L to the registers to depict "the structure of the subject" (333). In his second

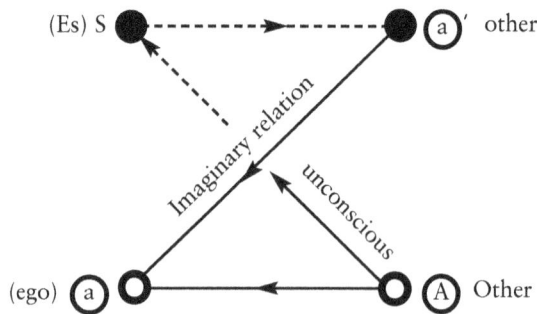

FIGURE 1.1
Lacan's Schema L: The Subject of the Unconscious

seminar on the Freudian ego and psychoanalytic technique,[15] Lacan suggests that a schema "would not be a schema if it yielded a solution. It isn't even a model. It's just a way of fixing our ideas, called for by an infirmity in our discursive capacity" (243). Each schema in its own way captures the decentering of the subject in a depiction of simultaneous relations between the registers, multiple structural relations that exceed the signifier's discursive limitations.

The more elaborate of Lacan's two presentations of his Schema L shows the relationship between the imaginary and symbolic registers as they distinguish the terms of subjectivity. Schema L, also called the Z-shaped schema, is presented in Seminar II as "a little schema . . . to illustrate the problems raised by the ego and the other, language and speech" (243). The ego and the mirroring other (*autre*) signify the imaginary relation and locate the imaginary register in the drawing while the Other (*Autre*) of language as such and the S or speaking subject locate the symbolic. It is clear from this simplest Lacanian schema that the speaking subject (*Es*, S) is not the ego (*moi*, a). It also clear that the mirroring other (a′) is not the Other (A). Lacan does not draw these relations because the necessary gaps between the Subject and the ego and between the other and the Other illustrate Freud's greatest discovery—the decentering of the subject of the unconscious. The Lacanian subject is not an *un*centered subject as is sometimes mistakenly inferred; the Lacanian subject is decentered vis-à-vis its own ego. The gap between the Subject and the ego in Schema L depicts Lacan's position contra the unified Cartesian thinking "I." The terms and relationships of Lacan's schema of the decentered subject of the unconscious are presented more fully in Schema R.

Schema R depicts both the structure of the three registers and the structure of the subject. On the upper left is the Imaginary triangle (whose corners are marked by e, i, and S). The register of the Real separates the Imaginary triangle from the Symbolic triangle on the lower right; the Real is denoted by a square with the corners e, i, o/M, and o′/I. The Symbolic triangle on the lower right is bounded on the inside by the letters o′/o/O and on the outside by the letters I/M/F. This simultaneous depiction of the three registers and the terminology of desire insinuates several ambiguities into Lacan's schema, suggesting that such simultaneous representation may be more that a simple two-dimensional drawing can handle. Perhaps the only thing that Schema R makes clear is that Lacan means to retain the gap between

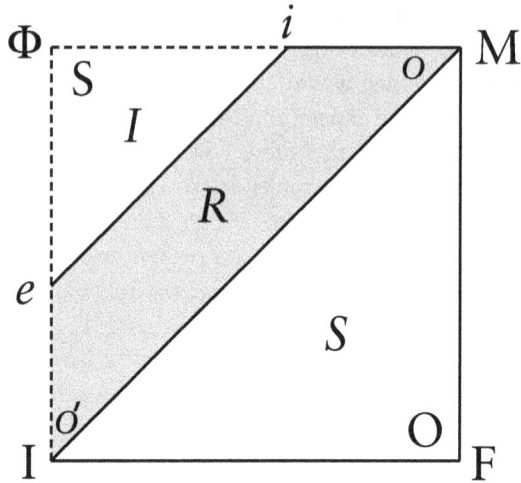

FIGURE 1.2
Schema R: The Three Registers

the imaginary and symbolic registers. The gap effected by the position of the real in Schema R reiterates the gap between the Subject and the ego in Schema L.

The structural paradigm applies even more loosely to Lacan's Schema R than to Schema L. In Schema R, terms change their value and meaning depending on their combination with other terms and depending on how many terms are considered simultaneously. The duplication of terms that occurs when the number of terms exceeds the number of available positions further reinforces the observation by Lemaire and by Miller that Lacan basically says the same thing in two different ways. As elaborations of earlier terms, the subject position (Φ), the *objet a* (M), the ideal ego (I), and the Other (as the F or Name-of-the-Father) contribute to the contradictions and inversions in the critical positions surveyed in this chapter.

Both Schema L and Schema R appear in Lacan's explication of the psychoanalysis of the psychotic in his essay "On the possible treatment of psychosis" (EE 179–225). In this essay, Lacan describes Schema R as a pattern composed of two triads. The first is an imaginary triad defined by "the two imaginary terms of the narcissistic relation, the ego and the specular image" together with the Subject's self-identification as third term. The second is the symbolic triad defined by the Oedipal relation. Another ambiguity enters here, however, when Lacan specifically distinguishes between the "third term of the imaginary triad . . . in which the subject identifies himself . . . with himself as a living being" (196) and the "fourth term . . . given by the subject in his reality, foreclosed as such in the system [e.g., the subject as the neither/nor position], and entering into the play of the signifiers only in the mode of death" (196). Symbolic existence through speech alone can be either a kind of death (the "fourth" term) or a set of positivisms ("third" terms), either the truth of the unconscious or the "empty speech" of the analysand. In fact, Lacan indicates that this speaking subject becomes the true subject "to the extent that this play of the signifiers will make it signify" (196), that is to say, to the extent that it abandons its self-defining certainties, giving up its third terms for its fourths. All in all, Schema R has introduced a number of redundancies and replicating patterns into Schema L's rather straightforward illustration of the dynamics of the decentered Freudian subject of the unconscious.

In spite of their differences, Schema R and Schema L share several characteristics. First, for all their complexities, both schemas are determined rather than overdetermined. In both, Lacan astutely avoids the overdetermination that would inevitably be entailed in any model whose relations exceeded its terms. Schema L, with its four relations and four terms depicts a circuit in which the imaginary and symbolic registers appear at cross purposes. The gaps that distance the subject from the ego and the mirroring other from the Other of language ironically rescue the model from radical polyvocality. Schema R avoids overdetermination by the sheer multiplication of terms. This does not in any way imply the failure of either model, but rather suggests that the models are far more complicated than they appear and that they do make quite specific assertions about the nature of the subject and the position of the unconscious. The strength of Lacan's theorizing and the reason why Lacan is both a structuralist and a post-structuralist reside in Lacanian theory's juxtaposition of the determined with the indeterminate. Finally, Lacan's "intersubjective" models should not be taken to imply interpersonal ones. The Lacanian subject, though certainly not the unified subject of the humanist tradition, does not suffer from multiple personality syndrome. The phenomenal otherness of the ego's imagoes and the linguistic Otherness of the subject's language provide the psychic resources with which the Lacanian subject confronts the brute alterity of its real. The grapplings of desiring subjects toward their missing parts provide the material for Lacan's own symposium on the unconscious.

Lacan's Symposium on the Subject of Desire

Though Plato's *Symposium* pretends to be a dialogue that is truly multivocal, the *Symposium* assimilates all its allegedly competing discourses to one reigning symbolic polarity: heavenly love/earthly love.[16] As John Brenkman notes, this core opposition is never in question, and all the differences Plato's participants seem so hotly to debate ultimately align themselves with the *Symposium*'s dominant opposition. Differences between soul/body, idea/matter, paternal/maternal, the permanent/the transitory, the one/the many, male/female, and good/bad merely question the best way in which to position each polarity in relation to the foundational binary heavenly/earthly. Like the positions in Plato's *Symposium*, critical positions on the Lacanian imaginary and symbolic registers align their critiques with a foundational binary and then argue for their alignments.

Lacan's response to Plato's *Symposium* combines his discourse on the registers with his discourse on desire, producing the rich and ambiguous blend characteristic of all his later theorizing. The very title of Lacan's response to Plato is ambiguous: "Position of the Unconscious."[17] Is the position of the unconscious synchronic and spatial like a schema of the registers? Or is it the position to which desire has brought the subject unawares? Language, the very basis of analysis and the *modus vivendi* of the unconscious "supplies warp and woof to what is woven between synchrony and diachrony" (264). Like Lacan's twinned theoretical perspectives, the alternative between language and speech "proposes itself as a disjunction" (264).

Lacan's essay on the *Symposium* emphasizes the disjunction between the imaginary and the symbolic registers, maintaining the decentering of the subject that prevents the categorical error of opposing the registers to each other or of opposing the unconscious to the conscious. The unconscious is something very different from the "not conscious" (260), a psychoanalytic fact that psychology refuses to acknowledge. Psychology's central error, like that of Descartes, is the attribution of a unifying, synthetic capacity to consciousness (261), yet the only "homogeneous function" of consciousness is the imaginary ego's capture by its own reflection which must be seen as disjunct from the symbolic presence of the unconscious that haunts every enunciation (263). "Everything . . . points to the distribution of consciousness . . . being heterotopic in terms of levels and erratic at each level" (261), and this complex and erratic interweaving of levels characterizes register theory through and through. Lacan concludes with another statement of the relationship between the registers and desire: As an effect of language, the subject of the unconscious is "born of this original split" between the registers; desire then beds down in the signifying cut Lacan concludes (265).

Lacan's desiring being has a less happy fate than Plato's: it seems caught between an imaginary paralysis and an inevitable symbolic lack. Freezing, the imaginary alternative, insists that the being is wholly what it imagines itself to be. Lack, by contrast, springs from the symbolic's organization around the "*vel*," the either/or that requires the subject to choose by eliminating one option or the other. The outcome of this forced choice initiates lack, and lack initiates desire. Thus, the *Symposium* is useful to Lacan because it demonstrates "this point of lack" (266). The *Symposium* illustrates and situates the libido, says Lacan, again pointing to the copresence of the situating registers with the dynamics of desire. In Plato's myth of desire, Lacan locates the registers of the imaginary and the symbolic not as categorical differences but as incommensurabilities. This disjunction between the registers, retained in Lacan's complex narratology of phallic potency and castration, has its genesis in his earliest theorizing and predominates in his early Seminars. Because register theory constitutes such a vital part of Lacanian reading practice, I will explore its genesis and then its full articulation before inviting Lacan's guests to return to the *Symposium*.

Page 20 blank.

2

The Master in the Mirror

Lacan's mirror stage theory is many things simultaneously: an epistemological critique of the autonomous subject of science, a developmental vision of the genesis of the *je* or speaking subject, a dialectical reinterpretation of Freud's concept of narcissism, a discussion of the role of
projective identification in the socialized ideals of the subject, and an
exposé of the tenuousness and vulnerability of fact-based knowledge.
Perhaps the sheer multiplicity of territories Lacan's mirror stage essay
sought to cover insured the vexed reception it has received, a vexation
made manifest in the running awry of the essay's citational afterlife.
Ironically, the fate of Lacan's mirror stage essay in subsequent scholarship so overwhelms the fact of its 1949 publication that this small *écrit*
does what it says; its fate exemplifies its argument. More than any other
single work of Lacan's, "The mirror stage as formative of the I" appears
to be where it is not. From the moment of its textual emergence in 1949,
it has been the victim of a continual mistaken identity—taken for a
seeming prior "self," the inevitable future of an anterior 1936 mirage.

The mirror stage essay's distinctively mirror-bound history begins
with the publication of "The mirror stage as formative of the function
of the I" ["Le stade du miroir comme formateur de la fonction du Je"]
in the French *Écrits*.[1] Originally a paper delivered at the sixteenth International Psychoanalytical Congress in Zurich on July 17, 1949, "The
mirror stage" essay's postwar genesis significantly links it to a precursor
essay, "Aggressivity in psychoanalysis."[2] However, the link established
between these two essays and between aggressivity and the mirror stage
by their simultaneous appearance in the French *Écrits* is immediately

severed by the appearance of a double in the chronological bibliography of that volume. The bibliography states, simply, the "facts" that "Le stade du miroir" had been read in the second scientific session of the Fourteenth International Psychoanalytic Congress at Marienbad chaired by Ernest Jones at 3:40 P.M. on the third of August, 1936 (917).

The future of the illusion of a 1936 mirror stage essay seems further assured by Sheridan's bibliographical note on the text of "The mirror stage as formative of the function of the I" which claims that this essay is "a much revised later version" of an "earlier version, entitled simply 'Le stade du miroir' . . . published in *The International Journal of Psychoanalysis*, vol. 18, part I, January, 1937, under the title, 'The Looking-glass Phase'" (EE xiii). So pervasive has the myth of the 1936 mirror stage essay become that *Le nouvel observateur*'s September 1993 review of Lacan's life and career merely adds to the long string of writings that persistently attribute to the fantasized former essay the ideas in the latter. "In 1936, in his essay on 'The mirror stage,' following a concept 'borrowed' from Henri Wallon, [Lacan] forged a theoretical lever to renovate the Freudian concept of the divided subject" (6) the *Observateur* writes, and then briefly describes the now familiar "jubilant" assumption by the infant of a mirror image which simultaneously gives it a consciousness of corporal unity and inaugurates a radical cut that separates it from itself.[3]

If there were, in fact, a 1936 mirror stage essay, the attribution of Lacan's later theorizing to it would simply be an instance of the tendency Lacan himself notes in his introduction to the section of the French *Écrits* containing the 1949 "version": "It happens that our students delude themselves in our writings into finding 'already there' that to which our teaching has since brought us" (67). But the delusion is not a misreading at all; it is a projection of a presence where no such presence exists—for the very being of the "prior" essay can only be attributed to the being of the latter. The address allegedly summarized in the report of the 1936 conference in *The International Journal of Psycho-Analysis* does not appear, and page 78 of the *Journal* bears only a brief line and title, "J. Lacan (Paris) 'The Looking-glass Phase.'"[4]

Nevertheless, Jean-Michel Palmier's guide to the reading of *Écrits* far exceeds previous missed histories of Lacan's project in attributing substance to the chimera of a preceding essay.[5] Palmier purports to "begin the study of the work of Jacques Lacan with the two texts that he devoted to 'The Mirror Stage'" (19), and in what can only be described as a textual hallucination, Palmier "reads" the prior text. "The first writing [*écrit*] of Lacan devoted to the Mirror Stage remains at certain points quite imprecise" (20), Palmier writes, noting that by contrast, "the second, despite the habitual difficulties relative to the Lacanian style, is of an incomparable richness" (20).[6] Here, Palmier's contrast between the two essays merely confirms the reality of the former—the virtual reality of the "imprecise" prior writing springs from the concrete and incomparably rich later *écrit*. The characteristic imprecision Palmier attributes to the phantasm seems remarkably apt all the same, since the hindsight of register theory shows its clear-cut distinctions to be muddied by the idea of the mirror stage as "The mirror stage" presents it. Though the borrowed ontology that the mirror stage essay itself exemplifies continues to mark the *moi* or specular ego as an imaginary fiction, the dynamics of specularity are by no means clear. Similarly, the temporal displacement between these marker mirror stage essays depicts the developmental illusion Lacan attributes to the mirror *stage* itself; development as a theoretical construct contradicts the structural differences that Lacan seems on the verge of hypothesizing. At this point, Lacan lacks a thoroughly articulated sense of the symbolic subject to contrast his grasp of the ego. His analytic world is monocausal.

Before the Mirror

All that we know of the 1936 "essay" is what we can tell from a title, yet the complete title of the 1936 address is revealing. "Le stade de miroir: théorie d'un moment structurant et génétique de la constitution de la réalité, conçu en relation avec l'expérience et la doctrine psychanalytique," or "The mirror stage: theory of a structuring and originary moment of reality formation, conceived in relation to psychoanalytic experience and doctrine,"[7] makes its political and intellectual positions explicit. The title alone implies a fusion of the synchrony of structure with the diachrony of development. Lacan has not, at this point, worked out the differences between the two, much less stated these differences in theoretical terms. The greatest discrepancy between this title and 1949's "The mirror stage as formative of the function of the I" concerns just what is formed during the mirror stage. Early on, the mirroring moment of realization yields a "reality," but by 1949 the moment of realization constitutes the birth of the *je*, the speaking subject. In the former, projection stands alone; in the latter, projection allies itself with introjection. Moreover, the larger philosophical contexts reveal a parallel difference. The emphasis in the former title is on the phenomenal, the psychoanalytic experience; the emphasis in the latter points to the importance of language and the dominant function of speech.

In a much later essay, Lacan suggests that the content of the unpublished 1936 address can be found in essence in his article on the family which appears in the 1938 *Encyclopédie française*.[8] The encyclopedia, edited by Henri Wallon, is arguably his first psychoanalytic publication of importance, a significant marker of his entry into the analytic community, and a concession to prevailing psychoanalytic opinion. In this early discussion of the mirror stage, mirroring is presented in familial, phenomenal, and experiential terms. A discussion of the "intrusion complex" illustrates the mirroring theme of recognition of the self outside itself. Here, the young child sees itself in its siblings or *"semblables"* and recognizes itself for the first time in the image of an other (Clark 127). The infant does not see these others as outsiders; rather, they comprise its own transitive extensions, they are its other selves. Consequently, the mirror stage is linked with infantile jealousy based on an identification with the other, a theme Lacan repeatedly exemplifies by borrowing Augustine's tale of the child who turns pale at the sight of its brother at its mother's breast.[9]

The relations emphasized in Lacan's article on the family seem clearly social, suggesting that readings of Lacan which attempt to equate entry into the symbolic with entry into the social are misguided. In fact, Lacan here points out that these mirroring relations between the infant and the other represent the "genesis of sociability and, hence, of consciousness [*connaissance*] itself insofar as it can be considered human."[10] Since *connaissance* also suggests "knowledge" in the context of Lacan's article, the link between the ego, knowledge, and mirroring identification with the other exists quite early in Lacan's work.

At this time in his theoretical writings, Lacan also postulates the *corps morcelé*, or fragmented body, as the prior state of psychic and bodily fracturing caused by the birth trauma that separates the infant from the mother and characterizes the infant prior to the mirror moment's unifying realization. As has often been noted, the awareness of fragmentation and the image of unity arise in the selfsame gesture. Knowing has its price. Seen straight on, the image in the mirror constellates the fragments into a vision of a whole self; viewed obliquely, the gap between the self and its mirror is the very measure of alienation, which Lacan depicts as the "temporary intrusion of a tendency towards alienation" into the "specular satisfaction" of the imaginary identification.[11] Lacan's distinction between his later theorizing and its early roots seems here not to ring true. The dynamic theory of the registers, though, will problematize what the mirror stage essay now accepts as definitional: a speciously unified, specular image providing the satisfaction of primary imaginary identification at the price of alienation. The accompanying ideas of fragmentation, rivalry, and jealousy point toward the accompanying theme of aggressivity and allow Lacan to critique the failures of contemporary analytic practices. Lacanian analysis has yet to be born. Given the issues raised in Lacan's early psychiatric, medical, and aesthetic writings, however, it is little wonder that he would be receptive to the theoretical answers offered by Hegel's powerful interpreter, Alexandre Kojève, since Kojève and Hegel explored themes that spoke to Lacan's earliest analytic questions.

Enter Hegel

Between 1933 and 1939, Alexandre Kojève presented his influential lectures on Hegel at the *École des Hautes Études* in Paris, pursuing the oral tradition of scholarship in which Saussure had preceded him and Lacan would follow.[12] Kojève is the first, critic Amié Patri insists, "to have attempted to constitute the intellectual and moral *ménage à trois* of Hegel, Marx and Heidegger,"[13] and it is precisely this trio of influences who cast their reflections on the intellectual scene from which Lacan's earliest mirror stage theory emerges. Of the three, it is Hegel who looms largest for Lacan, and it is Hegel's exemplary myth of the struggle to the death for pure prestige between the master and the servant that provides a continual touchstone for Lacan's early psychoanalytic theorizing.[14]

Not only did Alexandre Kojève give his popular seminars on Hegel at a time when Jacques Lacan was engrossed with those themes of doubling interaction and aggression so amenable to dialectical explanation, Kojève's collected lectures also saw publication in 1947, one year before Lacan's essay on aggressivity and two years before the "Mirror stage as formative of the I." This timing alone lends credence to Wilfried Ver Eecke's argument for profound Hegelian influences in Lacan's postwar essays.[15] Hegel is, Ver Eecke proposes, Lacan's "source for necessity"; in other words, Hegel provides Lacan with the philosophical and phenomenal grounding to claim a scientific status for the human subject of psychoanalytic study. More specifically, Ver Eecke sees Hegel's construction of the "Law of the Heart" at work in Lacan's 1948 essay on aggressivity and Hegel's "Dialectic of Lordship and Bondage" as the source of Lacan's 1949 mirror stage *écrit*. Within Hegel's larger argument, though, Kojève particularly stresses the fear of death, the Absolute master, and the transition from brute nature to human history (Inwood 9). Lacan's most explicitly Hegelian moments are marked by these same emphases.

In his pre-Seminar theorizing, Lacan struggles to define the nature of the ego by studying its formative moment. He defines the ego as a combination of the narcissistic and paranoid qualities articulated by Freud with the aggressive, competitive attributes postulated by Hegel. The aggressivity that psychiatry insisted was innate is not; instead, aggressivity is dialectically instilled in consciousness by the social struggles through which consciousness becomes a consciousness of self. Though Lacan never explicitly says what the subject before the mirror is, his mirror stage essay implies a raw subjectivity resembling Hegel's consciousness. This consciousness, perceiver of the Hegelian Thing, is less than self-conscious because it lacks the minimal requirement for the discovery of self—another self. For consciousness to become conscious of an "I," it must be "opposed to an other" Hegel says.[16] The consciousness must make the dialectical move of overarching the other "which, for the 'I', is equally only the 'I' itself" (104). Consequently, self-consciousness is reflective, it is, in Hegel's words, the "return from *otherness*" (105). When Hegel speaks of the difference between consciousness and its other as two moments that resolve into the illusion of a unified self, he articulates the gist of the mirroring moment as Lacan articulates it in his mirror stage essay. Eventually, Hegel's double object of consciousness, the negative object of sense-certainty and the "true essence" opposed to it, will metamorphose into Lacan's diagonal from o′ to o in Schema L's mapping of subjectivity. Still, it is Hegel who puts the agon in Lacan's diagonal.

The Lacanian ego as a self-conscious unity emblematized by the scenario of mirroring thus springs as much from Hegel's dialectic as Wallon's mirror stage. Hegel himself offers mirroring instances to Lacan. In one example of dialectical mirroring, Hegel explains the erasure of what would otherwise constitute an alienating gap between the ego and the other as follows: "Self-consciousness exhibits itself as the movement in which the antithesis is removed, and the identity of itself with itself becomes explicit for it" (105). In paragraph 179 of the *Phenomenology*, Hegel again articulates this mirroring motion which constructs a false self by obliterating an other. Since Hegel here explains the formation of a discrete self-consciousness, he offers Lacan a social genesis for the intrapsychic phenomenon of the ego. This is precisely the argument Lacan had been seeking since his thesis on paranoia in which he argued for a social and experiential rather than a biological cause for the psychosis of his patient Aimée.

Not only does Hegel's phenomenology of self-consciousness offer Lacan an explanation of the intrapsychic psychotic formations, Hegel's dialectic of mastery and servitude offers an interpersonal version of the same dynamic capable of explaining phenomena like Aimée's attack on her *semblable*, a famous French actress. Hegel's leap from the subjective to the intersubjective occurs in paragraph 181, where he writes of a double "supersession" in which the self becomes equal to itself in a unifying gesture that lets the other go free. Now, there are two self-consciousnesses. Now, there is the possibility of mutual recognition. Now, recognition as a middle term between two conscious beings can itself fracture into extremes yielding the impure recognition of lordship and bondage. Hegel's double supersession is thus a double bind for both the master and the slave, but particularly so for the master who ultimately loses by winning.

The double bind of the struggle between the master and the slave can be seen in H. B. Acton's summary of Hegel's exemplary myth of impure recognition:

> No individual will rest satisfied with a conquest that fails to secure the conscious acknowledgment of other men. Hence, there is a struggle for both power and recognition. In this struggle some will take greater risks than their competitors; those who risk the least will become the slaves or bondsmen of those who face death by risking their lives. In order to preserve his life, the slave submits to the master, who regards the slave as nothing but a means to his own designs. The slave is forced to work, whereas the master can enjoy leisure in the knowledge that the slave is reshaping the natural world to provide the products of his labor for the master to consume . . . the slave's work in transforming the natural world is a consequence of his fear of the master, who can kill him. Death is overcome by the works of civilization. The man who risks his life and becomes the first master breaks the bonds of nature and starts the process that will incorporate mind into it.[17]

Though Lacan frequently points out the inhumanity of the master's position, the double-bind of the master whose defeat of the slave leaves him bereft of the recognition of a self-affirming equal comes to characterize for Lacan the limitations of the ego and the failures of ego psychology. These two positions in fact go together since strengthening a purely fictional ego would constitute a misguided analytic practice. Consequently, the elements of Hegel's dramatization of the master/slave dialectic most explicit in Lacan's preregister theorizing are aggressivity and the mirroring relations manifest in the analytic phenomenon of primary identification. In "Aggressivity in Psychoanalysis," Lacan examines aggressivity as a formal and formative part of social recognition, a dialectical notch beyond the violence of life as mere brute existence. His mirror stage essay takes up the dialectical moment itself, presenting a critique of mastery aimed at therapists whose goal is to increase an analysand's ego strength.

These expressly Hegelian essays represent a culmination of Lacan's early theorizing; nevertheless, Hegel continues to put in occasional appearances at Lacan's Seminars. Sometimes the positions of the master and slave are implicit, as in Seminar II's passing reference to the problem of the mediating image as it contributes to a desire that cannot completely be fulfilled, leading either to an alienation from self or to a destruction of the other. This second Seminar on the ego in Freudian theory and practice reworks familiar Hegelian themes, themes that are addressed directly in Lacan's seminar on "Freud, Hegel, and the Machine."[18] With the famed French philosopher Jean Hyppolite in attendance, Lacan explores the Hegelian thrust toward absolute knowledge, particularly as knowledge appears to empower those who know (71). But Lacan's larger aim in his post–mirror stage use of Hegel is to refer to Freud's decentering of the subject, the touchstone for the Lacan of the Seminars. Thus, when Lacan positions Hegel at the limit of an anthropology from which Freud's radically antihumanist insights have broken free, it seems that analysis has trumped philosophy and that Freudian questions rule. For the moment, however, I want to return to the time when an Hegelian Freud defined Lacan's theoretical view.

"Aggressivity in Psychoanalysis"

In Lacanian theory as a whole, the roots of the idea of aggressivity are as historically deep as the roots of the idea of doubling. The two themes rarely appear separately in Lacan's earliest work. Before Lacan had even completed his 1932 thesis on his patient Aimée's violent attempt to murder the actress she felt occupied her own rightful spot in the community's regard, he had fused the themes of violence and semblance. In a cowritten article published in 1931, Lacan discussed two cases of mothers of illegitimate daughters whose social isolation resulted in delirium.[19] In the years immediately following the thesis, Lacan continued to focus on mirroring and disturbance, both in his psychoanalytic case study of a ten-year-old boy suffering from dementia, and in his *minotaure* essay on the sensational slashing murder of their employers by the Papin sisters.[20] Moreover, Lacan's discussion of biologism in an essay by Marie Bonaparte[21] and Lacan's early encyclopedia article on the family complexes postulate a "separation complex" in which fantasies of actual physical violation, dismemberment, and *morcellement* occur. This fragmented body imagistically links the idea of aggressivity to imaginary mirroring.

Lacan's essay on aggressivity comes as close as any of his early works to expressly addressing the idea of action, if only as an "acting out" of the psychoanalytic condition. His own position—that aggressivity expresses the idea of the Freudian death instinct—implies that psychoanalysis confronts the gaps and aporias in the psyche as they motivate an action towards death ("Aggressivity" 8). Lacan contrasts this position to two contemporary psychological projects heavily reliant on the mesh of action with psyche: behaviorism and psychodrama (9). Such therapies owe what successes they actually do have to their manipulation of underlying psychoanalytic principles related to aggressivity, he contends. To counter these psychological abuses of the idea of aggressivity, Lacan explicates in five theses the nature of aggressivity as it is revealed through the "psychoanalytic experience."

The first three theses establish the general terms in which aggressivity manifests itself in the psychoanalytic process. As the analyst attempts to maintain a neutrality in the face of the analysand's discourse, her tactic reveals the paranoid structure of the analysand's self-knowledge. Thesis 1, "Aggressivity manifests itself in an experience that is subjective by its very constitution" (9), simply asserts that the essential intersubjectivity of the psychoanalytic experience is a necessary condition for the expression of aggressivity. Thesis 2, "Aggressivity in experience is given to us as intended aggression and as an image of corporal dislocation, and it is in such forms that it shows itself to be efficient" (10), says that the aggressivity in psychoanalysis is visible in the analysand's discourse in the form of images of the fragmented body, of castration, of dismemberment. These highly charged imagoes comprise a sort of imaginary unity or "Gestalt" of aggressivity that serves the *moi*, the imaginary ego. Thesis 3, "The springs of aggressivity decide the reasons that motivate the technique of analysis" (12), points out the element of aggressivity in negative transference. The analyst's unresponsiveness evokes the display of aggressively charged imagoes in the analysand's reactions.

Thesis 4 explicitly ties aggressivity to Lacan's theory of the mirror stage as producing a formal, narcissistic ego structure based on primary identification. "Aggressivity is the correlative tendency of a mode of identification that we call narcissistic, and which determines the formal structure of man's ego and of the register of entities characteristic of his world," Lacan writes (16). The aggressivity apparent in the psychoanalytic dialogue springs from the series of dialectical changes that have shaped the analysand's *moi*. Thus Lacan here asserts the importance of human experience for the formation of the ego, a position he first maintained in his thesis on paranoia.[22] The stages Lacan points out in this portion of his discussion recapitulate the stages he discussed in his encyclopedia articles on the family. Thus, Thesis 4 presents a summary statement of Lacan's position on the formation of the ego as it had been theorized in his early professional career. Not surprisingly, discussion of Thesis 4 constitutes half the essay.

Aggressivity springs from the failure to adjust to the "shifting field"; it is a manifestation of human demand. Lacking all flexibility, ego and object become fixed, constituted as spatial and temporal categories. "This formal stagnation is akin to the most general structure of human knowledge: that which constitutes the ego and its objects with attributes of permanence, identity, and substantiality" (17). This paranoid, positive knowledge springs from a stage in the genesis of the ego, a stage in the development of "objectifying identification" (17), the mirror stage. At this point, Lacan summarizes the mirroring play of young children who recognize in their own mirror images (or in the mirroring presences of other children) images of bodily wholeness which anticipate the functional, physical unity of later development. The subject thus identifies with its own unified body image via the dialectical tactic of identification with the image of an other. The "broader co-ordination . . . will subordinate the functions of tonic postures and vegetative tension to a social relativity" (18), Lacan points out, recapitulating Hegel's dialectical leap from nature to society and indicating that the ego is socially structured. Here, Lacan speaks of the "normal transitivism" of children who themselves cry when they see other children fall, or who in striking an other say that they themselves have been struck (19). The transitive imaginary ego consequently feels with borrowed passions.

Significantly, Lacan connects the theme of aggressivity to the ego and to dialectic structure specifically when he writes about the "aggressive competitiveness . . . from which develops the triad of others, the ego and the object" (19). The ego so marked with "aggressive relativity" (19) cannot be reduced to its experienced identity, and especially in paranoia, the aggressive moments "when the subject denies himself and when he charges the other, become confused" (20). Indeed, this paranoid structure is the structure of all egos. Consequently, the subject must recognize the aggressive, "ambivalent" nucleus in experience, must own this ambivalence in aggressivity's contemporary manifestation as "resentment" (20).

Since the ego's knowledge is mirrored, borrowed, reflected, and relative, and since these dialectical structures are compositional of the ego itself, too close an evocation of the original formative imagoes can "*disconcert*"the subject's "voluntary functions" or sense of self-control. The formative imago of the primary identification always threatens to return to its original fragments. Thus, the ego is always vulnerable to the feeling that it is falling apart because it has fallen together, reflectively, in the first place. While analysts may emphasize the importance of the superego as a psychic ordering mechanism (Lacan here makes a concession to Freud's final model that he will later retract), it is also important "to isolate the notion of an aggressivity linked to the narcissistic relation and to the structures of systematic *méconnaissance* and objectification that characterize the formation of the ego" (21). To frame this attachment dialectically is to solve the theoretical difficulties Freud encounters because of "the mirage of objectification . . . constituted by the idea of the *perception/consciousness* system" (22). It is to replace, at the very heart of the idea of the ego, the rational with the relational.

This relational ego so kin to Hegel's dialectic of the struggle to the death and so exemplary of the phenomenon of mirroring means that aggressivity and narcissism are endemic in the evolution of subjectivity; thus, they are the precursors of normalizing, secondary identifications. While primary identification springs from an intrapsychic rivalry and is, thus, inevitably alienating, Oedipal identification "transcends" the rivalrous aggressivity that was necessary for primary individuation (23). Secondary identification, unlike the transitive fusion of primary identification, establishes a distance in which respect for "one's neighbour" can express itself. Lacan ties the two forms of identification together in a statement describing the transition from narcissism to its beyond, a transition that may be found in "all the genetic phases of the individual" (24). Here, again, Lacan makes concessions to a Freudian developmental model based on frustration and sublimation, a model his theory of the registers will expressly contradict. In this mirror stage model, however, primary identification bases itself on frustration, secondary identification on sublimation. Later, these distinct forms of identificatory "stages" will shed their developmental baggage and be reborn in formal and structural terms.

Lacan closes his discussion of aggressivity with a reminder that therapies insistent on developing the strong ego need to recall that the ego "represents the centre of all the *resistances* to the treatment of symptoms" (23). Also, Lacan reminds therapists that the ego so often invoked as the assistant to the analysand in resolving frustration *is* frustration in its core being: "This *ego*, whose strength our theorists now define by its capacity to bear frustration, is frustration in its essence. Not frustration of a desire of the subject, but frustration by an object in which his desire is alienated and which the more it is elaborated, the more profound the alienation from his *jouissance* becomes for the subject" (42). Thus Lacan's articulation of the link between the ego, frustration, and aggressivity as mirror-related social phenomena paves the way for his final thesis, a concluding "social thesis" (25).

Thesis 5's discussion directly bases itself on Hegel's dialectic of the master and the servant, and it is here that the aggressivity of the subject as person is writ large in the condition of the collective and of history. Lacan concludes that where aggressivity informs the fundamental constitutive condition of the human ego, space itself and every relation to it must be aggressively marked (25). Lacan here allies Kojève's Hegelian History with a capital H to Freud's broadest cultural/historical statement on the discontents of civilization. In Thesis 5, Lacan points especially to the ego as a spatial construct, or a construct formed in space, in order to demonstrate explicitly that the ego is "mapped socially," mapped into a geometric, "*kaleido-scopic*" space (27). The idea of a kaleidoscopic space recalls Lacan's early encyclopedia article on the family in which he first defines the other in the plural as *autrui*, others, suggesting that the *moi* or ego has a composite nature.[23]

As befits a postwar essay on aggressivity that is heavily indebted to Hegel, Lacan addresses war directly as the extension of the aggressivity that forms the ego, as the "inevitable" and "mutual adaptation of adversaries" (27). But Lacan concludes by turning back from the collective to the subjective, and finding there above all that "the fear of death, the 'absolute Master,' presupposed in consciousness by a whole philosophical tradition from Hegel onwards, is psychologically subordinate to the narcissistic fear of damage to one's own body" (28). Thus the subjective tensions generated by narcissistic aggressivity meet with the temporal anxieties so well elucidated by Freud. Years later, historically distanced from his immediate postwar theorizing, Lacan will expressly link the Hegelian scenario and the egocentrism of mastery to the German advance on Toulon (Sem II 72). For now, he takes a more apolitical position, pointing out that the death instinct inhabits this crossroads marked by the ego's formation in originary "splitting," and the subject's constitution of a world in a sort of perpetual "suicide" (28).

As a whole, "Aggressivity in psychoanalysis" persistently unites the idea of the ego with a variety of instances of aggressivity, and unites both with a dialectical formative mirroring stage that is cultural and intersubjective. Having already elaborated these themes at length, and having explicitly linked these themes to the idea of the mirror stage, Lacan would have little need to repeat his discussion of aggressivity the following year when he wrote an essay presenting the evidence for the mirror stage itself. But the significant link between aggressivity and mirroring is clear, not only from "Aggressivity in psychoanalysis" but also from the great variety of Lacan's early writings of which the 1948 "Aggressivity" essay is the culminating statement. Lacan makes a parallel culminating statement of mirror stage theory the following year. In both essays, the central hypothesis is of a recognition and a self-recognition that parallel each other; "other" and "ego" spring from one twin birth. Not surprisingly, the mirror stage essay unfolds a sequence of points recapitulative of the theses in "Aggressivity in psychoanalysis," suggesting that the mirror stage essay should be read as the other of the aggressivity piece and vice versa. The dialectical relation between the two essays seems an apt formal expression of the debt both postwar pieces owe to Hegel.

The Mirror Stage

No single Lacanian essay, not even "The signification of the phallus," is cited in the secondary literature as frequently as "The mirror stage as formative of the function of the I as revealed in psychoanalytic experience." Judith Butler's much-discussed critique of Lacan in *Bodies That Matter* emphasizes this essay. Moreover, the mirror stage essay is included in Routledge's recently published *Continental Philosophy Reader* as the single statement of Lacan's work. This briefest of the *écrits* presents both scientific and anecdotal evidence supportive of Lacan's position that the phenomenon of mirroring triggers a universal human developmental process essential to the formation of the specular ego. The specular ego or *moi*, in turn, alienates the seeming center of a seemingly unified identity from its point of speech. Thus "The mirror stage" asserts the idea of the decentered ego against Cartesian rationality, or, as Lacan states his thesis: "the conception of the mirror stage . . . leads us to oppose any philosophy directly issuing from the *Cogito*" (EE 1).

The first several pages of Lacan's mirror stage essay dispute the *Cogito* by positing, in the place of an autonomous, rational, and central consciousness, a relational ego based on mimicry. Much of Lacan's proof draws upon comparative psychology, and he cites developmental studies of the chimpanzee, the pigeon, and even the locust, the first for contrast, the latter two for comparison. Thus Lacan points out that the human infant's jubilant recognition of its image in the mirror differentiates it from the chimpanzee, which is only inclined to look behind the mirror for the source of the thing it sees reflected there (1–2); however, some species like the pigeon and the locust must see a mirror member of their species to reach developmental maturity (3). Not all readers are convinced by Lacan's scientific arguments. In fact, Raymond Tallis sees Lacan's comparative data as showing only how a human infant is more like a pigeon than a chimpanzee.[24]

Though Lacan's attempt to argue scientifically has been thoroughly critiqued both by Tallis, who disputes the uses Lacan makes of his data, and by François Roustang, who disputes the structure of Lacan's scientific argument altogether, Lacan's use of Hegel and the dialectic has met a more supportive reception.[25] Since Lacan's mirror stage thesis disputes the "philosophy" of the *Cogito* rather than the scientific basis for ego psychology, this essay evokes his essay on aggressivity, suggesting that Lacan's real vision of psychoanalysis is more philosophical than scientific at this point in his career. In fact, Lacan uses Hegel to reply to Descartes more directly than he uses comparative psychology to refute the assertions of ego psychology. When Casey and Woody argue that "It is probably best to see Hegel's analysis of the struggle for recognition and the master-slave dialectic as his substitute for the Enlightenment's myth of the origin of human civilization in a social contract between autonomous, rationally self-interested egos" (86), they reveal the primary idea at work both in Lacan's explicit use of Hegel and in his larger emphasis on mirroring, mimicry, transitivism, and the decentered self. Psychoanalytic philosophy rather than ethology seems key. Thus, Lacan sees in the "jubilant assumption . . . of the specular image" (2) by the still-dependent child "an exemplary situation" and this suggests that the mirror is not to be taken too literally.

The mirror realization reveals "the symbolic matrix in which the *I* is precipitated in a primordial form, before it is objectified in the dialectic of identification with the other, and before language restores to it, in the universal, its function as a subject" (2). The symbolic, or the universal organizing matrix here signified by the mirror contextualizes the experience of the primitive "I." While the mirror stage may indeed be a stage of narcissistic fascination with the reflected "I," it is preceded by the symbolic as matrix and will be succeeded by the symbolic as the speech of the speaking subject. Though Lacan seems to point out a sequence here, it is important to recall that the sequence can only be seen as such from the point of view of the child moving from symbolic obliviousness through the mirror stage into the dialectic of identification and finally to the normalizing secondary identifications language provides. What Lacan really shows here is that, for the subject, realization of the imaginary precedes realization of the symbolic, even though for the culture the two registers exist simultaneously. Register theory's components are here in an as-yet-untheorized form.

Next, Lacan specifically labels the "precipitated" ego the "Ideal-I" of Freudian psychoanalysis, stressing that the agency of the ego moves in a fictional direction even before social forces give it further subjective shape (2). In his argument here, Lacan's ego differs profoundly from the ego posited by ego psychology. It is to emphasize this difference that Lacan stresses the fiction of agency; the ego as center of conscious control is an illusion. The ego is a dependent rather than an independent construct because its mirrored, borrowed essence "will always remain irreducible for the individual alone" (2). This ego will reveal itself as decentered because the ego rejoins the subject only "asymptotically." Therefore, the ego persists as a decentered illusory fiction "whatever the success of [the subject's] dialectical syntheses by which he must resolve as *I* his discordance with his own reality" (2). Lacan will make this counter to the reality principle even more explicit in his concluding remarks. For now, he simply points out that the speech of the speaking subject cannot bridge the subject/ego split nor close the gap such a split inevitably opens up between the subject and reality.

Lacan next indirectly counters the idea of ego strength by revealing such "strength" to be the fixity of a gestalt, a frozen statue. The Ideal-I seems a whole because it is patterned on the body image, itself a *Gestalt*. This image is a fixed and inverted image whose efficacy comes from the fact that it is "human" in the sense of being species-bound rather than individual. The child takes this gestalt as a source of permanence and completion because the mirror image emphatically contrasts the fragmentation the still-dependent child finds within its own bodily movements and sensations. The frozen ideal ego and the fragmented *corps morcelé* are born of the same realization, the former distinguishes itself from the latter.

Lacan's strategy has been to establish the fictionality and fragmentation of the ego gestalt even as he establishes the ego as a mirage of wholeness. He offers this argument to counter the idea that the strong ego can willfully and functionally manipulate reality because this agentic ego implicitly affirms the Cartesian *Cogito*. Thus Lacan restates his position midway through the essay: "I am led, therefore, to regard the function of the mirror-stage as a particular case of the function of the *imago*, which is to establish a relation between the organism and its reality—or, as they say, between the *Innenwelt* and the *Umwelt*" (4). This relation seems more Hegelian than Freudian, however, and it is worth noting that the most frequently cited passage in Lacan's mirror stage essay begins with a clearly Hegelian statement:

> This development is experienced as a temporal dialectic that decisively projects the formation of the individual into history. The *mirror stage* is a drama whose internal thrust is precipitated from insufficiency to anticipation—and which manufactures for the subject, caught up in the lure of spatial identification, the succession of phantasies that extends from a fragmented body-image to a form of its totality that I shall call orthopaedic—and, lastly, to the assumption of the armour of an alienating identity, which will mark with its rigid structure the subject's entire mental development. (4)

This summary statement of the essential ingredients of mirror stage theory sets these elements—image, fragmentation, wholeness, alienation—within a temporal context. Here, the insufficiencies of the past measure themselves against the anticipated "orthopaedic" totality to come.[26] The mirror moment, in Jane Gallop's words, "produces the future through anticipation and the past through retroaction. And yet it is itself a moment of self-delusion, of captivation by an illusory image. Both future and past are thus rooted in an illusion" (80–81). For Lacan, time, like space, has a dialectical character.

The last line of Lacan's summary paragraph is frequently deleted, leaving no sense that the function of his midessay summary is to counter the reality principle. "To break out of the circle of the *Innenwelt* into the *Umwelt* generates the inexhaustible quadrature of the ego's verifications" (4) Lacan concludes, and then moves into a lengthy discussion of dream images and psychoanalytic symptoms. Lacan offers here an alternative version of the ego supportive of an alternative vision of therapy, a vision in which it is essential to frustrate the ego's "verifications" in order to free speech from the fortress of paranoid knowledge. Though the mirror stage essay makes its concessions at precisely this point, and though Lacan nods at both Anna Freud's study of the defenses and at Charlotte Bühler's work on infantile transitivism, the essay stops short of affirming less radical forms of psychoanalysis dependent upon a strong and stable ego. This small piece of diplomacy introduces the concluding portion of the essay which confirms, yet again, Lacan's Hegelian debt and which counters, yet again, the idea of an autonomous ego able to practice what reality principles preach.

The final pages of Lacan's mirror stage essay discuss the theme of negation that specifically recalls passages in his essay on aggressivity. Here, knowledge is Hegelian, mediated through the desire of the other by an interdependent ego that "constitutes its objects in an abstract equivalence by the co-operation of others" (5) hence perpetuating its dependence. Lacan elaborates his mirror stage position, finally, to throw light on the "dynamic opposition" between the destructive libido and the sexual libido "which the first analysts tried to define when they invoked destructive and, indeed, death instincts, in order to explain the evident connection between the narcissistic libido and the alienating function of the *I*" (6). But no such explanation is necessary given the mirror stage's dialectical vision of the normatively alienating process of ego formation itself—given an "essential negativity" (6).

Lacan's essay includes, at this point, an astounding break from Freud. He explicitly states the position he has implicitly held throughout: "all our experience . . . teaches us not to regard the ego as centred on the *perception-consciousness system*, or as organized by the 'reality principle'—a principle that is the expression of a scientific prejudice most hostile to the dialectic of knowledge" (6). At this moment when it seems Lacan has himself effected a Hegelian murder of Freudian theory, he returns to Anna Freud: "Our experience shows that we should start instead from the *function of méconnaissance* that characterizes the ego in all its structures, so markedly articulated by Miss Anna Freud" (6).[27] Though Lacan effects a seeming raprochement here, his position is, as Jonathan Scott Lee puts it, "shockingly at odds with numerous Freudian texts" (24), and it is clear that when Lacan discusses "the inertia characteristic of the formations of the *I*" (7) he has in mind the *imago* as his essay defines it rather than the defenses as Anna Freud defines them.

Taken as a whole, "The mirror stage as formative of the function of the I . . ." exhibits Lacan's philosophical freedom from traditional Freudian psychoanalysis. Thus, it prefigures the distinctly Lacanian work to come and is peppered with references foreshadowing Lacan's later theorizing. His discussion of the imaginary carefully situates itself within the larger symbolic matrix, he sees in the "veiled faces" of imaginary imagoes the "penumbra of symbolic efficacy" (3), he writes of the "guiding grid for a *method of symbolic reduction*" (5), and he ties together Hegel and Levi-Strauss in the essay's final paragraphs: "At this junction of nature and culture, so persistently examined by modern anthropology, psycho-analysis alone recognizes this knot of imaginary servitude that love must always undo again, or sever" (7). Each statement is a statement that parallels the symbolic and the imaginary; thus, each statement prefigures—but stops short of articulating—the emphasis on simultaneous registers in the decade to come.

Identification

Of the many topics covered under the umbrella of mirror stage theory, the topic most relevant to literary applications is the topic of identification. Though the idea of identification never takes center stage in the early theorizing, it is there pervasively, diffusely, throughout the early works. The mirror stage essay focuses its attention on the formation of the *moi*, the ego or specular identity, but there is a difference between the intersubjective process of identification and the psychological illusion of a unified identity.[28] Though the mirror stage essay foregrounds the production of the illusion of autonomous identity, it also persistently refers to the process by which that identity is precipitated.

The mirror stage involves both the process and the product formed by it, the *moi* or specular ego. Lacan describes the process explicitly as "identification" when he writes that "we have only to understand the mirror stage *as an identification*, in the full sense that analysis gives to the term; namely, the transformation that takes place in the subject when he assumes an image [*imago*]" (EE 2). Jacques-Alain Miller's index of Lacanian concepts restates this same process beginning with the symbolic and the signifier by showing that the signifier's path defines "the process of transformation (of mutilation) that makes a subject of man, through the obliquity of narcissism" (326). The mirroring merely foregrounds the midpoint—the narcissistic barrier—that deflects the signifier's progress through the many blind alleys and detours of the illusory identity that makes the subject a subject of an unconscious. The detailed and specific outline Miller provides stresses the idea of identification second only to the idea of the signifier itself. The production of the ego and its functional support via primary identification include the related concepts of mirroring, narcissism, aggressivity, and the ideal ego. The production of the subject, by contrast, involves the ego-ideal, the symbolic or dead Father, the Law, and the Oedipus—all of which provide normalizing identifications quite different in process and function from their primary precursors. The formal pattern Miller presents is the later version of the formative model Lacan earlier postulates. Twice in the mirror stage essay Lacan mentions primary and secondary identifications. Both times, he theorizes them as a developmental progression from primary to secondary, from narcissistic to normalizing.

The sequence from the primordial to the primary to the secondary is described in the mirror stage essay as a movement from "the symbolic matrix in which the *I* is precipitated in a primordial form" to the objectification of the I "in the dialectic of identification with the other" (2) to the linguistic restoration "in the universal" (2) of the I's symbolic function as a subject. Thus, from a naïve symbolic, to an imaginary, to a universal symbolic, the progression of development is set. Lacan's *progression* from primary mirroring to secondary normalizing identification casts the end of the mirror stage as a drama whose exemplary incarnation is the Oedipus complex (5–6). Here, yet again, primary identification—identification with an image that is both counterpart and rival—precedes the secondary identification with a generalized social standard.

In fact, Lacan says that primary identification "inaugurates" the social dialectic in which all of the ego's objects will be mediated via others' desires and all of the subject's knowledge will be cooperatively constituted. Thus, both primary and secondary identifications are deeply cultural. Self-identification and social normalization are both "dependent . . . on a cultural mediation" (6) of which the Oedipus is merely the final, universalizing stage.

Lacan's distinction between primary and secondary forms of identification recalls Freud's essay "On Narcissism," to which it is clearly indebted for its discussion of the relationship between narcissism and the ideal ego. The two identifications are suggested in Freud by the individual's "double existence" and this double existence takes on two forms, "one designed to serve [the subject's] own purposes and another as a link in a chain, in which he serves against, or at any rate without, any volition of his own" (35).[29] Lacan's debt to "On Narcissism" seems far greater than his debt to *Group Psychology and the Ego*, Freud's lengthiest and most explicit discussion of identification. In the Seminars, Lacan will cite the forms of identification Freud details in his later work, but at this early stage, the mark of Freudianism shows most clearly in the vision of the narcissism and aggressivity with which the fictional unity of the identifications constitutive of the Ideal-I are maintained.

Lacan's use of the analytic construct of identification gives him a way to talk about the developmental sequence; moreover, identification gives Lacan a way to assimilate other analytic concepts to that sequence as well. Consequently, the mirroring identification that Lacan exemplifies in the infant's jubilant assumption of the mirror image represents a primitive process that does not stop with the mirror moment. In fact, this mirroring identification is the essence of transference,[30] and transference is an essential part of the psychoanalytic process. The theoretical power that derives from thinking the process in reverse, by moving backwards from the normal to the primal, remains largely untapped in Lacan's mirror stage work. Later, thinking more structurally, Lacan will reverse his tactics; rather than using identification to postulate a developmental sequence from mirroring to socialization, he will use the disjunction between the symbolic and imaginary registers to analyze instances of identification in the analytic experience. With a Möbius logic, he turns his mirror stage theorizing inside out.

Breaking Out of the Mirror

Any exploration of the later essays in *Écrits*, essays written after Lacan's theoretical challenge to the international Freudian community in the "Discourse of Rome," will reveal the echoes of his postwar Hegelianism. Thus, Hegel is mentioned specifically in the "Discourse" itself several times, in the follow-up address "The Freudian thing, or the meaning of the return to Freud in psychoanalysis," and most importantly, in "The subversion of the subject and the dialectic of desire in the Freudian unconscious," which opens with a specific reference to Hegel's view of History in *The Phenomenology of Spirit* and provides a psychoanalytic narratology that yet again fuses Freud with Hegel. This essay, contemporaneous with Lacan's reading of *Hamlet*, provides the summary statement of Lacan's schema for the reading of the unconscious structured like a language. This essay so powerfully provides Lacan's solution to the problem of the synchrony of the structural with the diachronic that I will explore it at length in Chapter 5.

Identification, too, will remain an important psychoanalytic touchstone as Lacan goes on to elaborate his more complex vision of the subject of the unconscious. Lacan's subsequent emphasis on the registers of the psychoanalytic experience will restate primary identification as "imaginary identification" and secondary identification as "symbolic identification," retaining and clarifying the fundamental distinction between mirroring and normalizing identifications but recasting the distinction in structural terms. Both forms of identification must be accounted for in the theoretical process, in the therapeutic process, and in the reading process. Consequently, attending to the distinction between these competing forms of identification and the potential conflict between them keeps the reader from returning to a naïve symbolic in which facts seem self-evident—the kind of naïve symbolic at work in the undisputed "facts" with which this chapter began.

Though in this chapter I have emphasized the themes common to Lacan's early work and to his later theory of the registers, it is important to note that a closer examination of the dialectic, of aggressivity, and even of mirroring reveals their many and various mutations. Lacan quotes himself frequently, yet he recontextualizes his terms just as frequently. Sometimes the differences between earlier and later scenarios may be difficult or impossible to reconcile. Two examples of Lacan's central aggressive and mirroring scenarios will illustrate. First, let us return to Lacan's exemplary scenario of infantile transitivism, the scene in which the child who hits another says, without lying, "he hit me." Lacan offers this scene as an illustration of the mirror stage child's inability to differentiate itself from its other. Sometimes the scene is limited to the instance of the child who cries when it sees an injury to its *semblable*. In this exemplary scene of transitivism, Lacan is interested in the likeness of one mirror image to the other, the identity of ego with other.

The mirror stage essay's scenario of infantile transitivism with emphasis on the unifying power of the mirror image seems profoundly different from Lacan's use of a very similar scene in his first Seminar. Where the mirror stage essay offers the child's captivated unity with its other, the first Seminar's child has discovered its alienation in the imaginary. I offer the whole of the anecdote because it communicates the humor and charm of the Lacan of the Seminars:

> The little girl I mentioned earlier, who wasn't particularly awful, found refuge in a country garden, where she became very peaceably absorbed, at an age when she was scarcely walking on her feet, in the application of a good-sized stone to the skull of a little playmate from next door, who was the person around whom she constructed her first identifications. The deed of Cain does not require very great motor sophistication to come to pass in the most spontaneous, I must even say in the most triumphant, of fashions. She had no sense of guilt—*Me break Francis head*. She spoke that with assurance and peace of mind. Nonetheless, I still don't predict a criminal future for her. She simply displayed the most fundamental structure of the human being on the imaginary plane—to destroy the person who is the site of alienation. (Sem I 172)

This second fable, depicting our heroine's mastery over the hapless Francis, has turned the dialectic inside out and made the alienating difference rather than the unifying mirror the object of study. Since identification is again at issue, I will address identification in terms of the Seminars in the next chapter.

Similar mutations significantly alter the meaning of the mirroring moment itself. In the mirror stage essay, the infant sees and is captivated by its own image in the mirror. The moment reveals to the infant a wholeness, a specter of mastery (the ideal ego) that will from then on be formative for the ego. This scenario, too, changes in subsequent repetitions. By the eleventh Seminar, Lacan's only mention of the mirror stage is in a scene whose features barely resemble that of the 1949 jubilant infant before the mirror. Again, identification is the theme, and in a discussion of the role of the signifier in the primary identification and in the formation of the ego ideal, Lacan invokes the mirror: "I have described elsewhere the sight in the mirror of the ego ideal, of that being that he first saw appearing in the form of the parent holding him up before the mirror. By clinging to the reference-point of him who looks at him in a mirror, the subject sees appearing, not his ego ideal, but his ideal ego, that point at which he desires to gratify himself in himself" (257). The mythic mirroring cast of two has multiplied itself; seeing has become seeing oneself looking at oneself and being caught looking; fictional prospective agency contrasts factual parental support; the reflection of the parental ego ideal now overshadows the ideal ego so much so that the infant must work to cling to the gratifying point of self-reference. These shifts in core scenarios illustrate the reworking of early ideas that takes place throughout the Seminars, providing a caution against the urge to see a sequential, causal link between the Lacan of the mirror stage and the Lacan of the registers.

Borrowing Hegel's dialectic of lordship and bondage reveals—but does not simplify—Lacan's early theoretical ambiguities. Neither Hegel nor Lacan clearly differentiates the structural from the diachronic, though both offer a dialectical "solution" to the copresence of these two contradictory paradigms. Moreover, Hegel's move from consciousness to self-consciousness to the struggle over lordship and bondage provides a by-default leap from an intrapsychic consciousness to the interpersonal struggle to the death for pure prestige, a philosophical move that Lacan the psychoanalyst cannot afford to borrow. Hence, the ethnological evidence in the mirror stage essay. Ultimately, Lacan's use of Hegel achieves an elegant and detailed *description* of the decentering of the subject—but a description is not a solution, it is only a restatement, an elaboration. In order to offer an analysis that is effective, that does not repeat the errors of the ego psychologists or object relations analysts whose thinking he sees as deeply flawed, Lacan needs the distinction that has been waiting there in the Hegelian dialectic all along: the distinction between identity and difference, neither as content nor as form but as an interactive structural process. Once Lacan recasts identity and difference as the fusional and differential logics of the imaginary and symbolic registers respectively, he forges an analytic theory of great explanatory power, a theory that can inform an analytic practice capable of finding the analysand's truth. Lacan accomplishes his recasting in his early Seminars and it is to them that I now turn.

Page 44 blank.

3

The Poe-etics of Register Theory

While the mirror stage essay and its academic fate reflect the illusion of presence which creates some thing from an other, the Poe seminars exemplify the chief characteristic of the symbolic, of structuralism, and of later Lacanian register theory: recursiveness. "*The* Seminar on 'The Purloined Letter'" signifies not one but two seminars, each of which "fits" within the one signifying title's domain, each of which is determined by the titular signifier. But the seminars are nonidentical. As a result, speaking the facts about one seminar does not necessarily imply speaking the facts about the other, even though speaking of either seminar on "The Purloined Letter" unavoidably evokes the Other. Consequently, speaking of "*The* Seminar on 'The Purloined Letter'" does not exhaust that signifier's capacity to signify since that signifier, like the letter itself, is better thought of as an open signifying agency than a closed signified thing.

Both seminars on "The Purloined Letter" contribute to Lacan's teachings on the signifier's role in structuring subjectivity. Just how the subject of the unconscious relates to the geometry of the ego is the central topic Lacan explores in his 1954–55 Seminar on "The Ego in Freud's Theory and the Technique of Psychoanalysis," and it is midway through this year-long Seminar that Lacan's first seminar on the purloined letter appears, the seminar of 27 April 1955. "The letter is here synonymous with the original, radical, subject" (Sem II 196), Lacan says explicitly, pointing yet again to the decentered subject of psychoanalysis. What is this Lacanian subject? Lacan's supporter-turned-critic François Roustang suggests that the Lacanian subject is simultaneously a

Freudian critique of the philosophical conception of the subject (which denies that subject and object are correlative) and a linguistic critique of Freud (which replaces the psychoanalysis of the ego in its object relations with the analysis of the subject of an unconscious structured like a language) (*Delusion* 131).

The letter as subject and signifier remains the topic of the second seminar on the purloined letter, which repeats the first but elaborates its message. Now situated as the opening essay of Lacan's *Écrits*, the "Purloined Letter" seminar becomes, in Malcolm Bowie's words, "a ramifying fable of the analytic process and of the constitutive function of the signifier" ("Jacques" 141). Now the signifier "determines" the subject—both in the sense that the signifier defines the subject's position and in the sense that the signifier's movement causes subjects to occupy positions relative to other subjects with whom they are intersubjectively engaged in structured situations.

"*The* Seminar on 'The Purloined Letter'" thus sums up and instantiates the differences and duplications at work in Lacan's second phase of theorizing: one seminar, part of the explication of register theory in the teaching seminars; the other seminar, a summary of and introduction to the condensation of register theory in the theoretical epic *Écrits*. The title announces a seminar about interpretation—in this case, literary analysis. But the analysis seems continually interrupted by structural insertions. Aptly, Poe's tale of triangularity includes a vignette of mirroring identification, and Lacan's many uses of and additions to the literary text offer an overview of internalization, identification, and interpretation as these processes structure themselves according to register theory's various combinations of twos and threes, of less and more.

Register Theory

Critics who see Lacan's theory of the registers as a mere extension and elaboration of his earlier mirror stage theory place Lacan's fertile decade into a unified narrative of his theoretical career.[1] The strength of such a narrative lies in its evocation of similarities; however, narrative continuities mask the disjunction between the descriptive, dialectical focus of Lacan's earlier theorizing and the extraordinary explanatory power of his high structural phase. Each theory, if viewed independently, signifies a set of answers to those theoretical issues with which Lacan is continually engaged. While the fundamental question of how to read psychosis remains unchanged, Lacan's theoretical response to the problematic of reading psychosis alters radically from the 1930s to the 1950s. Lacan's theory of the registers may thus be seen as a better solution than mirror stage theory to the theoretical problems with which he had struggled throughout his career. Malcolm Bowie has pointed out that while Lacan's early work struggled with the "complex missing dimension" in prevailing discussions of psychosis, his later theory connects the structure of subjectivity with its linguistic dimension, explaining the "high evidential standing" which writing holds for Lacan and constructing "madness as a mode of meaning, an articulation of signs, in which the individual sufferer was held captive" (*Lacan* 107).

Mirror stage theory does, indeed, address the flaws in the prevailing psychiatric view of psychosis as an organic condition having little or nothing to do with the patient's experience and personality. The elements of mirror stage theory—the imago, the formation of the alienating ego, the fundamentally paranoid nature of all knowledge, and the aggressivity with which the ego defends its fictional coherence—all combine to connect a structure of personality to a phenomenal experience. Alone, however, these elements fail to capture the complex situation of psychoanalytic treatment with its emphasis on speech, the unconscious, and the elusive truth the unconscious conceals from the patient's history.

A theory adequate to the analysis of the unconscious could not rest on the claims made in "The Mirror Stage" and in "Aggressivity in Psychoanalysis," and philosopher Jonathan Scott Lee defines the repair of the defects in mirror stage theory as "one of Lacan's principal tasks in the 1950s" (30). Lee sees two significant limits of mirror stage theory: the too-great debt Lacan's early theorizing owes to phenomenology, and the need to get beyond the emphasis on feeling implied by the idea of alienation to a "radically antiphenomenological notion of the unconscious" (30). These are the theoretical limits that Lacan's structural and linguistic theory overcomes. Thus, there is no small irony in Lacan's insistence that "phenomenologically, the analytic situation is a structure" (Sem I 2) since structure is necessarily antiphenomenal, the copula here notwithstanding. While mirror stage theory explains what is there in the psyche's condition, the theory of the registers goes beyond mirror stage theory to offer an explanation of what isn't. The theory of the registers gives Lacan a way to talk about the patient's condition—the linguistic human condition—with all its repressions, omissions, condensations, and substitutions. Lacan's later theory transcends the dualisms and ambiguities of mirror stage theory by replacing mirror stage theory with a highly sophisticated, complex view of language as a set of inter-implicated structures.

What, then, is register theory in and of itself? Critics clearly differ in their definitions of it. For Ellie Ragland, Lacan's theory of the registers offers a philosophical theory of cognition, "the first epistemology since Descartes to locate the source of knowledge in a different place" (*Jacques* 130). Malcolm Bowie sees the registers as a sort of theoretical environment which serves "to position the individual within a force-field that traverses him" (*Lacan* 91). For Bowie, the Lacanian registers are explanatory principles which "together comprise a complex topo-logical space in which the characteristic disorderly motions of the human mind can be plotted" (*Lacan* 98–99).[2] Fredric Jameson feels that register theory offers the ability to think the discontinuities between the individual and the collective "in a radically different way" ("Imaginary" 349). Consequently, Jameson sees the registers as a "transcoding scheme" which allows the critic to construct a common conceptual framework for seemingly disparate theoretical stances, a process he exemplifies in the ability of the Lacanian notion of the symbolic to rec-oncile Freud's libido theory with linguistics.

Critical applications of register theory generally omit any discussion of the real, as does Lacan's own article "Fetishism: The Symbolic, the Imaginary, and the Real" which fails to address the real directly. The omission of the real is significant because the real operates as an ineffa-ble constraint on the free expression of the imaginary and the symbolic registers. The real "resists symbolization absolutely" (Sem I 66). Para-doxically, the feeling of the real is most salient in the "pressing manifes-tation of an unreal, hallucinatory reality" (67) because any encounter with the real bumps into the real as pure resistance to both symbolic dif-ferentiation and imaginary re-presentation, the stuff from which every-day experience constructs "reality." While the practicing psychoanalyst invariably encounters the real of the analysand, the critic using psycho-analytic register theory in textual analysis cannot address the real from which the text emerged nor encounter it directly. Thus, the real rarely constrains psychoanalytic reading[3] and its omission from titles like Jame-son's "Imaginary and Symbolic in Lacan" emphasizes its ineffability.

It is Jameson, more than any other critic, who focuses on the caveats of register theory in textual analysis. Thus, Jameson warns against the temptation to make the imaginary and the symbolic into binary categories that reduce analysis to mere classification. The methodological danger in register theory is that it tempts the critic to define the imaginary and the symbolic "relationally in terms of [each] other" as opposed functions ("Imaginary" 350). Instead, critics "ought to be able to distinguish Imaginary from Symbolic at the moment of emergence of each" (350). Critics must differentiate the registers to see the registers at work independently. In this manner, critics will be able to "form a more reliable assessment of the role of each in the economy of the psyche by examining those moments in which their mature relationship to each other has broken down, moments which present a serious imbalance in favor of one or the other registers" (350–51). This sensitivity to imbalances and disjunctions and this awareness of the breakdowns of structure recall Lacan's own theoretical description of the registers in his response to the *Symposium*. The technique for achieving just such a textual analysis will be explicated in Chapter 5 and illustrated in Chapter 6's analysis of the *Journals of Sylvia Plath*.

In order to use the registers in textual analysis, the analyst should be fully aware of the imbalances and disjunctions between the registers. Such an awareness can only be achieved when the registers are seen in their structural complexity, a complexity mapped by Lacan's many schemas and diagrams. To see imbalances, the registers must first be differentiated from each other. Lacan does just this in an exemplary reading of the variant significances of the color red within the real, the imaginary, and the symbolic registers: Red, in the real, is simply an "aberration of perceptions." In the imaginary, by contrast, red figures in the image of the robin's breast which acts as a signal to evoke preset responses in other robins. Here in the imaginary, red is part of a set of interrelations which evoke an understanding. Lacan refers, too, to the red of anger or of hostility, which has the expressive and immediate character in the human world closely analogous to the animal kingdom's display. Red in the symbolic order, by another contrast, is the red of the hearts and diamonds in a deck of cards in which the red signifies only because it opposes black in the card system. Here, red takes on the symbolic character of language; here, red signifies linguistically, that is to say, differentially (Sem III 9–10).

Making these distinctions *between* the registers does not absolve the analyst of the additional task of making distinctions *within* the registers. For instance, Ellie Ragland points out that the imaginary is not in itself a unified phenomenon; rather, it is a "set of processes and resulting 'self' myths" (*Jacques* 132). Though the function of unification clearly defines an imaginary process stamped by an imaginary "homogeneous, relational, and fusionary logic" (136), this process manifests itself in variant ways within the greater field of analytic practice. The imaginary's "sameness, resemblance and self-replication" (Bowie, *Lacan* 92) characterize the imaginary register's internalization of the imago, the imaginary mirroring identifications formative of the ideal ego, and the imaginary interpretive framework which yields the ego ideal. Though the imaginary's logic is persistently fusional and presentational, this logic infuses each of the processes of internalization, of identification, and of interpretation differently because each process is structurally distinct from the others. Thus, how the imaginary differs intrinsically within itself is as urgent a question as how it differs from the symbolic order extrinsically and structurally.

The structural applications of register theory clearly exceed the simplistic practice of assigning bits and pieces of experience or text to preset categories; the orders must be aligned, connected, or distinguished if they are to serve in the analysis of speech or text. Just such attention to the diverse possibilities of alignment, of interconnection, and of distinction characterizes Lacan's own interpretive use of the registers, and Lacan's frequent references to the registers as categories must be read in light of his parallel insistence that the symbolic and imaginary registers are dissymmetrical. Revealing structural disjunctions and replications in the Lacanian theory of the registers answers the riddles of the two and the three that puzzled the guests at the *Symposium*. The structural alignments and duplications which lead to the inverting and collapsing critical arguments explored there spring from structural reduplications within texts themselves, reduplications Lacanian theory addresses. If Lacan's own theoretical descriptions sometimes invite the confusions of registers, his application of the registers to critical problems in reading Freud's texts remains exemplary.

Lacan's Schemas L and R provide the structural paradigm for the following discussion; his *Écrits* and his early Seminars lay down the psychoanalytic processes that elaborate register theory's complexities. These structural schemas and Lacan's mathematical sense of structure define the importance of the one, the two, the three, and the four of fundamental structure against the ground of the psychoanalytic processes of internalization, of identification, and of interpretation. Structure and process must be read simultaneously if the replications of two and three central to Lacan, to Freud, and to critical theory are to be differentiated and the pitfalls such replications encourage are to be avoided in critical application.

Internalization

How does the subject acquire its vocabulary of signifiers? And how does the ego acquire its images and their cousins, the complex image-pastiches analysts refer to as imagoes? The term internalization will suffice to name this generic process for the sake of our discussion, though it implies a spatial metaphor of outside/inside, of container/contained that the very late twentieth century seems permanently to have deconstructed. Lacan himself foresaw the end of the homunculus-as-container of the entified subject and so, at times, refers to this internalization process as "assimilation." Internalization, as an analytic term, is frequently taken to be synonymous with introjection, though the latter most commonly refers to imagoes and can be considered a more limited expression of the former.[4] The process of subject formation and consequent function exploits both assimilated imagoes and signifiers; ultimately, these imagoes and signifiers are both the causes and the effects of subjectivity and signification. To paraphrase, in more strictly structural and Lacanian terms, the presence of both imaginary imagoes and symbolic signifiers generates the signified for the subject. Where there is full signification—where the imagoes and the signifiers combine—the subject will be possessed of and by meanings.[5]

Lacan, at many moments in his third Seminar, tempts the reader to align the symbolic with signification and the imaginary with meaning, yet the process is neither so straightforward nor so binary. Whenever the internalizations in both registers align, meaning results. The famous Lacanian "button" or "quilting point" that stitches together the registers links signifiers to other signifiers and to imagoes in such a way that a reliable meaning consistently emerges from the interaction—the button does not stitch the signifier to a signified directly.[6] If there is linkage there is also separation, and Lacan consistently emphasizes the bar that divides signifier from signified absolutely; "the relationship between the signified and the signifier always appears fluid, always ready to come undone," he notes (Sem III 261).

Lacan indicates that the process of signification at this structurally foundational level of internalization is polyvalent—though the signifier itself can be given a numerical, structural label. Meaning-making, like the internalization of imagoes and signifiers that enables it, is a process. Therefore, the internalized elements, the imagoes and signifiers—both unary and binary—are best thought of as part-processes in a psychoanalytic dynamic, as loci of the fusional imaginary and differential symbolic *logics* which combine to yield meanings that will be taken up into identificatory and interpretive structures of greater complexity. The fact that the following discussion must, necessarily, be linear should in no way be taken to indicate that the processes discussed are either sequential or developmental.

1: The Imaginary Unary Image

Lacan links the image to a number of mirror stage themes, stressing the need for images as the outgrowth of the infant's prematurity and vulnerability. The image, like the *moi* that it will come to compose, serves an "orthopedic" purpose. "This image is functionally essential for man, in that it provides him with the orthopedic complement of that native insufficiency, constitutive confusion or disharmony, that is linked to his prematurity at birth" (Sem III 95). Thus, the unifying image signifies, and like the binary symbolic signifier, it must be internalized for it is "the form of a foreign image which institutes an original psychical function" (95). As a result, the dependence of prematurity and the foreignness of the image combine to assure that the subject will "never be completely unified" (95) even though the drive toward unity and fusion remains. The prophylaxis of the image comes at the price of alienation.

The image at issue here is not a photographic re-presentation of the real, and Lacan spends much of his first Seminar distinguishing the former from the latter. "Don't think that . . . I am trying to . . . make you take optical images for those images with which we are concerned" Lacan says (76). Optical images "behave like objects and can be taken for such." Imaginary images, on the other hand, are like reflections in a glass. "Think of the mirror as a pane of glass," Lacan explains. "You'll see yourself in the glass and you'll see the objects beyond it. That's exactly how it is—it's a coincidence between certain images and the real" (141). Lacan also elaborates a set of classic Freudian images expressive of oral, anal, and genital realities, "images linked to the structuration of the body" (141). This structuring function characterizes the imaginary image and further distinguishes it from the real image. The most important distinction between the real image and the imaginary image involves memory—the camera that produces a real image never remembers; the imaginary images never forget.[7]

The imago,[8] structurally the simplest of all the processes of the psyche, captures the phenomenal through depicting it. The image's signifying function has been noted by a number of Lacanian theorists and analysts: The imago "acts as an Imaginary agent of mirror-stage primary meaning," Ragland notes.[9]Colette Soler defines the imago as "an image erected as something fixed which has the role of a signifier" (41); for Soler, the ego becomes "a totality of the imagoes assimilated by the subject."[10] For Muller and Richardson, the imago is form-as-function: "According to Lacan, the essential function of an image is 'in-formation,' which we take literally to mean 'giving *form* to' something— whether this be the intuitive form of an object as in knowledge, or the plastic form of an imprint as in memory, or the form that guides the development of an organism" (*Lacan* 28). The image is thus the signifying unit of the imaginary register, and while its logic is unary, it contributes to the structure of subjectivity and to the expression of subjectivity in speech.

Lacan speaks frequently of the primitive character of the unary internalized image, offering the somewhat surreal images of the subject as "the infantile doll that he once was . . . an excremental object, a scwer, a leech" (Sem III 165). Still, these images are capable of "a sort of barbaric poetry" (165). Lacan compares the image to Kant's schema-ideas (165), and though this world of the imaginary may be central to some philosophies, it is clearly not so to Lacanian psychoanalysis. "I have never said of this preconscious world . . . that in itself it has the structure of language. . . . But it retains its own pathways, its characteristic ways of communication" (165). Lacan's point in stressing the symbolic signifier over the imaginary is not that the image has no psychoanalytic value but rather than Freud's distinctive discoveries cannot be explained outside the terms and structures of the symbolic register. The imaginary is not the location of the unconscious structured like a language.

Lacan's depiction of the unary image in relation to the binary symbolic signifier identifies the first of many structural levels within Lacanian theory, the level of discursive elements themselves. Images function in discourse as "an inertia" (Sem II 306) or an "interruption" (319). Perhaps because images, like signifiers, are assimilated "there is something in the symbolic discourse that cannot be eliminated, and that is the role played in it by the imaginary" (306). The structural differentiation between images and symbolic signifiers—between the unary and the polar—expresses the dissymmetry of the registers. The decentering of subjectivity is implied in the incommensurability of the image with the symbolic signifier in this most elementary process of internalization. When Lacan points out that "the better we analyse the various levels of what is at stake, the better we will be able to distinguish what has to be distinguished and unify what has to be unified" (Sem I 109), he reminds the analyst of the necessary interimplication of analytic principles, structural properties, and interpretive practice.

2: The Symbolic Binary Signifier

The first seminar on "The Purloined Letter" appears in Lacan's Seminar II, the Seminar in which he introduces, at some length, the functions of the symbolic register and of the signifier. The symbolic universe that forms the beyond of the pleasure principle, and the symbolic register that forms the beyond of the imaginary, come down to the utterly symbolic question: Odd or even? Lacan borrows this question from Poe, who has embedded it in a child's game of marbles set within the dominant story line's detective game. The embedding aptly illustrates the locus of the signifier relative to the text.

Binarity is the fundamental attribute of the symbolic signifier. "In the symbolic order every element has value through being opposed to another," Lacan writes (Sem III 9). Elsewhere he speaks of the function of the signifier "as it polarizes meanings, hooks onto them, groups them in bundles" (292). Yet again, he writes of the binary signifier: "insofar as it forms part of language, the signifier is a sign which refers to another sign, which is as such structured to signify the absence of another sign, in other words, to be opposed to it in a couple" (167). These continually reiterated opposites, polarities, and couplings leave little doubt that the fundamental internalization of language rests on symbolic binaries.

Lacan stresses the linguistic as distinct from the experienced and uses the opposition day/night to show the difference between the phenomenal and the signifier: "Day and night are in no way something that can be defined by experience. All experience is able to indicate is a series of modulations and transformations, even a pulsation, an alternation, of light and dark, with all its transitions. Language begins at the opposition—day and night. And once the day is there as a signifier, it lends itself to all the vicissitudes of an arrangement whereby it will come to signify things of great diversity" (Sem III 167). Language is structure, not sensation, and structure begins at the opposition, at the differentiation. Lacan reiterates a set of familiar signifying distinctions: "day and night, man and woman, peace and war" and stresses that these opposites "don't emerge out of the real world but give it its framework, its axes, its structure" (199). Structure in turn provides the human with the "effect" of a reality in which she can orient herself. Thus reality emerges as a "web" of significations; the world is "cut across and constituted by a series of overflowings, of oppositional overdeterminations" (Sem I 54) as a consequence of the structuring properties of the symbolic binary signifier.

Lacan frequently speaks of the signifier as a "sign," thereby confusing concepts that Saussure makes distinct and, in the minds of some of his critics, begging the question of the sign itself. Nowhere is the confusion more explicit than in Lacan's Seminar III attempt to illustrate the founding feature of the differential signifier: negation. Lacan defines the symbolic signifier by contrasting it with the "biological" or "natural" sign, which he exemplifies by the red of the robin redbreast, and with the "trace," which he exemplifies as a footprint in the sand (Sem III 167). The biological sign acts as a referent that triggers the actions of its perceiver; the trace, conversely, separates sign from object. Finally the signifier or objectless sign "is a sign that doesn't refer to any object, not even to one in the form of a trace" (167) and is thus a pure negation, "the sign of an absence" (167).

Like the unary image, the binary symbolic signifier offers the raw material of structure *as process*. The signifier's work is the work of structuring. "The signifier doesn't just provide an envelope, a receptacle for meaning. It polarizes it, structures it, and brings it into existence" (Sem III 261). The signifier acts; the agency belongs to the letter. Thus, the signifier's capacity to determine the subject rests upon the signifier's capacity to move dynamically within a signifying structure, and the signified or meaning arises as the complement of the resulting signifying differences.

Lacan leaves little doubt that the active force of the signifier is determinant and causal, and that the signifier's causal function may seem paradoxical. "There is a real antinomy between the function of the signifier and the induction it exerts on the grouping of meanings. The signifier polarizes. It's the signifier that creates the field of meanings" (Sem III 291–92). Nor are specific meanings generally labeled as "affects" free from the differentiating force of the binary since "the elementary meanings we call desire, or feeling, or affectivity, these fluctuations, these shadows, these resonances even, have certain dynamics that can be explained only at the level of the signifier insofar as it is structuring" (260–1). At the level of the internalization, the signifier paints with broad differentiating strokes.

The fact that meaning is an effect of the signifier and its structural properties indicates that analysis must engage the symbolic register. Lacan insists on this. "Without an exact knowledge of the order proper to the signifier and its properties," he writes, "it's impossible to understand anything whatsoever . . . about psychoanalytic experience" (Sem III 261). The analyst must grasp the symbolic because analytic "phenomena"—the mistakes, the lapses, the jokes, the dreams marked by the unconscious—make themselves manifest within the realm of language. Consequently, the differential character of the binary signifier "essentially marks everything of the order of the unconscious" (167–68).

Lacan's exemplary symbolic binary day/night also illustrates a theoretical constant in register theory: the symbolic always precedes and articulates the imaginary. Only from the individual developmental perspective does experience seem otherwise, and Lacan appears to be speaking developmentally when he says that, "very early on, day and night are signifying codes, not experiences. They are connotations, and the empirical and concrete day only comes forth as an imaginary correlative, originally, very early on" (Sem III 149). Lacan's atypical reference to "codes" here aside, the symbolic binary as a precursor of its "imaginary correlative" reverses the pre-Oedipal/Oedipal language acquisition-based model advanced by the mirror stage essay. The ambiguity introduced into the Lacanian model here disappears when the temporal is replaced by the structural. Possession of the symbolic signifying couple day/night does not conflict with the possession of day and night as unary images of experienced day and experienced night (experienced day/night is an impossibility) located in the phenomenal imaginary.

While the imaginary and symbolic registers distinguish between discrete forms of internalization, they distinguish forms of identification as well, suggesting that a kind of structural replication is at work in Lacanian theory. According to Lacan, symbolic binaries define choices that preexist the subject; therefore, "the symbolic provides a form into which the subject is inserted at the level of his being. It's on the basis of the signifier that the subject recognizes himself as being this or that" (Sem III 179). The alternative, "this"/ "that," by which a subject knows himself to be himself replicates the signifying binary—it is true. But the identificatory gesture of self-recognition points toward an imaginary process; recognition is what the mirror stage is all about, and self-articulating self-recognition (talking to my self about myself) folds the symbolic differentiation back into the imaginary in a more complex and detached way.

Because of the structural replication of the binary signifier by the dualistic mirroring imaginary identification, absolute numerical distinction between the symbolic and the imaginary registers is impossible. Such structural replications actually encourage the categorical contradictions surveyed in Chapter 1. In a numerical sense, Lacan has invited the attributional inversions that assign code to both the imaginary (Althusser and the film theorists) and the symbolic (Garber and the cultural critics). Though Lacan's theory clearly and repeatedly associates duality with the imaginary, his theory just as insistently defines a binary symbolic signifier. Consequently, Lacan's high structural phase presents a theory in which "the two" is clearly not the exclusive structural property of either register.

Identification

Unless the distinction between internalization and identification is kept in mind, it is difficult to square Lacan's continual insistence on the binary nature of the signifier with his equally explicit position that "all two-sided relationships are always stamped with the style of the imaginary."[11] The "trick" of Lacanian reading as it employs the registers to explore textual problematics is the trick of perceiving both the raw number of terms that construct what is at issue and the psychoanalytic context of the problem. Issues of internalization are clearly not issues of identification—though both are important and both may overlap as they do in the Poe game-playing vignette that follows. In other words, simple duality in a text says little; the work the duality performs must be located as either a foundational symbolic signifying assumption or as an invitation for mirroring identification. Inversions inevitably arise when the necessary critical distinctions remain incomplete or when critics fail to specify either the relevant terms or the register of the terms in question.

2: Imaginary (Primary) Identification

The "unitary image" is perceived either in the mirror or in the "entire reality of the fellow being" (Sem I 125), Lacan points out, linking the image directly to the mirroring process of primary identification. The functional drive toward the unity of the *moi* replicates the fusional logic of the structurally simpler imago or unary image with which it shares a common process, even though *moi* identification shares a structural binarism with the linguistic signifier. There is no potential for fusion without distinction; or, as Lacan puts it, "the word identification, without differentiation, is unusable" (125). Yet the process of imaginary identification is a process of making-like; consequently, difference is what is done away with in the demand for mirroring likeness. This process of imaginary identification leads to a figure/ground, a this/not this distinction; thus the imaginary duality entails relationships of exclusion. Identification makes the pictorial positional since the in-forming images, oriented by patterned symbolic differences, emerge as mimetic behavior potentials at the level of imaginary identification.[12]

While the linguistic signifier as differentiation keeps both terms in play, the imaginary identification seeks a primary unity with an other who mirrors a self back to its self without discrepancy or difference. This narcissistic identification "enables man to locate precisely his imaginary and libidinal relation to the world in general," Lacan explains. "That is what enables him to *see* in its place and to structure, as a function of this place and of his world, his being" (Sem I 125). If the process is never perfectly accomplished, and the *moi* unity can never be freed from the dualism of the universe of signification, the process still retains its aim. Consequently, it is always with its structural parallels—the symbolic binary signifiers—that the ego's identifications ultimately war.

Imaginary identification is projective identification and whoever identifies with the other in a dualistic situation redefines the other in terms of the *moi*. Lacan's apt example of the danger of such an identification is that of the lover who accuses the loved one of the very infidelities the lover has committed; this transitive mechanism of projective disowning characterizes all such imaginary interactions. "Projection doesn't always have the same sense, but for our part we restrict it to this imaginary transitivism by means of which when a child hits his counterpart he can say without lying—*He hit me*, because for him it's exactly the same thing. This defines an imaginary order of relations that is constantly found in all sorts of mechanisms" (Sem III 145).

The aggressivity underlying capitulation to the image both recalls mirror stage theory and reflects the dualism of the imaginary identification. "All erotic identification, all seizing of the other in an image in a relationship of erotic captivation, occurs by way of the narcissistic relation—and it is also the basis of aggressive tension" (Sem III 93) Lacan writes in his third Seminar, deftly summarizing the whole of mirror stage theory. However, mirroring is structurally alienating because "the aggressive relation enters into this formation called the ego . . . is constitutive of it, because the ego is already by itself an other, and because it sets itself up in a duality internal to the subject" (93). Lacan again points out that imaginary identification involves exclusion: "In every relationship with the other, even an erotic one, there is some echo of this relation of exclusion, *it's either him or me*, because, on the imaginary plane, the human subject is so constituted that the other is always on the point of re-adopting the place of mastery in relation to him" (93). Which is why, Lacan concludes, relations based on imaginary identification are fundamentally unstable (93), making the imaginary duality of identification the structural antithesis of the fixed and dependable signifying binary opposites.

The structural similarity of binary signifier and imaginary identification and Lacan's sense that the symbolic signifier and the imaginary identification operate in different registers underlies his insistent critique of ego psychology's therapeutic shaping of adequate primary ego identifications. The level of imaginary identification is, in fact, pretherapeutic because it is preinterpretive. Therapy at this level is incongruous since imaginary identification is structurally confined to the binary, precluding the necessary analytic attitude and inviting the transitivism, aggressivity, and duplication whose aggressive deployment forces the capitulation of one of the two participants in the interaction. The only possible relation at the level of primary identification is the relation of master and servant in the struggle for pure prestige. The argument over identificatory issues in therapy is so important to the understanding of Lacan's project that it will be discussed at length in Chapter 5.

2 + 2: Imaginary Identification and
Symbolic Signification in "The Purloined Letter"

Though Lacan's general discussion of Poe stresses the "letter" as symbolic signifier, his first lengthy quotation from Poe's "Purloined Letter" offers a vignette in which the binary of the signifier competes as an explanatory device with the duality of mirroring identification. Lacan cites Dupin's tale of the crafty schoolboy who excelled all his peers at the game of "even and odd" which I paraphrase here:

> A "lucky" boy continually bests his friends at a game that involves guessing whether a player holds an odd or even number of marbles in his hand. The winner's "guessing" really involves the observation and measure of the "astuteness" of his opponent. If the lucky boy loses the first round by answering "Are they even or odd?" with the wrong guess "odd," a "simpleton" opponent will merely reverse himself, insuring his defeat in ensuing rounds of play. An opponent who is "a simpleton a degree above the first," however, transcends the tendency to reverse the number of marbles. This second simpleton has the second thought that the rival, having lost, might reverse his guess. So the second order simpleton keeps his second play the same as his first. The winning boy needs only to distinguish the second order simpleton from the first to insure his continued "luck." The winner does this, he confides to Dupin, by "identification"—he mirrors the opponent's expression and notes the sentiments arising in himself as a consequence of this self-refashioning. Dupin rejects the boy's logic as "spurious profundity."[13]

The distinction at work in Poe's exemplary vignette is not the distinction between two forms of identification as the boy would have it, however. It is, instead, the distinction between two binaries—the binary of the signifier and the mirroring of primary identification. The first-degree simpleton thinks only in terms of the rules of the game of odd/even. Thus, he never escapes the literal domain of the signifier and simply occupies one or the other of the poles that foundationally structure the game. The "simpleton a degree above the first," unlike the literalist, is capable of identification, of putting himself in the opponent's place. He conforms his play not to the rules of the game but to the imagined psyche of his opponent. Consequently, the winning boy in Poe's tale distinguishes not odd from even but rule-boundness from capacity for primary identification. He distinguishes one form of binarity from another, and, like an able Lacanian, he distinguishes between the registers.

3: Symbolic (Secondary) Identification

Lacan's discussion of identification in the embedded story of the odd/even marble game recognizes an additional stance toward the positions of subject and other, a stance from which it becomes "extremely difficult to pursue the same analogical reasoning" (Sem II 180). Separated from both the binary simplicity of the symbolic alternatives odd/even and the positioning of the ego as a pure reflection of the other there is a third possibility, a third that threatens to oscillate and return to the first unless a "fundamental bifurcation" is recognized (181). This new form of identification "lies in a completely different register from that of the imaginary intersubjectivity" (181). The new form of identification is nonreflexive, drawing on language and on language's combinatory logic (181), more mechanistic than humanistic (181), recognizing the element of chance and utterly dependent on the pact (182). Built from grouping and succession (185), and possessing a history (186), the alternative to the experiential immediacy of mirroring is secondary, symbolic "as if" identification.

Structurally, secondary symbolic identification is more complex than primary mirroring identification. The difference between the primary and secondary processes of identification, which Lacan distinguishes, parallels the difference between the defensive and nondefensive identifications Joseph Smith describes. Smith points out that "defensive, peremptory, or imaginary identification tends to be an in toto type, motivated by the necessity of disavowing difference" (59) while nondefensive identification recognizes difference and the differentiation of specific traits.[14] While Lacan would stress an aggressive element in defensiveness that Smith does not specify, Smith's description aptly distinguishes primary imaginary identification from symbolic secondary identification. Lacan further distinguishes relations of power (the master rules the servant) from relations of law (both master and servant find themselves equally ruled by the symbolic principle), and it is as relations of law that secondary identifications structure the subject. This transition from relations of power to relations of law constitutes the Oedipal realization.

Resolution of Oedipal conflict results in the assumption of secondary identifications. The capacity for secondary identification, in turn, comes with the gift of language in so far as language constitutes law as a pact between speakers. "Nothing touching on the behavior of the human being as subject . . . can escape being bound by the laws of speech" (Sem III 83), Lacan points out, and then adds that the "law is simply a law of symbolization. This is what the Oedipus complex means" (83). The paranoid knowledge of mirroring identifications, of jealousy, and of antagonism, gives way—with the resolution of the Oedipus and the accession to the shared order of speech—to a sort of role neutrality. "This rivalrous and competitive ground for the foundation of the object is precisely what is overcome in speech insofar as this involves a third party. Speech is always a pact, an agreement, people get on with one another, they agree—this is yours, this is mine, this is this, that is that" (Sem III 39–40). The Oedipus complex is psychoanalysis's archetypal instance of the struggle to reach the agreement that distinguishes what is yours from what is mine.

The Oedipal conflict ends in the acquisition of speech-based attributes, and these attributes require a higher order of thought, a capacity to abstract that structurally transcends the analogic of binary. Thus, the idea of "father," the name and not the person, exemplifies a symbolic order beyond the phenomenal, a rule-based order in which the secondary identifications find expression. Human relations—even the "natural" relations between man and woman—require a third, a "father"; such relations rest on "a law, a chain, a symbolic order, the intervention of the order of speech, that is, of the father. Not the natural father, but what is called the father. . . . The symbolic order has to be conceived as something superimposed" (Sem III 96). While the imaginary primary identification supports self-distinction by exclusion of difference, symbolic secondary identification supports a disjunct subjectivity shaped by inclusion within some overarching order of attributes. The Oedipus complex—an enmeshment of the two, resolves itself with the acquisition of the ability to think the three, to identify a subjectivity amidst all three positions in a sort of psychic simultaneity: "We are only able to express this complex, its triangular crystallization . . . insofar as the subject is at once himself and the other two partners. This is what is meant by the term *identification* that you are always using. Thus here we have intersubjectivity and dialectical organization" (Sem III 198–99). When identification itself incorporates the ability to think the three positionally, to see subjectivity relationally and *inclusively*—as a relation to a relation— the Oedipal conflicts between the imaginary and symbolic give way to secondary identifications.

Lacan's register theory writings continually draw on the idea of a secondary identification which demands "normalization" (EE 5) via "cultural mediation" (6), a secondary identification exemplified, in the case of the sexual relation, by the Oedipus complex (6). Secondary identification springs from "the need to participate" and is "that by which the subject transcends the aggressivity that is constitutive of the primary subjective individuation" (23). It creates a "distance" that allows for the realization of the affects of "one's neighbour" (23). So speaking, Lacan specifically defines symbolic secondary identification to differentiate it from imaginary aggression, mirroring, and fusion.

What Lacan does not do, directly, is differentiate triangular symbolic identification from triangular imaginary interpretation. These competing triplicities open the same potential for inverting and conflicting textual readings as do the competing binaries of symbolic signification and imaginary identification. Some of the variant readings of Plato's *Symposium* stem from this structural overlap and the textual ambiguity it creates. Variant interpretations of the Oedipal paradigm by different schools of psychoanalysis also originate in this structural replication. Even Lacan's own seminars on Poe employ both a symbolic set of identificatory positions paired with variant interpretive sets. Consequently, analysis of these complicated textual problems requires sensitivity both to replicating structures and to the differentiation of the registers.

Interpretation

The Oedipal myth, Freud's exemplary story, typifies the interweaving of registers that narrative entails. The structural complexity of the Oedipus is signaled by its characterization as a "dialectic of the imaginary and the symbolic" for Lacan (Sem III 175). To grasp the Oedipus's complexity, it is necessary to "highlight the dissymmetries that Freud always stressed in the Oedipus complex, which confirm the distinction between the symbolic and the imaginary" (172). These dissymmetries are a signal of dialectical process and whether the dialectics are Freudian and Oedipal or Hegelian and philosophical the dialectical triad reiterates a process where two opposed ideas at the moment of synthesis yield a "three-in-oneness" (Bowie, *Lacan* 96). But is the three-in-oneness of the Oedipal conflict structurally equivalent to the triangularity that yields the set of secondary identifications shaping a subject position? This question is a complex question, and to answer it, Lacan's discussion of the symbolic identification and its threefold structure must be weighed against his discussion of the imaginary triangle that introduces the notion of the phallus as a third term requiring the subject to both identify with and interpret a gender role.

3: Imaginary Interpretation

Lacan devotes a section of his elaboration of Schema R to a discussion of the imaginary triad in part as an explication of his schema itself, and in part as a response to the theories of object relations psychology. The points of the imaginary triangle are defined by the now familiar connection between o′ and o, the specular relation, with the addition of the S, the position in which "the subject identifies himself . . . with himself as a living being" (EE 196). Thus the terms of this triangle define the subject, the subject's ego, and the subject's specular image (197). Structurally, the imaginary triangle is the homologue (*not* the analog) of the familiar Oedipal symbolic triangle of the ego-ideal, the mother as object, and the Name-of-the-Father. At the level of the imaginary ternary, the subject "represents himself to himself" (333). The subject becomes self-interpreting.

The image undergoes a dialectical *Aufhebung* of simultaneous cancellation, preservation, and elevation in the structural sequence spanning the internalization of the imago, the mirroring *moi* identifications, and the interpretation of the subject's role in life as a pattern for action. Muller and Richardson describe this sequence: "Identification with a constellation of images leads to a behavioral pattern that reflects the social structures within which those images first emerged. It is this constellation that is called a 'complex,' a notion that is far richer for Lacan than that of 'instinct.' 'It is through the *complex* that images are established in the psychic organization that influence the broadest unities of behavior: images with which the subject identifies completely in order to play out, as the sole actor, the drama of conflicts between them'" (*Lacan and Language* 28). Thus the imaginary duality becomes an imaginary triad (the complex), and the complex accommodates the imaginary drive toward fusion with a role that must be sufficiently unified to provide a model for coherent action.

The workings of Lacan's imaginary triad are described by Ellie Ragland as the imaginary "in adult life," that is to say, the mature function of the imaginary. Ragland sees in this mature imaginary the continual "quest for sameness" that marks all imaginary processes. Even the adult urge to understand signifies a resistance to the "Oedipal injunction to difference"; in turn, difference resisted amounts to a denial of the castration attendant upon entry into the symbolic, a denial whose consequence is an imaginary empowering, a fictional agency.

The imaginary as a triad between the Subject, the subject's ego and the alter ego appears most commonly in adult life whenever the subject speaks of herself in the third person. This concept is represented on Schema L by the line of the imaginary, which disrupts the direct relationship between the speaking subject and speech's source in the Other of language. The triangular pattern "indicates triplicity in the subject, which overlaps the fact that it's the subject's ego that normally speaks to another, and of the subject, the subject S in the third person" (Sem III 14). Lacan calls the speech of the subject's ego "empty speech."

The speaking subject whose speech is less than full generates the discourse of the "official *ego*." Through such empty speech, the ego seeks the coherence between discourse, signifier, and signified "super-imposed upon one another" (Sem III 155). Unfortunately, this need for complete coherence, clearly the mark of the imaginary register, must be marred by its dependence on the recalcitrant stuff of signification. Thus, "the intentions, the plaints, the obscurity, the confusion in which we live" parallel the sense that "whenever we spell something out, we always have this feeling of discordance, of never being completely up to what we want to say. This is the reality of discourse" (155). This reality of discourse—this discordant inability to fully inhabit a position within the realm of imaginary interpretation—insures that the work of imaginary interpretation will always remain unfinished. Because the symbolic contextualizes the imaginary, and because the signifier inhabits the imaginary identification, imaginary interpretation's unity, its coherence, will always invite inversion. Still, because it belongs to the imaginary, imaginary interpretation of empty speech longs for the unity of confirmation.

Such an urge implies a "mature narcissism," according to Ragland, and a mature narcissism "implies a greater Desire to be 'right' than to 'know' the truth about oneself in the exchange of opinion or theory. . . . Imaginary logic stands behind the human tendency of moralizing (good or bad) and ethical judgments, therefore, as well as behind all binary and oppositional thinking" (*Jacques Lacan* 154). Thus a fundamentally imaginary logic is at work in all diachronic functions which define ideologies, beliefs, and convictions about the world (154–55). "The laws of narcissism and aggressiveness being inherent in its structure, the *moi* of Imaginary absolutism stands behind war, ideology, and religion" (155). Here, then, imaginary aggressivity reaches its cultural expression since it finds its interpretive backing, its justification.

Fredric Jameson, too, elaborates the imaginary's role in ethical interpretation and essentially agrees with Ragland's position. Jameson offers a complex and subtle reading of the interpretive imaginary that clearly indicates the interimplication of the imaginary's structurally simpler processes of identification and internalization. He writes of the assumption of the subject into language and the symbolic in such a way that the subject retains the mirroring imaginary: "It will be appropriate to designate this primordial rivalry of the mirror stage as a relationship of otherness: nowhere better can we observe the violent situational content of those judgments of good and evil which will later on cool off and sediment into the various systems of ethics. Both Nietzsche and Sartre have exhaustively explored the genealogy of ethics as the latter emerges from just such an archaic valorization of space, where what is 'good' is what is associated with 'my' position, and the 'bad' simply characterizes the affairs of my mirror rival" ("Imaginary" 357). While Jameson says that "the archaic or atavistic tendencies of ethical or moralizing thought . . . [have] no place in the Symbolic Order" (357), the ethical situation is more complex. The judgment of the good or evil of any position is not merely identificatory. Ethical judgment, as Jameson describes it, involves the act of interpretation, and because it does, the symbolic register becomes the prop for just such imaginary "valorizations" as Jameson describes (357). However, the symbolic order as the Other retains the capacity to negate all such fixed valorizations. Still, the duplication of the three of the imaginary interpretation by the three of the symbolic identification creates rich possibilities for reading. Just as clearly, the parallel threes invite the slippage of position that undermines any imaginary interpretation making reinterpretation a continual possibility.

3 + 3: Imaginary Interpretation and
Symbolic Identification in "The Purloined Letter"

When Lacan recalls his Seminar II discussion of the binary signifier in "The Purloined Letter," he emphasizes the complexity of the symbolic as a register in which the two of the binary signifier becomes less noteworthy than the three of the symbolic identification. "This is what I showed you last year in our probative exercises concerning symbols," Lacan writes. "Things became interesting, you'll remember, when we established the structure of groups of three" (Sem III 181). Simultaneous groupings of three designate the signifier's "synchronic coexistence," and synchronous threes pervade the "Purloined Letter" seminar, defining triplicities of characters, character positions, and intersubjective relations.

The *Écrits* elaboration on the "Purloined Letter" multiplies the many variants of the three, appending several essays which either diagram or discuss triadic mathematical patterns and the replicating sequences of such patterns. Lacan's own paraphrase of the tale's opening triadic or "primal" scene performed in the "royal boudoir" begins with the Queen's receipt of a letter, the unexpected intrusion of the King, and the subsequent entry of Minister D, who senses the Queen's vulnerability. Lacan summarizes Poe:

> At that moment, in fact, the Queen can do no better than to play on the King's inattentiveness by leaving the letter on the table "face down, address uppermost." It does not, however, escape the Minister's lynx eye, nor does he fail to notice the Queen's distress and thus to fathom her secret. From then on everything transpires like clockwork. After dealing in his customary manner with the business of the day, the Minister draws from his pocket a letter similar in appearance to the one in his view, and, having pretended to read it, he places it next to the other. A bit more conversation to amuse the royal company, whereupon, without flinching once, he seizes the embarrassing letter, making off with it, as the Queen, on whom none of his maneuver has been lost, remains unable to intervene for fear of attracting the attention of her royal spouse, close at her side at that very moment.[15]

Lacan's paraphrase provides ample illustration of the overlap between the structural symbolic three of identification with the positioned three of imaginary interpretation. As a prologue to the action, Lacan establishes and defines the roles of the characters in the scenario. Thus, he first introduces the person of rank, the exalted personage, the lady whose honor is in question, and then adds the entrance of the "other exalted personage" who is "in fact the King." The entry of the Minister D, the third character, begins the action that establishes the King's identity beyond a doubt. Thus, a symbolic triangle of characters presents itself, and their triangularity provides a set of positional identifications.

Lacan's discussion in the *Écrits* seminar on "The Purloined Letter" presents numerous variations on the threefold symbolic grouping of characters. The King, the Queen, and the Minister are succeeded by the Police, the Minister, and Dupin, who are in turn succeeded obliquely by Poe's concluding reference to the triangle of Atreus, Aerope, and Thyestes. Shoshana Felman explicates Lacan's triangular schematizations, constituting the "primal scene" as a triangle composed of: A the King (Not seeing), B the Queen (Seeing that the other does not see), and C the Minister (Seeing the letter). Felman constructs the second triangle of the Poe story in which the blind police ransack the apartment of the devious letter-concealing minister only to be bested in their search by clear-eyed letter-spying detective Dupin as a second structure composed of A the Police (Not seeing), B the Minister (Seeing that the other does not see), and C Dupin (Seeing the letter). Felman's analysis emphasizes the positionality of secondary identification at work in Lacan's analysis.

Lacan's identificatory triangles indicate that the letter's displacements define subject positions, and Felman's analysis underlines Lacan's point that such secondary positions may be occupied, in turn, by any character. Positions, not characters, are symbolically constructed.[16] The common critical conception of subjects forced into preexisting fixed roles fails to recognize the plurality, flexibility, and *impermanence* of Lacan's symbolic model as the "Purloined Letter" seminars present it.

The three points on the intersubjective triangle yield "the three places it assigns to the subjects among whom it constitutes a choice," writes Lacan, but he also points out that the same triangle also corresponds to "the three logical moments through which the decision is precipitated" ("Seminar" 31). Decision, in turn, implies interpretation and action, and Lacan's summary of the tale relates the identified positions to what can be known and done by the characters who inhabit them. The King's "glance that sees nothing" (32), the Queen's "glance which sees that the first sees nothing and deludes itself" (32), and the Minister's glance that "sees that the first two glances leave what should be hidden exposed to whomever would seize it" (32) all imply the imaginary. Together, these glances reiterate the three structures of the imaginary discussed by Muller and Richardson.

The King's imaginary involvement, unary and blind, is preidentificatory and preinterpretive; thus, the King sees nothing. The King's "imbecility"[17] takes the letter as pure image, nothing more. The Queen's "seeing that the other does not see" relates her own position to that of the other in an imaginary identification. She is, like the Minister who will come to inhabit her position, "trapped in the typically imaginary situation of seeing that [she] is not seen" ("Seminar" 44). The Queen's passivity and vulnerability well reflect the vulnerability of *moi* identificatory structures. By contrast, the Minister's position interprets the situation because the Minister alone grasps the meaning of the three roles and translates them into potential for action. The Minister sees the entire complex of his own position, the Queen's, and the King's and thus he "play[s] out, as the sole actor, the drama of conflicts between them."[18] The Minister behaves, here, with the "mature narcissism" that makes his role sufficiently unified to provide a model for action. Consequently, his glance initiates the theft drama, and the bulk of Lacan's narration of the primal scene describes the Minister's interpretation of the situation and his subsequent actions.

The mesh of symbolic and imaginary triangularities that compose the Poe scene and Lacan's analysis of it exemplify the complexity of the text. Structures more complicated than binaries afford larger patterns of identification and present internal interpretations. Lacan's seminar, though continually referring to the touchstone of triplicity, contrasts the many interpretations which characters offer of their own behavior with the position of the narrator of the tale. This contrast suggests a beyond of triangularity itself, a beyond in which symbolic identification and imaginary interpretation may themselves be placed within an analytic structure that employs and yet exceeds them both.

4: Symbolic Interpretation

Imaginary interpretation will always be superseded by a system of greater complexity when it has reached its own limits since the structural limits of imaginary interpretation preclude the search for truth. The symbolic appears beyond the interpretive struggles for understanding that constitute imaginary interpretations; the symbolic analysis is, thus, that "which all understanding is inserted into" (Sem III 8). While imaginary interpretation always runs the risk of getting caught up in the content of its object, and "content, the image's symbolism" (27) signifies a hopelessly blurred confusion of registers, symbolic analysis differentiates what Lacan calls the significant (or meaning-making) from the signifying (or that which causes the received message to be acknowledged). Lacan disregards what the message *says* in order to see what the message *does*. As a result, the purloined letter's movement and not its content guide the analytic interpretation of Poe's story.

Because imaginary interpretation contains the symbolic within the imaginary, imaginary interpretation can never free itself from the limits of the ego. It is inevitably productive of empty speech. Full speech, by contrast, establishes the "transindividual" nature of discourse. Full speech is the product of symbolic interpretation. The analyst's role of neutrality gives a clear picture of the position of the symbolic interpreter, and the analyst's role illustrates a clear transcendence of the imaginary either/or. The analyst's role in Lacan's famous schema resides in the position of the O, the Other of language, and this Other of language positions itself beyond all imaginary involvements. Unlike imaginary interpretation, which inevitably speaks from the position of the other and thus involves itself in the resistances and lures of the text, symbolic interpretation remains impartial and uninvolved. While imaginary interpretation sees itself in the subject (Sem III 162), and partakes in the "imaginary mechanisms that are obstacles to the passage of speech" (162), symbolic interpretation identifies interpretation itself *as* an interpretation rather than identifying *with* the interpretive position as such.

Lacanian reading privileges symbolic interpretation. The whole of the Seminars and the *Écrits* may be taken as the broad outlines of Lacan's argument for symbolic interpretation and his critique of imaginary ego-valorizing interpretation. The technique of symbolic interpretation, of "restor[ing] to speech its full value of evocation" (EE 82) requires for its learning an "assimilation of the resources of a language, and especially of those that are concretely realized in its poetic texts" (83). Thus, the texts of Poe and of Shakespeare figure prominently in Lacan's interpretations and teachings.

The very special significance of the letter in the Poe seminars makes of the letter a symbol of an absence. In the *Écrits* seminar on "The Purloined Letter" Lacan writes that "we cannot say of the purloined letter that, like other objects, it must be *or* not be in a particular place but that unlike them it will be *and* not be where it is, wherever it goes" (39). The allusion to Hamlet here at the very crux of Lacan's discussion of symbolic interpretation is no accident. In his Seminar II analysis of "The Purloined Letter," Lacan had earlier written that in the symbolic "everything comes back to *to be or not to be*" (192). While Lacan read Poe in order to illustrate the structure of register theory, he reads Shakespeare to depict Hamlet as the archetypal subject of the unconscious. Lacan's analysis of *Hamlet* thus exemplifies the practice of analytic reading as symbolic interpretation, the interpretation of the subject structured as a language, the interpretation of desire itself. "We shall not understand a thing unless we take this structure seriously," Lacan insists (Sem III 74). Consequently, I will take this structure seriously in Chapter 5, both as an example of Lacanian narratology and as the source of the rules for Lacanian reading. First, however, I want to return to the *Symposium* to explore the epistemological and theoretical implications of Lacan's complex structural differentiation of the symbolic from the imaginary.

4

Lacanian Epistemology

Lacanian psychoanalysis emphasizes language as the medium of subjectivity; consequently, Lacan honors Saussure's observation that "the mechanism of a language turns entirely on identities and differences" (107). Lacan's unique insight is that he sees identity and difference as two distinct processes, each of which functions as a "register" unto itself. The logic of the image and of the imaginary register is fusional. The logic of the signifier and of the symbolic register is differential. These processes and their related registers remain distinct in Lacan's writings, even though each register has points of structural analogy to the other. While duality is foundational in the symbolic register, duality in the imaginary defines the face-to-face immediacy of mirroring interaction whose ultimate goal is to achieve likeness—whether through fusion and synthesis or through Hegelian conquest and domination. Triplicity with its orthodox psychoanalytic incarnation in the Oedipal triangle defines symbolic identity, but at the moment the subject becomes self-interpreting, the self talks to itself about itself in a characteristically imaginary way. Formally, one register echoes the other. As a result, the registers describe identity and difference as complex processes, each of which can vary within itself while remaining distinct from the other.

When Lacan foregrounds desire and its interpretation in his later Seminars, the registers remain as a rich background resource for analytic reading. The registers define the forms, levels, and requirements of interpretability; desire provides the occasion. Before we explore the hermeneutics of desire—for interpretability is desire's raison d'être in

Lacanian theory—we will return to the questions left dangling in the *Symposium*, the undecided questions of the binary, of identification, and of code. These questions lie within the domain of the Lacanian registers as desire's other side because they pose issues concerning the relation of structure to process. The registers inform a Lacanian epistemology the more so because the function of truth positions itself within the registers. Lacan is not content to have a theory of markers alone—whether signifiers or images. Nor is he content to stop with the process of identification. Lacan pushes the structural system, shot through with gaps, overlaps, and incongruities as it is, to the point where the system's disjunctions themselves determine interpretation.

Lacan's epistemology of the registers seeks to position truth vis-à-vis the meaning-making process. At the beginning of his Seminars on the registers, Lacan claims that Freud's *The Interpretation of Dreams* "reintroduced" meaning to an age of science in a time obsessed with certainty. In interpreting a dream, "one is always up to one's neck in meaning" (Sem I 1). Meaning leads to a sort of metasubjectivity in which the subjectivity of the subject rather than the subject itself is at issue. In the process of meaning-making, the subject shows itself as a subject. The gap between the subject and its center of accrued, habitual, ego-invested understandings allows for a meaning that comes from beyond imaginary mastery. "What is the meaning of meaning? Meaning is the fact that the human being isn't master of this primordial, primitive language. He has been thrown into it, committed, caught up in its gears" (Sem II 307). Sounding at least as Heideggerian as Freudian at this moment, Lacan reveals the poststructuralism implicit in even his most structural moments. The subject does not make meaning; the subject is surprised by the meanings it has made.

Because Lacan's structure is both many layered and differentiated, it embraces positions that in and of themselves appear contradictory. Lacan is foundational and antifoundational, essential and constructionist by turns—but never ambiguously so. For Lacan, there are no binary answers to tertiary questions, no foundational answers to complex questions. Identification is not a substitute for interpretation—though in everyday life, and especially in neurosis, this is precisely the case. In fact, taking things personally (the everyday form of substituting identification for interpretation) is such a commonplace that this loss of interpretive distance is familiar to us all. Similarly, the reductive move from symbolic to imaginary is common: when subjects cease to respect the Law's positional definitions, they regress to Hegelian power struggles. Likewise, the loss of truth is commonplace since to refuse the leap into Truth's contingencies is to fall into imaginary reiteration of received constructions, constructions in which the ego is always alienated, always at stake. Such leaps and refusals, such substitutions and reductions contribute to the questions raised in Chapter 1's symposium on the subject: questions of the binary, of tertiary identities, and of interpretability.

Binary Logics

The most straightforward of the issues left dangling in Chapter 1 was the disagreement between Marjorie Garber and Kaja Silverman over the relation of the registers to the binary. Though Silverman appeals to Barthes and to *S/Z*, her conclusion that "it could be said that the symbolic code is entrusted with the maintenance of that order's dominant binary oppositions" (270) is entirely compatible with Lacan's emphasis on the binary basis of the symbolic order itself. In fact, the binaries that Garber offers—male/female, black/white, Jew/Christian, noble/bourgeois, master/servant, this/that, him/me—are classic symbolic distinctions in the sense that these kinds of differences are absolutely foundational for the Lacanian symbolic order. Lacan's emphasis on the oppositional signifier also confirms Silverman's sense of the symbolic as based on "antitheses, especially that variety which admits of no mediation between its terms" (270), and confirms Barthes's view of binary oppositions which set certain elements "ritually face to face like two fully armed warriors" as well (*S/Z* 27).

These "inexpiable" and irreconcilable opposites which found the symbolic order are definitional for Lacan. "Either/or" is the name of the symbolic at this simplest significatory level. This level, as we saw in the previous chapter, is preidentificatory and preinterpretive in structure. Thus Lacan uses the examples of day/night and red/black in the deck of cards (rather than the far more psychoanalytically complicated example of gender) to illustrate the moment of oppositional abstraction that gives birth to any symbolic realization. As binaries are realized they carve up the symbolic into a world of differences—an impersonal world of significatory distinction. The standard deconstructive claim that every binary contains a privileged term consequently exceeds Lacan's descriptive model. Something must be added to produce a privileged term—either the fusion of one term of a distinction with an imaginary image or the alignment of one binary with another to produce symbolic identifications of a higher level of intensity. Applied to a text, the binary signifier as it is foundational for Lacan, for Barthes, and for Silverman can answer little more than the question "What is this about?" And it can answer that question only in explicit either/or terms. "The film *Tootsie affirms* feminism." "The film *Tootsie subverts* feminism." "Plato's *Symposium* locates desire in *heterosexual difference*." "Plato's *Symposium* locates desire in the longing for *bisexual origins*." "Definitive" symbolic claims invert each other because the symbolic is foundationally structured as a binary. Because they are preidentificatory, symbolic claims present themselves as objective statements about some one or some thing. These simplest symbolic claims define which content is worthy of examination; such claims determine what signifies.

Lacan emphasizes the oppositional nature of symbolic abstractions in order to make it clear that entry into the symbolic entails the ability to abstract—to mediate experience via symbols or to provide a symbolic structure that can precede experience, assimilating experience to itself. The structural simplicity of foundational symbolic difference does not diminish either its creativity or its power. The abstract pair before/after constitutes the insight that confers history, causation, temporality. If/then institutes contingency. The symbolic pair above/below founds the more complex symbolic idea of hierarchy deployable in everything from tennis rankings to the order in a "to do" list. Parent/child, living/dead, good/evil . . . the list of mutually defining foundational terms is as endless as the symbolic register itself. Since symbolic terms are foundationally irreconcilable, Kaja Silverman's argument that any attempt to reconcile them is seen as "transgressive" (270) must include the notion that the transgressor of foundations commonly appears silly, sinful, mad, or naïve—not powerful in the sense of transgression as subversion. However, Lacan, like Hegel, privileges the dialectical leap in which binaries are both transcended and preserved. Such leaps are crucial to creativity, and for Lacan such leaps are the vehicles of truth.

Denial of difference in and of itself constitutes resistance, and resistance is a reduction of a symbolic difference to an imagined unity. This is why, in discussions of resistance, Lacan talks about the ego as "representing the ideational mass" (Sem I 23) that moves readily to what Freud calls the "pathogenic nucleus" (39). Because the registers of the imaginary and symbolic are both implicated in resistance, resistance "concerns the relations of the unconscious and the conscious" (23). For

Lacan, resistance appears in language as everything which "brakes, alters, slows up the blarney, or else completely interrupts it" (226). Since language defines the domain of truth, Lacan sees resistance as emanating from the subject's "impotence to end up in the domain in which his truth is realised" (50). Resistance reveals the ability of the imagined to deflect the symbolic at the preidentificatory, preinterpretive level of the content of speech itself. The idea of resistance is crucial to understanding how a term can achieve a "privileged" status. Consequently, the logic defining both the privileged term and the resistance says that all terms are not equal for a given speaker.

Definitional privilege employs resistance in a more complex way to make structural claims about "the world." Such categorical privilege rests on the alignment of one binary distinction with another. When Kaja Silverman gives the difference between male and female as the "most dominant and sacrosanct of all binary oppositions," she points to male/female as a binary that can assimilate other binaries to itself. Such alignments yield malignant categorizations of the strongmale/weakfemale variety, and malignant categorization is a combinatory masquerading as a binary "code." Where such a "code" informs cultural activity, weakfemales will be praised—though their conformity to expectation is more important than their literal performance of weakness. The oppression inherent in such constructions springs from the construct's resistance to strongfemales and punishment of weakmales—both of whom are entirely thinkable within the available terms but "unthinkable" as cultural practices. Resistant readings of opposites sometimes present themselves as egalitarian by denying the very basis of difference, as when Sartre suggests that negritude is an insufficient antithesis to white supremacy since "it is intended to prepare the synthesis or realization of the human in a society *without races*" (emphasis mine).[1] Such dominant and sacrosanct opposites can become tools for creative political statements, however. Toni Morisson exploits the possibilities of the black/white symbolic distinction to label the characters in *Beloved* "blackpeople" and "whitepeople." Thus, Morrison uses the symbolic at the foundational level of signifying difference to coopt the resistant obliteration of racial distinction by a privileged imaginary "unity," to prevent the reductive conclusion that people are just people after all.[2]

Lacan's symbolic register entails the attributes Saussure gives to the signifier itself, one of which is *arbitrariness*. "Arbitrariness is a question of the relationship between a particular *signifiant* [signifier] and a particular *signifié* [signified]: it has nothing to do with the range of the possible inventory of *signifiants* available," Saussure's translator points out.[3] It is arbitrary that 1997 is labeled "nineteen ninety-seven" in one language and "*dix-neuf cent nonant sept*" in another. It is not arbitrary that 1997 follows 1996 which follows 1995 which follows 1994 and so on. Arbitrariness valorizes the gap between the signifying marker and what it signifies; arbitrariness is not a function of the relations between symbols within a symbolic system. Marjorie Garber's constructionist claim that the transvestite functions to expose the fictional basis of symbolic distinction appears to place arbitrariness within symbolic distinction itself. If the Lacanian symbolic distinction male/female were to be made consistent with Garber's "fictional" gender construction, then the question "male or female?" posed at birth would have to be answered by the toss of a coin. Consequently, Garber's critique of difference is neither a critique of foundational symbolic difference nor an exposé of the fictionality of male/female. Instead, Garber's transvestite reveals the work of identification in the maintenance of difference—a distinction between the foundational and identificatory formations within the symbolic register itself.

The Lacanian symbolic order is unique in its arbitrariness, just as language is unique among cultural systems. Saussure compares linguistics to economics regarding the arbitrariness of each and points out that certain elements of economics are founded on natural connections between things. The economic value of a piece of land can be traced through time "bearing in mind that it depends at any one time upon the relevant system of contemporary values. However, its connexion with things inevitably supplies it with a natural basis, and hence any assessment of it is never entirely arbitrary. There are limits upon the range of variability. But, as we have already seen, in linguistics these natural connexions have no place" (81). Similarly, for Lacan, extrasymbolic constraints limit the free play of language in constructing human experience (as distinct from subjectivity). As we have already seen, the inertia of the imaginary limits the free play of the symbolic. However, the kinds of constraints on the economic values of land which Saussure describes more closely parallel what Lacan calls the "real." The real limits the symbolic by its brute resistance to it. If, at birth, the answer to the symbolic question male or female is "I don't know, what do you think?" the sexed symbolic has suffered a blow from the real. This blow from the real is not a failure of the symbolic register; nor is the birth that does not fit "transgressive." The blow from the real shows the limits of the symbolic distinction, rather than its fictionality or even its arbitrariness. The register of the real turns the other registers into unfree null hypotheses, fragile and contingent and pathetically vulnerable.

Combinatory Logic and Third Terms

Marjorie Garber's "transvestite as transvestite" shares a critical complexity with the problem of the deconstructive "privileged term" of a binary since both concepts exceed the foundational level of simple symbolic difference. Every imaginary identification can produce a privileged term where the image overlaps the signifier of the subject. The privilege of the "privileged" term in this instance lies less in its claim to intrinsic qualities than in its masking of the imaginary identification that gives it its weight. The privileged term is thus an identification presenting itself as an objective fact about the world of difference. It is an identification pretending to be a construction. Garber's "transvestite as transvestite" reverses and exposes the logic of the privileged term by situating its privilege in a related combinatory.

How can two become three? How can identification inhabit a world of difference? The "transvestite as transvestite" provides the answer, since the transvestite relies on the simplest symbolic combinatory: FF, MF, and MM as do the female, the androgyne, the male—the *Symposium*'s children of the earth, the moon, the sun. The "splitting" that each "whole" undergoes to become a desiring part is implied in Aristophanes' denial of the androgyne's interior difference—situating the androgyne on par with the privileged unity of the male and the female creatures. But, as Lacan is fond of pointing out, the only way to get a rabbit out of a hat is to put a rabbit in the hat to begin with, and the way to arrive at heterosexual difference is to make a claim for androgeny at the more complex level of the combinatory in which attributes appear to inhere essentially "in" some one or some thing. For Lacan, the third term in the symbolic order is not, as Garber argues, "something that challenges the possibility of harmonious and stable binary symmetry" (12). The third term relies on the foundational binary, expands it into a combinatory, and exploits the consequent possibilities.

That three-termed relations and the combinatories productive of them contribute as much to stability as subversion should be clear from

Freud's emphasis on the Oedipal triangle. The child's Oedipal realization is, in part, that it has a relation to a relation. It is neither the rivalry with the father nor the desire for the mother that defines the Oedipus symbolically. It is the child's ability to see the relationship between the mother and the father as a relationship that both excludes it and yet defines its possibilities. Relation to a relation makes the Oedipal realization what it is for Lacan—the archetype of introjection. In introjection, "something like a reversal takes place—what was the outside become the inside" (Sem I 169). A relation comes to define a position. The reproductive relation yields a child. Or a heterosexual difference yields a transvestite. Lacan sees the larger structural implications of the Oedipal formation: "if the foundation of the inter-analytic relations is truly something that we are obliged to represent as being triadic, there are a number of different ways of choosing two elements from out of this triad. You can put the accent on one or other of the three dyadic relations that are set up within it. As you will see, this furnishes a practical means of classifying a certain number of theoretical elaborations concerning technique" (Sem I 12). Consequently, Lacan's reading of Oedipal relations suggests that the triangle can be read as a set of constructions (paternity, maternity, or reproduction) yielding essential positions (*the* Father, *the* Mother, *the* Child). Or is it the positions that yield the relations? The duplication of relations by positions—or vice versa— is what gives introjection its power, but the ambiguity between constructions and positions makes little difference in the Lacanian structural scheme of things.

The idea that introjection—whether of relations or positions—is somehow tied to the nature of the combinatory does make a difference, since it is at the heart of a dispute between Lacan and those branches of analysis that presume (as social constructionists do) that introjection is a structurally simpler and historically prior process to projection. Constructionists hold that ideas (or ideologies or codes) are introjected, taken in, internalized, and then projected onto the world where they construct what passes for "reality." Lacan argues the reverse, that the subject must be able to alienate its position in a projection before it has the ability to enact specific identificatory attributes. Prior to projection, the world of difference is radically disjunct from the subject. In a study of subjective self-fashioning, Stephen Greenblatt refers to a similar relation of imaginary to symbolic, claiming that the subject needs a mirror site or point of "histrionic entry" into any symbolic system of roles.

Lacking such a point of histrionic entry, the subject is unable to grasp what is symbolically expected of it.[4]

Secondary symbolic identification, attributing some quality to some one or some thing, is itself situated within the greater combinatory logic that turns the binary into a grid. Lacan refers frequently both to the combinatory and to the grid, taking as a granted Saussure's dictum that it is a positivist oversimplification to claim that a speaker utters a word because it stands for the idea the speaker wants to express. "In reality, the idea evokes not just one form but a whole latent system, through which the oppositions involved in the constitution of that sign are made available. The sign by itself would have no meaning of its own" (128) writes Saussure. The signifier "run," for instance, is meaningless. Outside of either context or combinatory, it is impossible to tell whether "run" is a noun or a verb—much less what it "means." Thus Lacan points out that what characterizes language is "the system of signifiers as such" (Sem III 119). Signifiers as such in turn imply "a complex relationship of totality to totality, or more exactly of entire system to entire system, of universe of signifiers to universe of signifiers" (119), systems so vastly in excess of the subject that they yield the unconscious.

The Lacanian unconscious structured like a language "covers all human lived experience like a web . . . it's always there, more or less latent, and . . . it's one of the necessary elements of human adaptation" (112). Even the simplest linguistic element in the unconscious, the phoneme, participates in a vast set of combinatories. In the language system, /p/ is consonant/not vowel, unvoiced/not voiced, anterior/not coronal, labial/not affricate and so on incorporating a host of binary differences into what appears to signify the essence of the phoneme itself.[5] What appears to be an independent free-floating signifying unit in the unconscious is a signifier in suspension. Such "unary" signifiers signify in combination with other signifiers. In other words, the unary signifier in the unconscious participates in the simplest of all linearities: it becomes the signifier for another signifier. Consequently, the unary signifier participates in the combinatory of combinatories that defines the unconscious as a series of displacements. For Lacan, the end of analysis is "the realisation of the subject through speech which comes from elsewhere, traversing it" (Sem II 233). This elsewhere—of the overdetermined signifier in the unconscious with its contradictory logic of plurality in linearity—frames simpler combinatory relations, secondary identifications, and foundational symbolic distinctions, exceeding them all.

Lacan himself suggests that a "quadripartite structure" is required to depict the unconscious (French *Écrits* 774). This is because, logically, four terms are necessarily overdetermined. Lacan does not see the fourth term in the general structural way, however, and his schemata illustrate his avoidance of simple spatial overdetermination. Instead, Lacan sees the fourth term as the letter in Poe's tale which transits from one position to another, marking each position in succession as it moves from the Queen to the Minster and finally to detective Dupin. Recall that the letter which initiates the action in Poe's story is never opened or read. From the beginning of the story till the end, we do not know the contents of the purloined letter. The letter's position, its motion, and its ability to mark whomever possesses it (or is possessed by it) makes the letter the very emblem of an unconscious discourse. Any unconscious discourse will appear as an unopened letter in the pattern of identifications and positions it supports. The movement of the unread letter from hand to hand adds linearity, temporalizing the combinary of positions and making them into a series.

In his hypothesis of the unconscious structured as a language, Lacan embraces the second Saussurean characteristic of the symbolic order, this principle of the linearity of the signal. The linguistic signal has a temporal characteristic, Saussure writes. The signal *"occupies a certain temporal space"* (69–70). Lacan complicates Saussure's basic idea of temporality considerably, emphasizing a linearity that involves tempo and discontinuity: "There are properly symbolic laws of intervals, of suspension, and of resolution, there are suspensions and scansions that mark the structure of every calculation, the effect of which is that it's precisely not in a continuous manner that this internal sentence, lets say, gets registered" (Sem III 112). Lacan's Saussurean space is *"measured in just one dimension*: it is a line" (70). This, too, Lacan complicates, and in emphasizing the musical metaphor so characteristic of his vision of subjectivity, Lacan writes of discourse that "it is not quite exact to say that it is a simple line, it is more probably a set of several lines, a stave" (Sem III 54). The act of speaking, like the discourse of which it is a part, "is not deployed on one lane alone" (Sem I 130).

Lacan's definition of discourse adds the idea of linearity to the combinatory, a vision he finds in Freud who "quite straightforwardly takes the discourse to be a reality in its own right . . . a bundle of juxtaposed discourses which overlap, follow on from each other, forming a dimension, a layer, a dossier" (Sem I 22). Consequently, Lacan sees cultural life as divided into "several planes" whose "multiplicity . . . does not make life very easy for the individual, because conflicts ceaselessly are bringing them into opposition" (198). Here, in the midst of symbolic multiplicity, the idea of opposition still persists, as does the triad of the law as the simplest structure of the combinatory: "In as much as the different languages of a civilisation gain in complexity, its tie to the most primitive forms of the law comes down to this essential point . . . which is the Oedipus complex" (198). Given the persistance of binary oppositions and triadic complexes in the music of discourse, Lacan logically sees the analyst's task as that of discerning the "various levels of what is at stake" (109). Thus, he sees the analysand's discourse as a "cryptogram," and it is the analyst's job to translate the whole of it "in the guise of a restoration of the past" (13–14). Lacan's evocative description of the universe of discourse is worth quoting in full:

> You know only too well the everlasting disputes there are on every theme and on every subject, with greater or lesser ambiguity depending on the zones of interhuman action, and the manifest discordance between the different symbolic systems which prescribe action, the religious, juridical, scientific, political systems. There is neither superposition, nor conjunction of these references—between them there are gaps, faults, rents. That is why we cannot conceive of human discourse as being unitary. Every emission of speech is always, up to a certain point, under an inner necessity to err. (Sem I 264)

Speech is thus an exercise in omission that makes error inevitable.

Given the complex overlapping of discourses, to translate the combinatory of combinatories into something like a linear history of the subject is no small task, yet this is the impossible function of speech as it joins the registers interpretively. Speech is the subject's demand for recognition. Speaking subjects wish to be believed, to be heard and understood "on the plane of knowledge" (Sem I 168). In the previous chapter, we saw that Lacan depicts this everyday speech as a search for recognition in his "imaginary triangle" of Schema L, the three-termed interpretation which illustrates that "it's the subject's ego that normally speaks to another and of the subject . . . in the third person (Sem III 14). The ego system and its knowledge comprise "a whole organisation of certainties, beliefs, of coordinates, of references, which constitute in the strictest sense what Freud right from the beginning called an ideational system" (Sem I 23). Lacan locates what is intellectual at the level of "the *ego*-phenomena" and relates this intellectualization both to defense and to resistance. Speech, as the central feature of psychoanalysis, must be understood within a three- rather than two-termed relation. Lacan uses the "Purloined Letter" with its trio of participants to illustrate the triangular logic implied by imputing knowledge to others, seeing such third-person knowing "in this double gaze whereby I see that the other sees me, and that any intervening third party sees me being seen. There is never a simple duplicity of terms. It is not that I see the other, I see him seeing me, which implicates the third term, namely that he knows that I see him. The circle is closed. There are always three terms in the structure, even if these three terms are not explicitly present" (218). Thus, thinking in the third person is quite literal for Lacan.[6]

Just as the path of the purloined letter can be traced through echoing patterns of interaction, everyday "elementary" interpretation "comprises an element of . . . repetitive [meaning], it proceeds by reiteration" (Sem III 22). By repetition and reiteration, empty speech creates and perpetuates its misrecognitions. Misrecognition is Lacan's term for the "organisation of affirmations and negations to which the subject is attached" (Sem I 167). To get beyond the analysand's habitual misrecognition, the analyst looks to "the knowledge which guides and directs the misrecognition" (168). The analyst is a formalist, capable of being "formative for the subject" (278); the analyst is not the subject who knows, not the one who substitutes understanding for misrecognition. Lacan is careful to point out that the analyst doesn't guide the subject to knowledge but rather engages with the subject in a dialectic that reveals the paths by which access to knowledge is gained. The point, he says, is not that the subject's empty speech is wrong—that is a given. The point is to show the subject "that he speaks poorly . . . without knowing, as one who is ignorant, because what counts are the paths of his error" (278).

The subject as analysand is not particularly interested in achieving full speech or in rising above error. The subject wants answers, wants the analytic "fix." Consequently, at the interpretive level, transference expresses the same reductive movement from symbolic to imaginary expressed in simpler logical levels as resistance and aggressivity. In fact, Lacan asks us to realize that "the apparent contradictions regarding transference, simultaneously resistance and motor of the analysis, can only be understood within the dialectic of the imaginary and the symbolic" (Sem I 284). Thus, Lacan says, transference is "plurivalent." Transference creates an illusion of presence that stuctures the subject's perception of its world.

Just as Lacan positions transference and resistance between the registers, Daniel Dayan positions "code" and "ideology" in film between the imaginary and the symbolic. Rather than trying to assign the idea of code categorically to either the imaginary or the symbolic as Althusser, Silverman and others have done, Dayan makes the Lacanian move of using the registers to deconstruct the means by which codes construct versions of reality. Dayan explains referentiality in terms of the interaction of the registers:

> What Lacan shows is that language cannot function outside of the imaginary. The conjunction of the language system and the imaginary produces the effect of reality: the referential dimension of language. What we perceive as "reality" is definable as the intersection of two functions, either of which may be lacking. In that language is a system of differences, the meaning of a statement is produced negatively, i.e., by elimination of the other possibilities formally allowed by the system. The domain of the imaginary translates this negative meaning into a positive one. (25)

In other words, a statement about "reality" that is meaningful and referential can only arise from the interaction of the symbolic and the imaginary registers.

In spite of his many comments denying the value of the theoretical concept of the code, Lacan does invoke an idea of code quite like Dayan's in his first attempt to explain the subversion of the subject by its linguistic unconscious. Thus, Lacan's seminars on desire and its interpretation presented in late 1958 outline the discourse of desire in a sequence of three schemata.[7] Schema 1 introduces the topology of the relation of the subject to the signifier as this relation is observable in the linguistic act. This simple drawing expresses the paradox of diachrony and synchrony at work in the discursive line which moves forward along a vector of discrete linguistic elements while being retroactively hooked by a reverse vector expressive of the subject's intent, an intent grounded in need. Lacan labels the points at which the vectors intersect the "code" [C] and the "message" [M], defining code as a "synchronic system of signifiers that commands for the subject the access to the sought-after satisfaction and therefore retroactively imposes on need a broken structure" (264). The following Schema 2 replaces the locus of the code with the Other [Autre] and a final Schema 3 develops the pattern with the addition of the imaginary register's elements. A much-revised version of these drawings appears in Lacan's essay "The subversion of the subject in the dialectic of desire" which I will discuss in detail in the next chapter. Though Lacan retains Schema 1 in "The subversion of the subject," renaming it the "elementary cell" of language, he deletes the points marked [C]ode and [M]essage. This unmarking allows Lacan to expand on the double discourse of desire in terms of the registers, whose signifying capacity now emerges from the combined dynamics of the imaginary and symbolic registers, the imaginary acting as a retroactive drag against the forward progression of symbolic signifiers. Taken together, however, Lacan's earlier patterns struggle to define a view of the combined effect of the registers as "code" that Daniel Dayan articulates in the debates over subjectivity and film.

While Lacan would insist that the imago be separated from the referent, Lacan's own readings are consonant with Dayan's move to suggest that a referential world is part and parcel of the subject's reality and that reality is a composite of the imaginary with the symbolic. The codes of a filmic image, Dayan insists "are organized by the system of representation: it is an image designed and organized not merely as an object that is seen, but as the glance of a subject. . . . Certainly classical narrative cinema . . . is founded upon the representation system . . . the perceptual system and ideology of representation are built into the cinematographic apparatus itself" (28). Codes would thus constitute self-interpreting systems. As such, codes become analyzable in their positioning of the imaginary vis-à-vis the symbolic. For Dayan, code, representation, narrative, ideology, and apparatus compose the "reality" known as the film system. The effectiveness of film depends on the ease and invisibility with which the film system reduces symbolic plurality to a positive imaginary expression—thus, the film system is a transference machine. Film's illusory depth creates the kind of stereoscopic perception of several planes that Lacan evokes throughout his lectures on the registers in psychoanalysis.

The High Price of Subversion, or Hegel Goes to the Movies

Garber's "transvestite as transvestite" Michael Dorsey/Dorothy Michaels and Aristophanes' man-woman moon creature participate in a sequence that resembles Poe's trio of king, queen, and minister. The sequence, for Poe, locates power in the king even as it reveals the blindness of the king's position. The sequence of he (king), s-he (the queen as the king's opposite), and s/he (the "third" position vis-à-vis the opposition itself) does not indicate a failure of distinction. Far from it. The third here uses the opposition to its own advantage with the implication that such use will in fact enmesh it in relations of a lower structural order if it succeeds. Unlike Garber's "third" which initiates "a failure of definitional distinction" (16), Lacan's third actually reinforces a distinction and exploits distinction to its advantage. But the advantage is necessarily short term. The permeable boundary is the "boundary" between the symbolic and imaginary registers where border crossings from the former to the latter, from "one (apparently distinct) category to another," inevitably involve the kinds of reduction explored earlier in this chapter. The distinction Garber makes between the male/female binary and the transvestite is actually a distinction between a foundational gendered difference and secondary introjection of symbolic identity—a distinction within the levels of the symbolic order itself rather than between the symbolic and the imaginary.

As an exposé of introjection, the "transvestite as transvestite" expressly articulates the fact of secondary identification. The film *Tootsie* relies on its identification of Michael Dorsey/Dorothy Michaels *as transvestite* for most of its comic moments. Failing to hail a cab in her contralto, Dorothy booms out "taxi!" in Michael's baritone. Lunching in drag with his agent George, Michael is simultaneously male to his horrified agent (playing Dorothy is "a great acting challenge" he insists) and female to the waiter ("I'll have a Dubonnet with a twist" she flirts). The reduction of Michael to Dorothy is inevitable, however, when Michael's use of Dorothy to master his unemployment succeeds. When Dorothy wins the battle for pure prestige, the price of mastery for Michael is imaginary servitude. As the master, Dorothy is alienated in a primary identification for which there is no adequate mirror; or, as Michael's agent explains it: "There are no other women like you— you're a man!" The dilemma of the Hegelian master is that, in a world of slaves, there is no longer anyone from whom genuine recognition can be forthcoming. Dorothy's dilemma is the same. Little wonder, then, that as Dorothy's slave Michael eventually wishes for her death; "I've got to get back to my life," he demands.

The reduction from secondary to primary identification constitutes a reduction from identification "as" to identification "with" the alter-ego. Much of the film's insistence on Michael Dorsey's transformation from a self-absorbed know-it-all to a person capable of compassion comes from its location in Dorothy of the qualities of tact and integrity that Michael lacks. The more he identifies with Dorothy, the better person he becomes.

The humor in *Tootsie* relies on a multiplication of possibilites far exceeding those which Aristophanes imagines at his *Symposium*. The combinatories of gender and sexuality created by *Tootsie*'s characters move the film's narrative line, creating the kind of overdetermined discourse Lacan equates with the unconscious. Michael Dorsey's girlfriend Sandy misreads his interests and assumes he's gay—despite their one sexual encounter. Dorothy Michaels, unable to contain her affection for fellow actress Julie, attempts to kiss her—leading Julie to assume Dorothy is a lesbian. Since Julie has been trying to encourage a relationship between Dorothy and her father, she demands that Dorothy come out to father Les. The whole of the combinatory reveals itself in the film's crisis as Michael tries to convince his agent to let Dorothy "die."

M: She thinks I'm gay . . . I told her about Julie. She thinks I'm gay.

A: Julie thinks you're gay?

M: No. My friend Sandy. I mean, it's crazy.

A: Sleep with her.

M: I slept with her once. She still thinks I'm gay.

A: Oh that's not so good Michael.

M: Look. I've got to get my life back. . . .[8]

With this irruption of the unconscious combinatory into the narrative, the film comes as close to full speech—to the truth of sex and gender—as it ever gets. Here, the "I" as a shifting locus of subjectivity and the gaps and disjunctions between the "I," the ego "me," and the third person ("Dorothy") illustrate the impossibility of enforcing anything like a unified subjectivity in the face of an overpowering combinatory logic. Though Michael talks about killing Dorothy, he expresses concern for the feelings of the others who have become enmeshed with her. This causes his agent George to remark on the changes Dorothy has wrought in Michael's character:

A: Since when do you care so much about how other people feel?

M: I mean, if I didn't love Julie before, you should have seen the look on Julie's face when she thought I was a lesbian.

A: Lesbian? You just said gay!

M: No. No. No. Sandy thinks I'm gay—Julie thinks I'm a lesbian.

A: I thought Dorothy was supposed to be straight.

M: Dorothy *is* straight. Les, the sweetest nicest man in the world tonight asked me to marry him.

A: A guy named Les wants you to marry him?

M: [Stammering] Yes. No. Not . . . he wants Dorothy to marry him.

A: Does he know Dorothy's a lesbian?

Michael's confused dialogue shows how the many-levelled line of speech punctuates itself, since "the moment when the subject interrupts himself is usually the most significant moment in his approach towards the truth" (Sem I 52). In this case, the truth is a good deal more homosocial than the film in general is willing to admit, and the scene concludes with Michael's announcement of Les's marriage proposal: "He gave me a ring."

The film moves rapidly to contain the polyvalent sexualities released by the irruption of the combinatory into its discourse. Where Dorothy had received a ring from Les, Michael returns it—in an inordinately homophobic scene that applies a heavy-handed beer-swizzling, sports-viewing, bar-bonding stereotypy to the work of instant reduction to the reproductive sexual foundations the film has all along sought to rein-force. What we see when *Tootsie* regresses so rapidly to its heterosexed conclusion is an attempt to contain desire within the strictest limits pos-sible, an attempt to let the film's viewers know, with Cartesian certainty, that Michael is meant for Julie—not Les.

The subversion of the subject of transvestism by its dialectic of desire has been evaded. The master's death means the victory of imagi-nary servitude. *Tootsie* has refused the meanings available to it, all but the most reductive. However, in its most Lacanian moment, the film has displayed the "beyond" of meaning. "A meaning is an order, that is to say, a sudden emergence. A meaning is an order which suddenly emerges. A life insists on entering into it, but it expresses something which is perhaps completely beyond this life, since when we get to the root of this life, behind the drama of the passage into existence, we find nothing besides life conjoined to death" (232). The drama of Michael Dorsey/Dorothy Michaels, like the drama of analysis, comes down to the familiar life and death quandry: to be or not to be. The complex epistemology of the registers explored in this chapter provides the necessary context for Lacan's narrative of the phallus and castration. The epistemology of the registers is, thus, the other side of desire.

5

The Discourse of Desire
and the Registers in *Hamlet*

Lacan's pointed statement of the symbolic register evokes Hamlet directly: "Everything comes back to *to be or not to be*," he remarks (Sem II 192). For Lacan, as for Freud and for the analysts who followed Freud, the archetypal subject of the unconscious is Hamlet. Hamlet's "to be or not to be" punctuates the seminars on the "Purloined Letter." Moreover, Lacan concludes his discussion of *Oedipus* and *Oedipus at Colonus* with a return to Hamlet's soliloquy (Sem II 233). This "to be or not to be" is "an entirely verbal story" (233), an alternative statement of "the primordial couple of *plus* or *minus*" (192) offering Lacan the prototypical instance of the signifier. Thus in Seminar III, where the structure of the subject is at issue, Lacan again discusses the "Other of speech" as the locus from which the subject "recognizes himself and gets himself recognized" (168), pointing out that this locus is "the level of the signifier, of the *to be or not to be* . . . the level of [the subject's] being" (168).

Since references to Hamlet pervade the early Seminars in which Lacan formulates his register theory, it is not surprising that the registers ground Lacan's discussion of desire and his interpretation of Hamlet. After putting at issue the reading of Freud, Seminar I explicates the imaginary and Seminar II relates the imaginary to the symbolic. Seminar III (1955–56) develops the crucial connections between register theory and language with particular emphasis on the dominance of the signifier. Seminar IV (1956–57) on object relations and Freudian structures initiates a discussion of desire; here, the general notion of the signifier is replaced by the specific concept of the phallic signifier. Consequently, the Oedipus complex, reproductive difference, and castration redefine the language of register theory. Seminar V (1957–58) on unconscious formations elaborates these themes stressing the role of the symbolic Name-of-the-Father and its connection with the signifying phallus.[1]

Having labored to merge register theory's structure of subjectivity with a narratology of desire in the first five Seminars, Lacan concludes this project with his Seminar on desire, on desire's interpretation, and on the exemplary instance of desire in *Hamlet*.[2] His choice of Hamlet as the archetypal desiring subject is far from serendipitous, since Lacan's lengthy battle to put the decentering of the subject rather than the centering of the ego foremost among Freud's psychoanalytic discoveries implicates Hamlet. From his 1953 "Discourse of Rome" through his first Seminars, Lacan's "return to Freud" has been an explicit polemic against variant—or, notoriously deviant—interpretations of Freudian doctrine. Thus, he disputes the analytic practice of the ego psychologists, especially ego psychology as it is practiced in America, and though he grudgingly respects Melanie Klein, he resists the maternal orientation of object relations as well. Lacan's constant emphasis on the decentering of the subject as it is expressed by the gap between the imaginary and symbolic registers leads him to oppose theories grounded in a good object/bad object or a good breast/bad breast dichotomy, just as he opposes any analytic practice based on a weak ego/strong ego epistemological foundation.

Recapitulating as it does Lacan's break from the International Psychoanalytical Association, Lacan's *Hamlet* may be taken as a politics of praxis. Thus, William Kerrigan characterizes the *Hamlet* seminars as Lacan's own "revenge play in the theater of psychoanalytic thought," arguing that the territory of an English play ruled by Freud's English heir apparent suggests a signifying chain that "moves from Hamlet and Claudius to [Ernest] Jones to Anna Freud of Hampstead, the International Psycho-Analytical Congress, and the famous wound Lacan suffered in 1953."[3] Though Kerrigan's analysis is characteristically witty, his emphasis on Lacan's feelings toward the man Lacan once termed "this master's brat" (Sem III 316) misdirects attention from the very significant differences between Jacques Lacan and Ernest Jones on the interpretation of the Oedipus complex, the phallus, and castration—differences *Hamlet* brings into sharp focus. In surveying the ruptures between Lacanian analytic reading and Jones's application of psychoanalysis to *Hamlet*'s text, I will emphasize the distinctions between Lacan and Jones in order to illustrate the controversy over the practice of "applied analysis," the relationship between the castration complex and the Oedipus complex, Lacan's alternative textual paradigm of the dialectical subversion of the subject's speech, and his consequent reading of desire in *Hamlet*.

Lacan and Jones and Hamlet and Oedipus

Ernest Jones's Oedipal reading of *Hamlet* provides the venue for Lacan's confrontations with ego-oriented approaches to therapy, approaches that recenter Freud's decentered subject in a way Lacan finds unacceptable. Freud himself had staked out that particular Shakespearean territory in a footnote to the first edition of *The Interpretation of Dreams* when he noted that *Hamlet* "had its roots in the same soil as *Oedipus Rex*," an observation Freud elevated from footnote to text in subsequent publications of his volume.[4] Freud defines the question of *Hamlet* as its tragic hero's hesitation in the face of enacting his revenge; thus, Freud finds the answer to Hamlet's delay in Hamlet's own repressed Oedipal wishes. Ernest Jones extends Freud's basic thesis in his 1910 essay "The Oedipus Complex as an Explanation of Hamlet's Mystery," in an expanded 1923 "applied psychoanalysis," and in an elaborate 1949 book-length treatment, *Hamlet and Oedipus*.[5] Jones's claim that an Oedipal answer to the problem of Hamlet's delay was necessitated by literary criticism's failure to account for the play's central plot element triggered a hostile response from literary critics, providing an early instance of the resistance to theory.

To set up his argument for the necessity of psychoanalytic explanation, Ernest Jones extensively reviews the critics' positions on the issue of Hamlet's delay, dividing them into temperamental and situational explanations. He notes that one group of critics attribute Hamlet's delay to "some general defect in Hamlet's constitution" (*Hamlet* 26). This explanation—that Hamlet "was inherently incapable of decisive action of any kind" (27)—Jones refutes from the text, using the many examples of Hamlet's strong actions to counter the image of his character as naturally weak. Jones also presents the literary counterargument—that Hamlet's delay results from his difficult political situation—and then argues against this position as well, pointing to Claudius's tenuous political footing and Hamlet's popularity with the Danish masses. Jones's willingness to argue content against the critics exemplifies the kind of imaginary involvement with the speech of the other against which Lacan perpetually cautions.

Lacan's own review of the criticism points out imaginary invest-ments, noting with humor that the intellectualism of Goethe's Hamlet produces a Hamlet who is "properly speaking, goethean" ("Canevas [fin]" 21), while looking into Shakespeare's Hamlet causes Coleridge to "[do] nothing but find himself there" ("Other" 26). Such imaginary pro-jections are insufficiently critical, since "it isn't enough to say that Ham-let is a mirror where each one sees him in his own fashion" ("Canevas [fin]" 14). In the midst of an attempted Jones-style review of the popu-lar critical solutions to Hamlet's mystery, Lacan's typical attraction to the bizarre and the outrageous manifests itself in his greater interest in two "extravagant" responses to the play: an 1860 *Popular Science Monthly* article entitled "Impediment of Adipose," which attributes Hamlet's delay to his weight problem, and an 1881 article by "a certain Winting," which argues that Hamlet is really a woman disguised as a man who makes up the entire story to seduce Horatio.[6]

Digressions aside, Lacan valorizes Jones's proposed third alternative to the critics' either/or as the properly analytic solution: Against the tem-peramental and the situational explanations, Jones argues that Hamlet's delay is caused by his repugnance at the task of revenge itself. This repugnance shouldn't be attributed to the kinds of conscious conflicts literary critics point to—conflicts between Hamlet's ethical or Christian values and the task the ghost has asked him to perform—since Hamlet's ruminations and "false pretexts" (*Hamlet* 48) exclude conscious conflict as an explanation for his delay. Here, Jones's implicit refutation of the *Cogito* agrees with Lacan's explicit position on the unconscious; their disagreement arises over the relationship between the unconscious and Hamlet's Oedipal situation. Jones basically elaborates Freud's own Oedipal explanation of Hamlet's delay, arguing that Hamlet can't kill Claudius for doing what Hamlet himself unconsciously wishes to do: kill his father and appropriate his mother. Thus, Jones sees a pattern of repressed Oedipal longing in Hamlet's behavior: Hamlet continually sees his duty and continually shirks it and this inaction causes him remorse and self-reproach (52). He then makes shallow excuses for his hesita-tion, excuses that change from one circumstance to the next (53–54). His outbursts of remorse signify reactions to external reminders of the duty he so wants to forget (55). All this points to "a *tortured conscience*, to some hidden ground for shirking his task, a ground which [Hamlet] dare not or cannot avow to himself" (57). This is Oedipus by the Freudian book, a necessary and sufficient explanation of "the core of the mystery" for Jones (48).

Having reached the heart of the mystery of Hamlet, Jones says, almost as an aside to his argument, that perhaps readers find it hard to understand Hamlet because even Shakespeare did not understand him (*Hamlet* 50). Jones's use of Hamlet to put Shakespeare on the couch evokes Freud's own foray into the psyche of Leonardo with which Jones's original essay is contemporaneous.[7] Where *Hamlet* provides the voice of Shakespeare's unconscious, Hamlet provides a stand-in for the Bard, allowing Jones to psychoanalyze Shakespeare in absentia. Jones takes greater and greater liberties in each elaboration of his analysis, drawing on the equally imaginative literary biographies of Frank Harris.[8] From Harris, Jones borrows a supposed William Shakespeare/Mary Fitton/William Herbert love triangle to explain Shakespeare's vivid depiction of Gertrude's "faithlessness," a faithlessness that impresses Shakespeare's audiences "simply because Hamlet-Shakespeare had identified her with Miss Fitton" (*Hamlet* 61). Hamlet's excess can only be Shakespeare's; this is a clear-cut case of underdetermination. The origin is obvious: "Behind Queen Gertrude may stand Mary Fitton," Jones concludes, "but behind Mary Fitton certainly stands Shakespeare's mother" (61).

Once he has invented a biography for Shakespeare, Jones creates a childhood for Hamlet, stamped from the same Oedipal mold. Jones's supplementation of Shakespeare's play grows with every revision of his article until in 1949 he confidently writes, "as a child Hamlet had experienced the warmest affection for his mother, and this, as is always so, had contained elements of a disguised erotic quality, still more so in infancy" (*Hamlet* 80). Jones concocts a childhood in which Hamlet had "bitterly resented" having to share his mother's affections with Old Hamlet. Hamlet would have repressed this rivalry and covered over the repression with a veneer of filial piety until Claudius's murder of Old Hamlet stirred Hamlet's repressed wishes. Repression, Oedipal longings, and delay go hand in hand since "to Hamlet the thought of incest and parricide combined is too intolerable to be borne. One part of him tries to carry out the task, the other flinches inexorably from the thought of it. . . . He is torn and tortured in an insoluable inner conflict" (70). Here, Jones's emphasis on diachrony and on historical cause culminate in the kind of argument Lacan find inadequate since Lacan situates "cause" beyond the Oedipus as a fixed structure, in the limits of language itself.

Since Jones and Lacan differ over the role of the Oedipus complex in *Hamlet*, they offer two distinct readings of the mother's role in the play. While Lacan's analysis centers on Hamlet as a drama of desire foregrounding Hamlet's relationship with Gertrude, Jones's revisions suggest that he sees Gertrude as the weak point in his conventional Oedipal analysis. Though he pays minimal attention to Gertrude's position in his early drafts, Jones's book adds an entirely new section on "the theme of matricide" (92) in order to better explore and account for Hamlet's complicated responses to his mother. However, all Jones's explanations draw Gertrude back into the original Oedipal matrix, and Jones points out that "actually matricidal impulses . . . always prove to emanate from the Oedipus complex of which they are one facet, or—to change the metaphor—for which they are an attempted solution" (98). In spite of continual references to Gertrude's incest and her luxuriousness (actresses generally fail to capture Gertrude's "outstanding characteristic" of sensuality, Jones complains in an addendum [159]), Jones ultimately subordinates all references to the queen to Hamlet's Oedipal enmeshment with Claudius. Jones's Oedipal answer to Hamlet's mystery is an answer Lacan ultimately rejects,[9] finding guilt over primary identification between Hamlet and Claudius insufficient because of that argument's openness to the very kind of inversions we saw earlier in readings of the *Symposium* and *Tootsie*. Hamlet might just as easily punish Claudius as torture himself, Lacan points out, since this kind of self-justifying punitiveness is a Shakespearean staple, both in the dark comedies and in the tragedies.

Finally, Jones's Oedipal explanation of Hamlet's delay relies on a sociologically shaped idea of repression with which Lacan takes issue. Though Lacan praises Jones for taking an analytic position toward the interpretation of *Hamlet*, and though he calls Jones's essay on *Hamlet* a "monument" ("Canevas" 19), Lacan sees Jones's limitation as his need to plead for the fundamental psychoanalytic concepts of repression and censorship themselves (19). As a result, Jones's work takes on a sociological emphasis leading to a sociogenetic view of repression. The "needs of the group aren't the only explanation for the interdiction from which the unconscious emerges" ("Desire" 19), Lacan insists, emphasizing his own theory of unconscious repression as the inevitable outcome of the entry into language itself. Jones commits "a deliberate error, apologetic, the error of someone who wants to convince, to conquer an audience of psycho-sociologists" (20). Lacan's central complaint against Jones is, in the end, characteristically structural: Jones's Oedipal explanation is limited because it is "a non-dialectical scheme" (19). Jones fails to take into account the dialectic of desire; Jones centers the decentered subject of psychoanalysis. In contrast to Jones's theory of Hamlet's repressed Oedipal longings, Lacan reads the subversion of Hamlet's subjectivity in the play's dialectic of the Mother's desire.

Desire and the Subversion of the Subject

Lacan's essay on the subversion of the subject is of a piece with the psychoanalytic politics of *Hamlet*. Thus, Lacan presents his model of the subversion of the subject as a polemic against the "notorious deviation in analytic praxis . . . in Britain and America" (EE 293), the deviations of object relations and ego psychology. His interest in illustrating desire's dialectical subversion of the subject lies in this model's refutation of the possibility—much less the desirability—of creating the "strong ego." Creating the strong ego inadvertently affirms the knowing, centered Cartesian subject of humanism; thus, creating strong egos is a goal Lacan rejects as insufficiently analytic. For Lacan, knowing can play no part in Freudian practice since analysis should open the ego to the interrogative voice of the unconscious (295). This unconscious poses its questions through the gap between the imaginary and symbolic registers, between the ego and the subject. These gaps emphasize Freud's Copernican decentering of the subject, a decentering Lacan feels the ego psychologists particularly have forgotten.

Lacan borrows the Hegelian dialectic to illustrate unconscious truth's "constant re-absorption into its own disturbing element . . . a real crisis in which the imaginary is resolved, thus engendering a new symbolic form" (296). Symbolic form, in turn, houses desire. Consequently, desire inhabits the disjunction between truth and misknowing. *Desire* expresses Freud's idea of the *wish* more forcefully, since the German *Wunsch* like the English *wish* connotes "individual, isolated acts of wishing" (Sheridan viii). Lacan's term *désir* "has the much stronger implication of a continuous force. It is this implication that Lacan has elaborated and placed at the centre of his psychoanalytic theory" (viii). Thus, though biological needs come and go, amenable to biological satisfaction, and wishes find substitute fulfillments in dreams and in fantasies, desire—because it is constructed by language—is implacable, "excentric and insatiable" (viii). Desire is the price of admission to the symbolic order; for Lacan, the subject's dues are never fully paid.

In "The Subversion of the Subject in the Dialectic of Desire," Lacan uses a sequence of graphs to connect his theory of the registers to his theory of desire. The result is a psychoanalytic narratology in which the narrative line as a sequencing of signifiers operates paradoxically. On the one hand, the sentence is read forward, through time; on the other hand, meaning is conferred retrospectively, in the "aha" that comes with the punctuation of the sentence. Lacan illustrates this paradox of signification in a sequence of four graphs depicting the "practical structure" of analysis. Practical here should be taken to mean "in practice" since analytic practice itself is ultimately at issue whenever Lacan's discussion focuses on interpretation.

The graphs in "Subversion" situate the subject in relation to desire and show how the subject is articulated "by the signifier." Note the agency attributed to the signifier rather than the subject, the anti-Cartesian and antihumanist constants in Lacan's work. The speaking subject of analysis is surprised by meaning rather than deliberately productive of it. The simplest graph of the subject's discourse is the "elementary cell" depicting the sentence. The elementary cell illustrates the interruption of the "endless movement" of anticipatory signification by the retrograde motion of an anchoring point, the period. At the period, the diachronic line works forward and backward; meaning is simultaneous and temporally paradoxical. In the sentence, each term anticipates "the construction of the other" yet inversely seals the meaning of the sentence by "retroactive effect." The elementary cell thus depicts the march of the symbolic sentence as a signifying line moving from left to right; this line is "hooked" by a backward vector of punctuation looping over it.

Lacan adds a sequence of complications to Graph 1's elementary cell, a sequence that builds toward his complex depiction of the discourse of desire. Consequently, Graph 2 inscribes an imaginary circuit within the simple symbolic diachrony of the elementary cell. The familiar terms from Schema R return in a new arrangement. The Other as the unconscious treasure of signifiers is positioned on the signifying line that moves from Signifier to Voice. The symbolic subject of the unconscious is now slashed through by a bar reflective of the bar that divides the signifier from its signified. This barred subject is distanced from its meanings. Thus it appears on the fishhook of retroaction where it is the last to know:

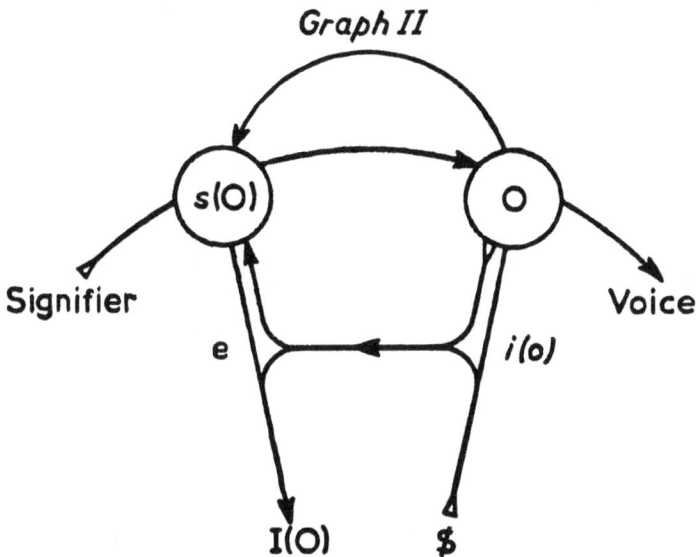

FIGURE 5.1
Graph 2

Note that Lacan depicts the imaginary relation between ego [e] and specular image [i(o)] as a double drag against the forward motion of signification. Nested inside the elementary cell of the symbolic, the imaginary barrier remains. Just as Schema L showed the imaginary alienation as a barrier between the Other and the subject's speech, Graph 2 shows the imaginary as the retroaction of entrenched knowing in competition with the retroaction of significance for control of the I's signifying line. The speaking subject cannot know in advance whether the punctuation will yield inanity or truth.

The imaginary triangle discussed in Chapter 3 finds expression through Graph 2's circuit linking the subject of the unconscious to the ego Ideal [I(O)]. By speaking, the subject hopes to confer its own wished-for image upon itself. "This is the retroversion effect by which the subject becomes at each stage what he was before and announces himself—he will have been—only in the future perfect tense" Lacan explains (EE 306). Thus, the alienating leap of the imaginary identification is a part of the foundation of desire. The identification created by the leap into the mirror image repeats itself in the subject's leap into its idealized self-story. Lacan's point is, once again, to reveal the folly of strengthening such an ego, tempting though the cunning of its reason may be.

The tendency for the subject to become fixed in the ideal ego lends the ideal ego a deceptive air of presence. It appears to possess the "function of mastery." The duplicity of the alienation in the mirror is masked by this illusion of self-presence. The ideal ego assures the subject of an "incontestable existence"; the ego seems "immanent" even though it is not. The relation of the imaginary ego to its immanent ideal is continually threatened by the symbolic, since speech cannot force this presence into words. Thus, Graph 2 indicates how the "ego is only completed by being articulated not as the *I* of discourse, but as a metonymy of its signification" (307). The ego's presence is the part of the discourse that is always missing.

Thus far, the elementary cell and its elaboration as the line of speech in Graph 2 have shown us the relation of the ego to the speaking subject and the relation of the imaginary to the symbolic register. Graph 2 is Schemas L and R rearranged. It still remains for Lacan to position desire in relation to the registers. This is the work he begins in Graph 3. Graph 3 illustrates Lacan's famous dictum that the unconscious is the "discourse of the Other." In desire, the Other asks the subject what it wants. This question from the unconscious inhabits a line that parallels the line of speech, merging the discourse of desire with the speech of the subject in a portrait that resembles the musical staff to which Lacan makes continual reference.

Together, the discourse of desire and the structure of the registers work to produce the illusion of the ego as an ongoing presence, as an historical being. This production is a masterpiece of inversion in which impermanence and permanence exchange places. For Lacan, desire is a permanent and implacable force. The ego, by contrast, is a flickering image in the mirror, the subject an ephemeral verbalization. In a dialectical move, the subject transfers the permanence of its desire to the intermittence of its ego. Now the ego seems to be the stable, ongoing essence of self whereas its desire seems intermittent. This leap of the dialectic is illustrated by Lacan in the double discourse of the Completed Graph of Desire:

The bottom arc of the Completed Graph illustrates the line of speech moving from signifier to voice. This lower arc comprised of the elements of Graph 2 includes the terms that have occupied our discussion up to now—the imaginary and symbolic registers, the ego and the subject. The image in Graph 2 has been doubled here and the line of speech paralleled by the discourse of desire in the unconscious. Running from jouissance

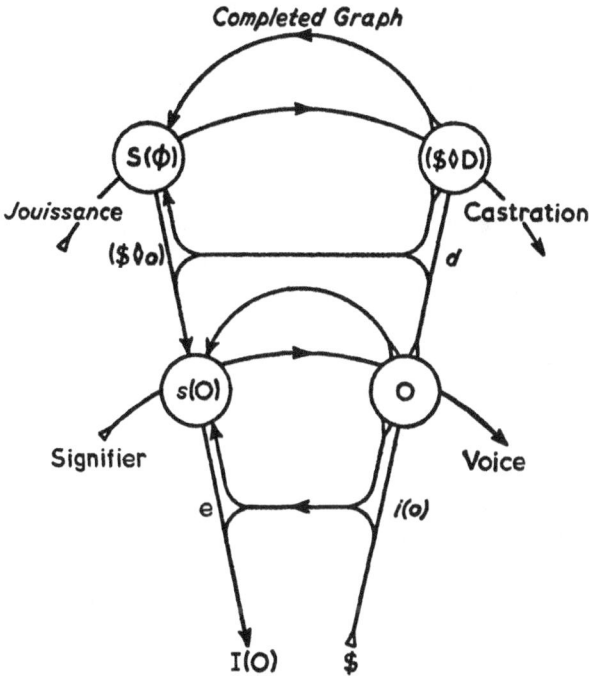

FIGURE 5.2
The Completed Graph of Desire

(enjoyment) to castration (lack), the discourse of desire situates the phallic investment in speech in relation to the locus from which castration inevitably threatens. The Completed Graph weds the more conventional Freudian dynamic of phallic potency and castration fear to Lacan's own distinctive theory of the registers. The analytic language of desire has been added to the theory of the registers, elaborating rather than replacing the function of the imaginary and symbolic in Lacanian analysis and interpretive reading. The merger of the theory of the registers with the dynamics of desire creates a narratology driven by phallic dynamics. Thus, before I turn to Lacan's *Hamlet*, I want to review the role played by the phallus in Lacan's drama of signification and castration.

Triangulations on the Phallus

To understand why Lacan does not directly identify Hamlet's delay with Claudius's crime (as Freud and Jones do) is to understand the role of the signifier and the function of speech as the product of an unconscious structured like a language. Lacan's reading of *Hamlet* follows the same fundamental approach Lacan takes toward other texts, that of an unraveling of psychoanalytic complexities via the differentiation between the imaginary and the symbolic registers. Register theory's structural matrix of signification and identification nested within complex patterns of interpretation prefigures, in toto, the role of a structural symbolic Oedipus homologous to an imaginary castration complex. Interpretation requires both the Oedipus and the castration complexes to fully define the function of the signifier phallus in desire.

As a statement of the position of the subject, the phallus constitutes a paradox in the fully realized pattern of Lacan's completed graph of desire. The phallus is to subjectivity what Lacan's *objet a* is to objectivity—a mathematizing, relativizing marker capable of stitching down a nexus of overdetermination to a meaningful signified. As the ultimate indicator of entry into the symbolic register, the phallus signifies the quantifying, hierarchizing, temporalizing outcome of the Oedipal experience, the point at which humans, for good or for ill, become comparators. This is a difficult concept, which I will discuss at length in the final chapter of this book. For now, it is enough to understand that the phallus is more like a situation than a "thing." For example, the phallus generates positions on the normal curve of weight distribution of American first graders, in *Burke's Peerage*'s mapping of British aristocracy, or on the time line of events in the French Revolution—though it is not "forty-five pounds" nor "earl" nor "the beheading of Marie Antoinette." The phallus is not the symbolic specificity itself but rather the *condition of possibility* that allows a specificity to signify.

The "phallus" is a theoretical construct, not a body part. That Lacan is far more interested in a pattern than a penis seems clear from the virtual absence of references to the phallus in the early Seminars that articulate the registers specifically. Seminar I (the imaginary) does not refer to the phallus at all, while Seminar II (which elaborates the symbolic and its relation to the imaginary) only mentions the phallus once in a brief discussion of Freudian penis envy (272). It is not until Seminar III that Lacan discusses the phallus in detail, but even there, the discussion centers on the role of the Oedipus in feminine hysteria (174–77) and on the supplementarity of the father to the Oedipal resolution that generates the linearity of the signifying chain (319–20). Moreover, throughout the early Seminars and the *Écrits*, Lacan differentiates his structural designation of the "phallus" as a theoretical function from the phallocentrism of patriarchal culture.

To better distinguish Lacan's theoretical construct of the phallus from the cultural meanings attributed to the phallus in other contexts, it will be helpful to recall Lacan's distinction between the image and the signifier. As an imaginary imago, the phallus has a rich and diverse cultural history. In its many incarnations—as lingam, as May pole, as "the simulacrum that it represented for the Ancients" (EE 285), this image of a phallus provides the ultimate surface, "bereft of all inwardness" (Bowie, *Lacan*, 128). The phallic image does not depict the male organ; it depicts visible erection, the lot of *homo erectus*, the "power and height, the ability to stand upright, on one's own legs, that fascinates the infant" (*Lacan* 216). The phallic image reflects what every infant, primordially, hopes to be. Against this imaginary image, Lacan contrasts a signifying binary: penis/clitoris. Thus, in "The Signification of the Phallus," he insists that the phallus is not "the organ, penis *or* clitoris, that it symbolizes" (EE 285, emphasis mine). The phallus is not an organ that anyone has. Consequently, for Lacan, the term "phallus" is distinct from any imaginary phallic image and from any foundational sexed difference.

These common cultural meanings attributed to the phallus make referential claims about the world, stopping short of the much more Lacanian distinction between the states of *being* and *having* the phallus. Lacan, by contrast, distinguishes between two conditions of self-identification, describing the subject's ways of defining who and what it is. Point of view is crucial here, since from the point of view of the narcissistic child, cultural differences do not exist in any personally meaningful way—until language as a symbolic Father introduces a world of mediating difference. In the immediate experience of imaginary mirroring interaction, the child experiences itself to be its mother's satisfaction—the child, living in a world of "same," mistakes itself for the phallus. In taking itself to be the phallus, the child alienates itself in the object of the mother's desire. That is to say, this mirroring identification with the source of the mother's desire constitutes the child's imaginary and narcissistic sense of itself; the child's satisfaction lies in believing itself to be the satisfaction of the other. The child's sense of being the phallic satisfier is terminated by the Oedipal injunction instituting a mediate world in which particularizing nominal identity replaces projective mirroring. Phallic matters are no longer matters of being, they are matters of having, and it is the father who has the phallus the mother desires.

Though Lacan persistently criticizes object relations, he turns to Melanie Klein's famous case study of little Dick to differentiate the registers in his Seminar I discussion of the Oedipus.[10] Klein's case is exemplary for Lacan because it expresses the triadic "totality of the situation" (Sem I 84). "She slams the symbolism on him with complete brutality, does Melanie Klein on little Dick! Straight away she starts off hitting him with large-scale interpretations" (68). What Klein, using the toys common to play therapy, actually says to the autistic little Dick that yanks him into the symbolic is: "Dick little train, big train daddy-train. . . . The station is mummy" (Klein 85). Though Lacan refers to the incident as a "brutal verbalisation of the Oedipal myth" (Sem I 68), he emphasizes the resulting "palpitating cell of symbolism" (69) precisely because the set of relations between the imaginary representative objects ultimately introduces quantifying, hierarchizing, and temporalizing symbolic relations. Klein's symbolic message states, unmistakably, that Daddy is bigger than Dick, and more powerful than Dick, and that Daddy's relation to Mommy comes before her relation to Dick. This Oedipal capacity for comparison is the child's structural achievement; thus, Lacan concludes of the Oedipus complex that its "triangular system . . . requires us to see in it something quite different from this solid mass summed up in the classic formula—sexual attraction for the mother, rivalry with the father" (Sem I 66).

The dialectic of desire that Lacan illustrates in his graph of subversion suggests that the conventional family triangle is inadequate to explain the Oedipal crisis. In order for the palpitating cell of Oedipal symbolism to emerge in the symbolic register, a parallel interpretive structure must incorporate the negation implied by castration in the imaginary register where the child once indulged its wish for presence. When Lacan associates symbolic interpretation with the motor of desire signified by the illusion of having the phallus and the threat of its loss, he elaborates a linguistically derived Freudianism utterly at odds with the developmental paradigm on which Ernest Jones relies. Against Jones's monocausal historical sequence, Lacan argues for a castration complex that parallels the Oedipus structurally, a move Bowie characterizes as Lacan's wish to make Freud's Oedipus and castration complexes "fully compatible" (125). Against Jones's developmental biologism, then, Lacan offers the mediated entry into language. The Oedipus is a structure, Lacan insists, and the castration complex is homologous to it. Consequently, for Lacan, the phallus only begins to signify for the subject at the moment that the subject becomes self-interpreting.[11]

Taken literally, the phallus reduces Lacan's best structural orchestration to a monotone for many critics. A phallic investment could be designated by any image the culture erects; the dollar sign, the manor house, or the television interview—all have the power to produce positions of mastery and servitude when combined with their respective signifying binaries of rich/poor, aristocratic/common, or famous/anonymous. Mastery is nothing more than the illusion of private significance produced by an hallucinatory presence; slavery, by contrast, must labor to signify, must struggle with the discrepancies between the imaginary and the symbolic. The Oedipal realization that the subject occupies an interpretable position creates a conditional self-awareness. The news of mastery arrives simultaneously with the threat of mastery's loss. The awareness of lack also introduces the fantasy of restitution. Hegel's description of this state as that of "unhappy self-consciousness" seems painfully apt.

An ambiguous overlapping of the interpersonal with the intrapsychic inflects Lacan's comments on the Oedipus. For instance, when Lacan speaks of the Oedipus and its failure, he says "the father is present only through his law, which is speech, and only in so far as his Speech is recognized by the mother does it take on the value of Law."[12] This is clearly not the Freudian Oedipus confronting the child with the irrefutable evidence of a relatedness between its parents in which it plays no part. Here, by contrast, the Lacanian Oedipus seems to be imposed on the *mother* since it is she who must affirm the symbolic relation of legitimation obtaining between the father and the child. Lacan continues in this vein, adding that "if the position of the father is questioned, then the child remains subjected to the mother" (Lemaire 83), suggesting that the interpersonal is foremost in his mind. If the mother refuses to participate in the mediate world of symbolic relations, allowing immediate relations to dominate, she will not pass on patterns of distanced mediation that reorganize parent-child relations around greater symbolic structures. The child will remain subjected to present power rather than abstract authority.

This scenario has tempted some of Lacan's readers to ally the mother wholly with the imaginary and the father entirely with the symbolic. Such a simplistic binary alignment would be a misreading of Lacan, however, since the imaginary father and symbolic mother also play crucial roles in the dynamics of Oedipal longing and of castration. In Lacanian theory, the mother who can recognize the father's law and reinforce the child's symbolic orientation clearly differs from the mother who can subject the child to a world of duality by questioning the value of the symbolic order. This pivotal Oedipal mother plays her role in both registers. Though Lacan does not point to the imaginary father in the Oedipal scenario above, he often writes of the experienced father, contrasting this imaginary father with the father's symbolic name. The best way to illustrate the multiple roles of the mother and the father in the work of Jacques Lacan is in the examples to which he frequently turns, instances where the imaginary father and the symbolic mother respectively dominate: the case study of Judge Schreber's psychosis and the narrative analysis of Hamlet's desire.

Schreber's Father and the Symbolic Mother

Lacan writes of the "profoundly dissymmetrical character" of each of the dual relations included in the Oedipal triangle's structure. Thus, he points out that the relationship linking the subject to the mother is distinct from the relationship linking the subject to the father. Moreover, the "narcissistic or imaginary relation to the father is distinct from the symbolic relation" to him (Sem I 66). In his second Seminar Lacan goes on to say that the function of the father is important in analysis because the paternal function inhabits "several levels." Lacan points to Freud's case study of the Wolfman as the place where analysts can see "what distinguishes the symbolic father, what I call the name of the father, from the imaginary father, the rival of the real father, in so far as he is endowed, poor man, with all sorts of layers, just like everybody else" (Sem II 259–60). Lacan uses the faithful married couple to exemplify these layers in the man and the woman, distinguishing their symbolic pact-drawn relations from their interpersonal relation with its "imaginary vicissitudes." The wife's symbolic vow does not change her relationship to one man, her husband, but rather changes her relationship to *all* men, just as the husband's vow changes his relationship to *all* women (260). Their vows illustrate the "universal" function of the symbolic order (261). To further distance the symbolic name of the father from the imaginary father of childhood experience, Lacan jokes in his third Seminar that "nobody is aware of being inserted into the father" (321). The father's name and not his person interpellates the child into the symbolic order.

Lacan frequently turns to the case of Judge Schreber when he needs to distinguish the symbolic father's name from the imagined father or from the father's real function. Daniel Paul Schreber was the second son of a distinguished father, Daniel Gottlob Moritz Schreber, a German physician and best-selling author whose theories of child-rearing emphasized physical exercise. His *Medical Indoor Gymnastics* preached the virtues of health in eight languages through more than thirty editions over the latter half of the nineteenth century, making Daniel Gottlob Schreber the latest name in a chain of achieving Schreber fathers—lawyers, professors, scientists, scholars—all with the Christian name Daniel. Lawyer Daniel Paul Schreber brought a different kind of attention to the Schreber name, however, when in 1893 he advanced to the Presidency of Dresden's Court of Appeal. Unfortunately, Schreber's promotion exacerbated his "nervous illness." Only six weeks after his election, Daniel Paul Schreber was admitted to the psychiatric clinic of the University of Leipzig as a patient of Professor Paul Flechsig from whom he had received treatment for "severe hypochondriasis" a decade earlier. Soon after his admission to the clinic, Schreber was transferred to a public asylum where he remained for more than nine years. During this stay Schreber kept the scraps and notebooks eventually published as *Memoirs of My Nervous Illness*.[13]

Schreber's *Memoirs* express his desire to have scientists observe his transformation into a woman, a process Schreber refers to as his "unmanning." This unmanning was effected on Schreber by a God that was itself "only nerve," yet nerve with the capacity to transform itself into rays, and rays with the capacity to transform themselves into "all things created" (46). Schreber's two-part God required of impure souls that they learn God's own language, which Schreber calls "basic language"(49–50). Even the rays speak this language, for Schreber notes that God's law "was expressed in the phrase 'do not forget that rays must speak,' and this was spoken into my nerves innumerable times" (121). Thus, Schreber felt his body "temporarily damaged by miracles" (131) as the upper God Ormuzd used the rays in repeated attempts to unman him and turn him into a "female harlot." During this process, God's speaking rays mocked him, calling him "Miss Schreber" (119). Macalpine and Hunter note that Freud "seized upon the opportunity provided by the *Memoirs* to apply his method for the first time to the case material of a mental hospital patient" (*Memoirs* 10). Thus, in 1911, Freud published "Psychoanalytic Notes upon an Auto-biographical Account of a Case of Paranoia." In his case study, Freud saw the Schreber *Memoirs* as evidence of a negative Oedipus in which, under threat of castration by the father, Schreber had abandoned his desire for the mother yet identified himself with her position.[14]

Where Freud foregrounds the role of the Oedipus itself, Lacan uses Schreber's delusion to elucidate the differences between the registers as they relate to the Oedipus complex and the paternal function.[15] Lacan notes that the Oedipus can have two resolutions. In the Oedipus that runs by the Freudian book, the child achieves symbolic integration "by way of an imaginary conflict" (Sem III 212), that is, via an aggressive relationship. Thus the emphasis falls on a "symbolic realization of the father by way of an imaginary conflict"—a situation whose neurotic reversal constitutes an "imaginary realization of the father by way of a symbolic exercise of conduct" (213). In the latter, fear of conflict leads to the veneer of good behavior. Schreber's delusion, however, belies an interest in the *real* father's function of generation, an interest revealed in a delusional proliferation of small, fantasmatic Schreber men, the real father function being captured "in an imaginary form, at least if we accept the identification analysts make between the little men and spermatozoa" (213). Lacan illustrates Schreber's imaginings of the real in a complex schema that depicts quite vividly the bracketing off of the symbolic Name-of-the-Father and of the phallus (EE 212). With the paternal function asymptotically detached from Schreber's schema, the drawing's borders are defined by the two relations that implicate the mother, the imaginary specular relation and the symbolic Oedipal relation between the mother and the ego ideal.

In his discussion of the Schreber case, Lacan differentiates the registers of the father function just as he distinguishes the registers of the mother-child relation. The boundaries of Schreber's schema represent elaborations on Lacan's Schema R, a schema that involves the mother in both her imaginary and her symbolic incarnations. Thus, the "polar relation, by which the specular image . . . is linked as a unifier to all the imaginary elements of . . . the fragmented body, provides a couple that . . . serve[s] as a homologue for the Mother/Child symbolic relation. The imaginary couple of the mirror stage . . . provide[s] the imaginary triangle with the base to which the symbolic relation may in a sense correspond" (EE 196). In Lacan's Schema R, the symbolic triangle includes a line that runs from I (the ego ideal) to M (the mother as primordial object). Lacan associates this relation between the child and the symbolic mother with the famous Freudian fort/da game, a game in which the child symbolizes the mother's absence by tossing away a spool (her symbolic stand-in). In Schema R this line marking the symbolic Mother/Child relation precisely parallels the line denoting the imaginary specular relation (197). Thus, it takes two relations between the mother and the child to articulate their interaction, and to use their interaction to illustrate Lacan's maxim that human desire is the desire of the Other. The child is dependent on the mother not only vitally, physically, but also symbolically. Since the child desires her love, the child desires the mother's desire. Consequently the child identifies itself "with the imaginary object of this desire in so far as the mother herself symbolizes it in the phallus" (198).

The absent symbolic mother of the fort/da game establishes the place in which the paternal metaphor or Name-of-the-Father eventually finds itself positioned (EE 200). The vanished mother recaptured in the fort/da game resembles the absent real father who is "more than compatible with the presence of the signifier" (200). Both absences are crucial to the child's Oedipal accomplishment, to its ability to structure a symbolic order rather than merely re-presenting its world in iconography. This is why the mother must symbolize her desire, must put symbols on her desire so that her child can do the same. The mother's function in the Oedipal situation does not imply her obedience to the person of the father; rather, the mother in the Lacanian Oedipus must honor her symbolic pact with the father. The mother needn't bow to the authority of a real father; she must, however, demonstrate her comprehension of his symbolic words, her understanding of his author-ity.

Lacan cautions against searching for the "environmental coordinates of psychosis" in the real parents, the "frustrating mother" or the "dominating father, the easy-going father, the all-powerful father, the humiliated father" and so on (218). He points to the ironic collapse of the registers when the father's Law happens to be a literal fact, the "paradox by which the ravaging effects of the paternal figure are to be observed with particular frequency in cases where the father really has the function of a legislator or, at least has the upper hand" (218). The posture of a "paragon of integrity and devotion" provides the father with "all too many opportunities" to be found inadequate, even fraudulent, thus "excluding the Name-of-the-Father from its position in the signifier" (219). This foreclosure of the Name-of-the-Father is the lot of the psychotic, and so it is with Schreber. For Hamlet, however, the former problem—that of symbolizing the mother's desire—dominates.

Hamlet's Desire Is the Desire of the mOther

The relation between Hamlet and Queen Gertrude provides Lacan with the quintessential instance of his maxim "man's desire is the desire of the Other. Since desire, its channels, and its subversion of subjectivity are at issue, the symbolic register dominates Lacan's reading of the play with its focus on the encounter between Hamlet as subject and Gertrude as the Other of language, specifically, the mOther. Throughout the play, Hamlet speaks to Gertrude as Other, to "his mother, but beyond herself" ("Le désir" 23), and he is all the more a subject because he speaks "not with his own will, but with the will . . . of the father" for whom Hamlet is only the "support" (23). Were Hamlet human, he would be doubly dispossessed—his subjectivity captive to the moral imperatives of his father's ghost and his link to his maternal object severed by the her discourse as it emanates through her from the beyond of Otherness. To grasp the dispossession inherent in subjectivity as it informs Lacan's reading of Hamlet is to grasp what it implies to be a construct in the symbolic. Lacan notes that Hamlet and Gertrude provide particularly apt illustrations of the dynamics of symbolic desire because they are fictional characters, not people. The audience's perception of an enacted Hamlet illustrates the function of the unconscious since the hero Hamlet is present only in the discourse delivered by the actor playing the Hamlet role. Just as Hamlet exists as subject only by virtue of his discourse, Gertrude's Otherness is discursive as well. Gertrude, the symbolic mOther, is not an entity.

The symbolic mOther's desire, the desire that recursively determines Hamlet's desire, provides Lacan with a symbolic, significatory explanation of Hamlet's mystery utterly at odds with Jones's Oedipal interpretation. The difference between the two readings can be seen most clearly in the closet scene since Hamlet's encounter with the queen in her bedchamber invites the most literal of Oedipal readings. Not surprisingly, a bed has become a prominent prop for the closet scene's mother/son battle over desire. Lawrence Olivier's oscar-winning Oedipal version of the play—powerfully influenced by Ernest Jones's *Hamlet and Oedipus*—puts Hamlet on Gertrude's bed, not merely in her boudoir. Olivier's literal, conventional Oedipal staging accentuates the difference between traditional Freudian reading and Lacanian analysis since the lust for the mother in the former contrasts with the lust of the mother in the latter. As Lacan explicitly notes, "it isn't [Hamlet's] desire for [*pour*] his mother, it's the desire of his mother" that drives the narrative encounter in the closet scene as well as the plot of the play.[16] Hamlet cannot act because he cannot come to terms with Gertrude's desire.

According to Lacan, Hamlet confuses Gertrude's desire with his own. Hence, the apt ambiguity of the French "le désir de la mère" in which the desire of the mother positions the mother both as desiring subject and as the desired of another subject. The mother's desire and the mother's being desired consequently define two lacks. These overlapping lacks illustrate the negation implied in Lacan's linguistic revision of the Oedipus with its emphasis on castration. Unlike Jones's Oedipal child who knows what he wants but is forbidden to have it, Lacan's Oedipal subject does not know what it desires. The object consciousness invited by the former theory is utterly negated in the latter, making it clear why the subject of the Lacanian Oedipus is the subject of the linguistic unconscious and why the Oedipal achievement of the subject of the linguistic unconscious is separation rather than some sort of hydraulic libidinal repression. The lack in the Lacanian subject of the unconscious and its relation to the ambiguously lacking mOther is elucidated by Bruce Fink: "The mOther must show some sign of incompleteness, fallibility, or deficiency for separation to obtain and for the subject to come to be as [barred S, the Subject of the unconscious]; in other words, the mOther must demonstrate that she is a desiring (and thus also a lacking and alienated) subject, that she too has submitted to the splitting/barring action of language, in order for us to witness the subject's advent."[17] The mOther's symbolic lack initiates the awareness of lack in the subject; the mOther's desire models desirousness for the subject. Thus, the Lacanian subject's tendency to confuse its desire with the desire of the Other, a confusion endemic to the symbolic order.

Lacan tells his auditors that the "ins and outs of the play Hamlet will enable us to get a better grasp of the economy—very closely connected here—of the real, the imaginary, and the symbolic" ("Desire" 39). He point out the symbolic register of desire as it appears in two distinct ways in the play's Act 1. First, the ghost as the dead symbolic father gives Hamlet a message about the betrayal of love ("Other" 30), disrupting Hamlet's illusion of the beauty of his parents' relationship. Second, the symbolic as such is presented in the play's emphasis on rites, and what are rites "if not the total mass intervention . . . of the symbolic register" in the narrative ("Desire" 38). The symbolic rites of mourning have, however, been cut short by the mOther's desire, trapping Hamlet in a paradoxical position from the outset. In order to understand why Hamlet delays, we must "ask what significiance the killing of Claudius has for him" ("Canevas" 15). Killing Claudius means doing away with the object of Gertrude's desire. In desiring Gertrude's desire, Hamlet cannot fulfill the mandate to kill Claudius; the revenge demanded by the ghost encounters the obstacle of the mOther's desire ("Other" 27). Recall that successful entry into the symbolic requires that the mother and the father articulate each other. But Hamlet's mother and Old Hamlet (the imaginary, remembered parents) are embattled, at odds, presenting him with mutually canceling messages. Consequently, the mOther's desire presents a problem.

Once Lacan has situated the driving force of *Hamlet* in Gertrude's desire, he reads the narrative of Hamlet's subjectivity in relation to the signifier of the mOther's desire: the phallus. Recall that the child's options in relation to the phallus are two: to deny alienation by "being" the phallus, or to remedy separation by "having" it. Lacan restates Hamlet's phallic question as "*to be or not to be* the phallus" ("Canevas" 7), linking a narratology of desire to the theory of the registers. Hamlet could act if he could believe he had the phallus, if he could occupy the symbolic position of the parent of the same sex, but Claudius has "cut off" the imagined Old Hamlet and now occupies his symbolic position. Conversely, Hamlet could act if he could be the phallus, if he could see himself in the mirror of a rival, but he does not see himself in Claudius. Even worse, the dead father's castration presents Hamlet with a clear message about the phallus: not even the symbolic father has it. Thus, Hamlet has been subjectified; he has had a brutal slamming on of the symbolic register.

Knowing he lacks the phallic signifier of the mOther's desire but unwilling to admit the fictional status of the phallic construct, Hamlet is vulnerable to the phallus's every seeming incarnation. "The phallus is everywhere present in the disorder in which we find Hamlet each time he approaches one of the crucial moments of his action," Lacan notes ("Desire" 49). It resides in the contempt Hamlet continually casts on Claudius, though the contempt has "every appearance of denegation" (50). Hamlet castigates his usurping uncle because he calls upon Claudius to embody the phallus (50), misrecognizing the phallus in Claudius's "real phallus" which for Hamlet is "always somewhere in the picture" (50). (Lacan does not point out the irony that Hamlet's misrecognition of Claudius's penis as the phallus is paralleled by the Polonius family's misrecognition of Hamlet's penis as the phallus.) A phallus that appears to be everywhere but is in fact nowhere aptly signifies Gertrude's desire. Claudius's elusive position as the phallic investment of Denmark accounts for Hamlet's failure to strike in the prayer scene where he has the clear opportunity to carry out the dead father's command. Hamlet does not strike "because he knows that he must strike something other than what's there," Lacan says ("Desire" 51). He must strike his mOther's desire, but he cannot do so until he abandons his narcissistic attachments, until he assumes his own desire. At this point in the play, however, Hamlet's desire remains the desire of the Other.

The question Hamlet poses to Gertrude in the closet scene is the question of the mOther's desire. How is it that you could turn from your Hyperion husband to this "garbage, this pimp?" How is it that you "roll in the filth" with this man? ("Le désir" 21). The impure nature of Gertrude's desire implicates Hamlet's desire, so Hamlet cannot act because of the recursive complicity of his own subjectivity. In this scene, the audience knows that Hamlet is "fixated on his mother" (20). Because Hamlet is enmeshed in Gertrude's desire, he calls for her reform, for her to assume an appropriate mourning, for her to eschew her sexuality. In doing this he submits his need to the "caprice, to the arbitrariness of the Other as such" (20). Hamlet appeals to this Other, the mOther, not as a unified, entified Gertrude but as a complex of discursive structures, all decentered in relation to her image as Queen. Given the closet scene's extraordinary emphasis on desire and the symbolic register, Hamlet's killing of a substitute for the king seems particularly apt.

The slippage in the symbolic invites an imaginary duplication in which Hamlet finds his "customized double" ("Desire" 34). In the graveyard scene, Hamlet sees himself in an other, and through the mirror of Laertes is able to assume his mourning "as a narcissistic relation of the *moi* with the imago of the other" (24). Laertes is, for Hamlet, "the model role, of support, against which Hamlet hurls himself with a passionate embrace, and from which he comes out literally other" (25). Where Hamlet had been the prisoner of the desire of the mOther, he now "recovers possession of his desire. And it's there the point towards which are drawn all the avenues of articulation of the piece" (25). The doubling of Hamlet and Laertes continues into the final duel, and Lacan points to the punning use of the signifier "foil" as it implies both the mirroring of characters and the threat to mortality associated with aggressivity. The relationship between Hamlet and Laertes illustrates the

Lacanian emphasis on symbolic integration by way of an imaginary conflict. As a result, Hamlet's "customizing job" at the hands of Laertes is the "consequence of the immanent presence of the phallus, which will be able to appear only with the disappearance of the subject himself" (34), at the moment when Hamlet is mortally wounded.

Hamlet's fate is the generic fate of the linguistic animal. In the play that bears his name, Hamlet-as-Lacanian-subject locates the reader's ignorance, composing from an empty playing space a location for what the reader does not know ("Desire" 17). "A situated ignorance is not something purely negative. A situated ignorance is nothing other than the 'presentification' of the unconscious" (16), Lacan points out, emphasizing the structural implications of the linguistic unconscious. What the reader does not know, what the linguistic unconscious withholds, is a signifier. This is the pathos of Lacanian subjectivity to which Hamlet gives a local habitation: "There is a level in the subject on which it can be said that his fate is expressed in terms of a pure signifier, a level at which he is merely the reverse-side of a message that is not even his own" (12). Lacanian analysis sets as its task the unearthing of the subject's mortal message; consequently, language itself takes on a tragic dimension. Lacan has, throughout the early Seminars, constructed a process for the analysis of the "presentification" of the linguistic unconscious in text. Before I conclude this discussion of *Hamlet*, I want to use the play to make explicit the analytic reading techniques implicit in Lacan's early Seminars and *Écrits*.

Rules for Lacanian Reading

Rather than bringing a ready set of answers to the text, the best theory—as William Kerrigan points out—asks questions. "To . . . [make] psychoanalysis and literature illuminate each other, one must derive from psychoanalytic texts, not just theory, but theoretical questions" ("Unbound" 199). Shoshana Felman offers a similar observation when she replaces the concept of application of theory to literature with the idea of "implication" that "[brings] analytical questions to bear upon literary questions" ("Open" 8). Lacanian reading practice takes these suggestions one step further since, for the Lacanian reader, text poses and answers its own questions.

Distinguishing the register of the symbolic from the register of the imaginary in a discourse reveals the question of the text's desire. In dis-

course, castration inevitably threatens a tragic revelation that the possession of the symbolic phallus is only an illusion produced by the empty
speech of the imaginary *moi*. However, the threat of castration is usually
dimly perceived, if at all, by the speaking subject since "the signified is
sufficiently captured by our discourse for everyday purposes" (Sem III
155). Most of life's ego-driven meanings find their confirmation, and
everyday life becomes a dream of potency; everyday interpretation—
imaginary interpretation—takes the *moi*, the ego, at its word. "It's when
we want to do a bit better, to get to the truth, that we are in total disarray," Lacan notes (155). Then, we are forced into the realm where being
and not being meet, where castration snips the sutures holding empty
speech together and the contents of the unconscious spill out of the
wound left behind. Ultimately, the analyst reads the wound and not the
discourse. In order to do so, the Lacanian analyst follows certain rules
for reading made explicit in Lacan's *Écrits*:

First, *the analytic reader must refuse to validate the textual ego by
participating in its demands*. Lacan repeatedly emphasizes that the analyst must, above all, refuse to engage the imaginary ego, the *moi*. Just as
the analysand wants—expects, even demands—participation in his
symptom, text demands the participation of the reader. Text, like the
analysand's discourse, has its own aggressive moments when it attempts
to provoke imaginary identification and strong reaction, moments of
"opposition, negation, ostentation, and lying" (EE 14). Just such aggressive ostentation makes Hamlet's first soliloquy a vivid invitation to
respond to Hamlet's suffering:

> O that this too too solid flesh would melt,
> Thaw, and resolve itself into a dew!
> Or that the Everlasting had not fix'd
> His canon 'gainst [self-] slaughter! (1.2.129–32)

The analyst who refuses to participate in the textual ego refuses to validate the content of these lines, resisting the temptation to speculate
about whether or not Hamlet is feeling suicidal. Looking past the content, the analyst sees the first suggestion of what Lacan calls the characteristic "[mode] of agency of the ego in dialogue" (15), Hamlet's pen-
chant for self-dramatization.

Second, *the analytic reader recognizes empty speech for what it is*.
The problem of a text, like the problem of psychoanalysis, is signaled by

empty speech. Empty speech—the discourse of the ego—attempts to conceal the subject's frustration by its own imagined coherence. In empty speech, text confronts the limits of being nothing more than a construct (EE 41), a construct that "disappoints all certainties" (41) even as the text attempts to reconstruct these certainties for the imaginary other, the implied reader. No textual imaginary can escape the fundamental alienation imposed by the borrowed constructs which disjoin it from its own desire, the desire it pursues, the desire with which it can never be at one (45). Thus, text rambles on, or continually rectifies itself, in a floundering attempt to pin down real meaning; thus, text reiterates and elaborates to prop up its tottering constructs; thus, text fills with gaps and pauses. All these attributes of empty speech come to life in Hamlet's reiteration, chronological rectifications, and elaborations, afflicting his perception of time and allowing him to magnify Gertrude's crime in his first soliloquy:

> That it should come [to this]!
> But two months dead, nay, not so much, not two.
> So excellent a king, that was to this
> Hyperion to a satyr, so loving to my mother
> That he might not beteem the winds of heaven
> Visit her face too roughly. Heaven and earth,
> Must I remember? Why, she should hang on him
> As if increase of appetite had grown
> By what it fed on, and yet, within a month—
> Let me not think on't! Frailty, thy name is woman!—
> A little month, or ere those shoes were old
> With which she followed my poor father's body,
> Like Niobe, all tears—why, she, [even she]—
> O God, a beast that wants discourse of reason
> Would have mourn'd longer—(1.2.137–51)

The analytic reader's response to Hamlet's first offer to take the reader into his confidence determines whether the reader will engage the play from a complicitous acceptance of Hamlet's demands, the textual imaginary, or whether the reader will maintain an analytic distance—whether the reader will be seduced into a condemnation of Gertrude's inappropriately brief period of mourning (or any discussion of mourning, for that matter), or whether the reader will read the shrinkage (two months to "not two" to "within a month") from which this condemnation is constructed.

Lacan's third maxim suggests the way in which the reader avoids enmeshment in the textual imaginary: *the analytic reader remains detached.* The reader must be patient, must be depersonalized and impassive. The reader attempts to efface her own imaginary directions by showing no private interest, no sympathy for the positions the text offers, no individualizing reactions, and no personal tastes (EE 13). This does not mean that the transference, or primary identification, does not take place. This means, instead, that when the transference takes place, the analytic reader recognizes the engagement and distances herself from it so as not to impose her own imaginary limits on the discourse.

The analytic reader does not look for her position in a text; therefore, she does not identify with the text in the mirroring imaginary fashion of projecting herself into it. The analyst sees the text's position as a position—refusing to identify *with* the text in order to identify text *as* text. Discourse reveals its unconscious only to the extent that the analyst remains the detached, indifferent Other of language. Thus the analyst's position is the position of death, since the analyst "must be dead enough not to be caught up in the imaginary relation, within which [s]he is always solicited to intervene" (Sem III 162). Thus, the analytic response to Hamlet's demand that others lionize Old Hamlet, condemn Gertrude, and impugn Claudius, is silence: the analyst withholds judgment. The analyst willing to forego the complicit pleasures of primary identification explores a more complex discursivity via some further rules:

The analytic reader allows the text to reveal its own truth. Discourse contains truth that can never be imposed upon it by a set of prescriptive anticipatory meanings. The analytic reader can note that truth and reply to it only when the text's questions and not the analyst's assume their form in full speech. The analyst need not supply an answer to the text's questions since "true speech already contains its own reply" (EE 95). The analyst's role is merely to confer on the text its "dialectical punctuation" (95)—to note its registers, and to separate the text's truth from the empty speech of the textual imaginary.

What would constitute textual truth? Lacan does not say, specifically, but he does point out that the place to learn analytic technique is in the "concrete realization" of truth in "poetic texts" (EE 83). Perhaps Lacan would agree with André Green's vision of analytic reading as "unbinding" since the text, because it is a work of fiction and governed by desire, contains "scattered traces of the primary processes on which it is constructed" (18). At the level of signification, the scattered traces of primary process arrange themselves as repeating signifiers. Lacan points out, for example, that the bell chiming one when Hamlet sees the ghost and grasps his fate, albeit unconsciously, finds its echo in Hamlet's last act comment to Horatio that "A man's life's no more than to say 'one'" (5.2.74). This "one" reverberates in Hamlet's first hit against Laertes when he cries out "One!" (5.2.280). Hamlet's "one" even echoes in Lacan's own overture to his teaching Seminars when Lacan speaks of the Freudian ego as "that which says no or me, I, which says one" (Sem I 3). This reiterated "one" so evocative for both Lacan and Hamlet points to Hamlet's tragic truth, the truth of Hamlet's mortality.

The analytic reader reads the registers within the web of recurrent signification. Consequently, the analyst contrasts the symbolic *je* of speech to the imaginary *moi* of text in order to locate the meaning of a discourse rather than attempting to derive a meaning from the content of the discourse itself (EE 90). The analytic reader remains aware of the difference between text that directs its questions to the symbolic Other of language and text that seduces imaginary others, discerning upon whom the discourse makes its demands (140). The reader recognizes the two separate registers in operation in order to see the interpretive points of opportunity, the moments for "punctuation." Then, the analyst intervenes in the text (140). Most of Lacan's practice and much of Lacan's discourse remind analysts of the discrepancy between the registers that is always at play in any text.

Signification and identification meet in Hamlet's punning use of the signifier "foil." The pun allows Hamlet to identify himself both as Laertes's mirroring rival and as his symbolic instrument. Their mortal contest, too, relies on the interpretive disjunctions between the symbolic and imaginary registers. On the one hand, the contest is only playing, mock battle, a mere dream of antagonistic passion. Symbolically, Hamlet plays for honor only, enacts his fatal contest even for an eggshell. Since nothing in the symbolic stays put, Hamlet gets caught in Claudius's mousetrap. It remains only to ask what truth has been punctuated by the catching.

To read Hamlet's truth, *the analyst identifies the text's full speech.* The text's own truth has a self-orienting quality that no prosthetic application of theory could provide. At the moment of its truth, a text can be seen in the "solitude" of its immediate and ultimate outcomes as a unique expression of desire. The extent to which a text's truth lives for its reader equals the extent to which that text's drive to fulfill itself constitutes a sort of mortal awareness. Lacan calls this the text's "being-for-death," putting the analyst in the role of mentor/companion to it. The reader can only "accompany the [discourse] to the limit of the *Thou art that* of [its] awareness of mortality and destiny" (EE 7). Here, the role of accompanist should be taken in the sense of the musical metaphor that dominates Lacan's work. This willingness to accompany the text distinguishes symbolic analysis from imaginary interpretation.

Most significantly, the analytic reader discerns the manner in which the text's full speech "reorders past contingencies by conferring on them the sense of necessities" (EE 48). In his reading of *Hamlet*, Lacan's tracing of the path of the signifier "one" illustrates this symbolic reordering of incidentals into necessary pieces of the puzzle of Hamlet's destiny, of Hamlet's mortal awareness. Lacan concludes of *Hamlet* that "death is in sum the pivot-point of the piece" ("Other" 26). Hamlet's death renders all the play's contingencies necessities. It isn't that Hamlet chanced to see his father's ghost on the castle ramparts. It isn't that the first player happened to speak of Hecuba. It isn't that Hamlet accidentally met Fortinbras. It is that Hamlet had to see the ghost, had to hear the player, had to encounter Fortinbras in order to die as Hamlet did. In the end, *Hamlet* illustrates the temporal thrust of the discourse of desire toward its own hour. "For Hamlet . . . there is only one hour, the hour of his destruction. The entire tragedy of *Hamlet* is constituted in the way it shows us the unrelenting movement of the subject toward that hour" ("Desire" 25).

Like the unrelenting movement of *Hamlet* toward the hour of death, the *Journals of Sylvia Plath* have their own momentum expressive of their own truth, a truth marked by perfection rather than by death. In order to more fully illustrate the rules for Lacanian reading that I have presented here in brief, I offer an in-depth analysis of the question of perfection posed by Plath's unique discourse of desire. By allowing the signifier "perfect" to punctuate Plath's text, Chapter 6's analysis listens for the truth of the *Journals* since it is Plath's perfectionism that renders her *Journals'* seeming contingencies necessities.

Page 118 blank.

6

Symptomatic Perfectionism
in *The Journals of Sylvia Plath*

Sylvia Plath crafted her last poem, "Edge," on 5 February 1963, six days before her suicide.[1] Its bald, bold opening assessment, "the woman is perfected" comes like the last word in an argument, assertion and conclusion in one blow. "Edge" is an instance of creative speech whose status as mark and as mirror interests both the aesthete and the analyst. What the artist listens for in the poem is, in the words of Ted Hughes, "the direct speech of a real self" (Foreword xiv).[2] Here, Hughes's humanistic assumptions are clear. There is a "real" self from which speech can emerge directly; the source is a human center. By contrast, what the Lacanian analyst listens for in the poem is "full speech." Full speech allows the real of the subject to find symbolic expression free from the distortions and demands of the ego; full speech voices the history of a decentered subject.

Though Hughes and Lacan are opposed in their underlying attitudes toward humanism, they are agreed on speech's rootedness in the real as the measure of its truth. For Hughes, the real self may be silenced, may remain mute, "shut away beneath the to-and-fro conflicting voices of the false and petty selves" (xv). Note the implied centeredness at work in the notion of a real self buried within, covered over by a false veneer of other voices. Lacanian analysis would not look for the subject's truth buried deep within since truth resides in speaking. For Lacan, full speech delineates a speaking that is as "devoid as possible of any assumption of responsibility" and free from "any expectation of authenticity" (Sem I 108). Lacan's point is not that speech can never emerge authentically; his point is that authenticity cannot be produced on demand—especially on the demand of the ego. Full speech can never be determined in advance. However, neither artist nor analyst will hear the voice from the real until the Self or subjectivity frees itself from the a priori claims of false selves and expectations.

Interestingly, the artist and the analyst agree that ideals pose significant barriers to authenticity. In his introduction to Plath's journals, Hughes writes that "The impulse to apprentice herself to various masters and to adapt her writing potential to practical, profitable use was almost an instinct with her. She went about it, as these journals show, with a relentless passion, and yet in a fever of uncertainty and self-doubt. This campaign of willful ideals produced everything in her work that seems artificial" (Foreword xiii). Hughes's description of Plath's modus here situates the issue of her "campaign of willful ideals" squarely in the Freudian field, since the symbolic ideals of which he writes—the ego ideals defined by "various masters"—are never free from the censoring agency of the superego, are ever accompanied by "uncertainty" and "self-doubt." An even clearer strain of analytically relevant idealism plays at the edges of Hughes's assessment of Plath's journals, hinted at in his passing observation of her "relentless passion" and willfulness. Such signatures of the imaginary ideal ego's exuberance and relentlessness contrast with the superego's uncertainty, pointing toward a paradox centered in Plath's perfectionism itself.

There is no small irony that Hughes—who clearly sees the drama of Plath's idealism—comes to serve as the psychic prop for Plath's ideals. As a mirroring other in whom Plath saw her ideal ego reflected, as an idealized poet whose professional success measured the distance between Plath and her own aspirations, and as the voice of the superego whose disapproval struck her speechless, Hughes's presence stitched together the gaps between the registers of Plath's experience. As a suturing presence, Hughes joined the imaginary to the symbolic of Plath's reality, their marriage a premature solution to her dynamic Oedipal problem of negotiating an artistic self through speech. This substitution of suture for solution, this fantasied happy ending to the permanent problematic of real life between disjunct registers is the wish well captured in Plath's relentlessly self-analytic journals—the "nearest thing to a living portrait of her" that remains ("Sylvia" 153).

The Kid Colossus

Sylvia Plath's *Journals* record her struggle to find a true voice; over and over again the *Journals* confront a wall of silence where Plath feels that speech itself eludes her, where Plath feels not-speaking as "paralysis." To explore the perfectionism and the paralysis recorded in Plath's texts, this analysis follows the rules of Lacanian reading, guided by Fredric Jameson's injunction that the critic "ought to be able to distinguish Imaginary from Symbolic at the moment of emergence of each" ("Imaginary" 350). This analysis stresses the emergence of the voices of the ideal ego, the ego ideal, and the superego as they inflect the reality Plath records in her *Journals*. Consequently, I here emphasize what Jameson aptly calls the "economy" of the psyche, by examining the moments in which the mature relationship between Plath's ideal ego and ego ideal breaks down, "moments which present a serious imbalance in favor of one or the other registers" (350–51).

To read the *Journals* is to read the story of symptomatic perfectionism. Like the letter in the "Purloined Letter," the symptom is "a fourth element, which can serve . . . as *signum*" (Sem I 280). Thus the symptom operates to link the registers of the imaginary and the symbolic into signs which figure against the real of "the organism as ground" (280). Slavoj Žižek[3] points to the element of repetition involved in the Lacanian symptom when he identifies the symptom as "a particular signifying formation which confers on the subject its very ontological consistency, enabling it to structure its basic, constitutive relationship to *enjoyment* . . . if the symptom is dissolved, the subject itself loses the ground under his feet, disintegrates" (155). The element of consistency conferred by the symptom is characteristic of what Lacan earlier called the "narcissistic *Bildung*" and related to the repetitious character of empty speech. For Freud, symptom and repression are connected since "substitutive formations and symptoms . . . are indications of a *return of the repressed*" ("Repression" SE XIV 154). Since the dynamic of repression and return provides a narrative impetus in Freudian theory, and since the unravelling of the subject's empty speech provides the narrative impetus of Lacanian analysis, the ties of both to the symptom indicate the symptom's connection to the structure and function of the analysand's story. Thus Plath's *Journals* are, perhaps, the most logical place to trace the symptom that names itself "perfect."

The first mention of ideals and the first definition of perfection appear in Plath's *Journals* during her early years as a Smith college coed.

In September 1951, she writes that she is not "strong enough, or rich enough, or independent enough to live up in actuality to [her] ideal standards" (35), an adolescent banality that is disrupted the minute it is recorded by a fascinating conversation between an "I" and a "you":

> You ask me, what are those ideal standards? Good for you. The only escape (do I sound Freudian?) from the present setup as I see it is in the exercise of a phase of life inviolate and separate from that of my future mate, and from all males with whom I might live. I am not only jealous; I am vain and proud. I will not submit to having my life fingered by my husband, enclosed in the larger circle of his activity, and nourished vicariously by tales of his actual exploits. I must have a legitimate field of my own, apart from his, which he must respect. (35)

"The present setup" from which Plath seeks escape remains undefined, and here Plath's speech is more interesting for what it does than what it says. This tale of the ideal requires two voices for the telling. That the "you" is as much a part of Plath as the "I" expresses the psychic distinction Lacan has captured in his schemata. This distinctive intrapsychic dialogic pattern will be reiterated in a journal entry one year later, an entry which turns from the ideal to perfection.

On August 9, 1952, Sylvia Plath left her summer babysitting job to drive into Chatham to the Bookmobile where she spoke with a professional writer, Val Gendron, about writing as a career (52). Plath's record of this meeting concludes "I will be no Val Gendron. But I will make a good part of Val Gendron part of me—someday" (53). The secondary identification is clear—it is Gendron's attributes Plath hopes to attain; Plath does not see herself in Gendron nor does she see herself living Gendron's life. Significantly, the female image of successful professional writing Plath draws from her "first author" includes elements of independence—living alone, keeping cats, not having a telephone—that Plath rejects with a questioning "Signs of loneliness?" (52). A later journal entry writes of Plath's visit to Gendron's home as a "pilgrimage—to my First Author." The entry begins with a self-differentiating survey of Plath's own attributes (tan, tall, blondish, brainy, "intuitive," willing to work hard) and goes on to include a listing of her recent publications in *Mademoiselle*, *Seventeen*, and *Christian Science Monitor*, each meticulously recorded with the amount of money she was paid.

Plath's first explicit mention of perfection comes in a parenthetical aside to her description of the Gendron visit. It is worth noting in full:[4]

> Can't stop thinking I am just beginning. In 10 years I will be 30 and
> not ancient and maybe good. Hope. Prospects. Work, though, and I
> love it. Delivering babies. Maybe even both kinds. Val grinning at me
> in the faint light, face in shadow, tough talk, but good to me. I will
> write her from Smith. I will work, maybe drive down wintertime and
> visit. Maybe take Dick even. God, she has been great to me. Tonight
> best yet. All the boys, all the longing, then this *perfection*. *Perfect love*,
> *whole living*. (55, emphasis in this and subsequent citations mine)

An extraordinary change of tone follows the remembered visit and the
planned return. A break, and the "I" and "you" of the earlier idealization return: "Hell, you deserve more than being in *The Ladies' Home
Journal*. If only I could get you in *The Atlantic*: 'The Kid Colossus'"
(55). This deserving mirroring "you" of the other, this literary "Kid
Colossus," is entitled to make its demands on the symbolic "I." From
now own, the ideal ego has a name. Remember it.

The voice of Plath's imaginary ideal ego dominates a fascinating
journal entry following the sale of three poems to Russell Lynes of
Harper's, an accomplishment she labels her "first real professional
acceptance" (75). "Shut up, oh ye of little faith" the voice orders and
then speaks of how "one mortal imperfect Eve" came to be filled with
"a fierce full rightness, force, and determination corresponding to the
ecstasy experienced by the starving saint on the desert who feels the
crackling cool drops of God on his tongue" (75). This ecstatic unexpected literary success was followed almost immediately by the additional success of Plath's winning a *Mademoiselle* guest editorship. Significantly, the Smith college junior felt moved to justify her successes in
a later journal entry: "I am at Smith because I wanted it and worked for
it. I am going to be a Guest Editor on *Mlle* in June because I wanted it
and worked for it. I am being published in *Harper's* because I wanted it
and worked for it. Luckily I could translate wish to reality by the work"
(78). Here, Plath's self-assessment seems the very voice of the reality
principle, acknowledging both the effort, effort's limits, and the beyond
of luck. If there is any danger here, it can only be the emphasis Plath
places on attributing her newfound successes to her own conscious
choices and the false sense of control this perception might nurture.
However, nothing in the entry insists on such control.

Too much of the "infinitely unexpected" was not a good thing for
Plath, and the hindsight of history has shown that she was unable to
accommodate her being to her new life circumstances or to assimilate

her ego to her radically improved subject position. Aurelia Plath describes the "tired, unsmiling" Sylvia who returned from the *Mademoiselle* month in New York to the news that she had not been accepted into Frank O'Hara's Harvard summer school short-story writing class.[5] "I knew Sylvia would see it as a rejection of her as a competent or even promising writer, despite all the writing honors and previous publication" Aurelia writes. "I could see Sylvia's face in the rear-view mirror; it went white when I told her, and the look of shock and utter despair that passed over it alarmed me" (*Letters* 123). The extreme shock induced by the single failure suggests that Plath's successes were in fact premature, processed largely in the all or nothing manner of the imaginary ego—the only psychic agency to which the single blow could be so fatal. The bright exhilaration of the ideal ego find its contrast in the dark demands of the superego, and in Sylvia Plath's case, the dark side poured out "an endless stream of self-deprecation, self-accusation" and even self-recrimination over the very prize-winning stories that had netted her the guest editorship (123).

The events of Sylvia Plath's subsequent suicide attempt in the summer of 1953, of the botched electroshock therapy she received, and of her return to Smith little more than a year later are too well-known to need reiteration. Though she seemed mature in the distanced perfection she attributed to the meeting with her "first author," Plath proved premature in her responses to her own success. Such imaginary prematurity, aggressivity, and vulnerability go together, exacerbated by the totalizings of the ideal ego in the mirror. By contrast, genuine maturity—which Lacan defines structurally as access to the symbolic register—should be signified in Plath's case by the language of the ego ideal/superego polarity. Plath's *Journals* record her struggle to rewrite perfection in terms she might endure.

The Perfect Mirror

Symptomatic perfectionism plays a prominent structural role in Sylvia Plath's psyche as a nexus of her writerly ideal ego, the publishing goals of her ego ideal, and the punitive recriminations of her superego with its inability to countenance failure. Meeting, courting, and rapidly marrying Ted Hughes seemed to satisfy the symptom, providing the perfection Plath sought and giving her the mirror, the goal, and the censor all rolled into one. In her relationship with Ted Hughes, Sylvia Plath encountered the kind of captation that Lacan confines to his description of mating in animal species, the distinctive combination of fascination and seduction by which the individual becomes the captive of a type. It is a relation in which identity is annihilated, Lacan warns (Sem I 146). But the headlessness implied by the term "captation" aptly expresses the human condition of being head over heels in love, and the imprisonment to type that occurs in mirroring automaticity is reflected in Plath's honeymoon journal entry:

> Never in my life have I had conditions so *perfect*: a magnificent handsome brilliant husband (gone are those frayed days of partial ego-satisfaction of conquering new slight men who fell easier and easier), a quiet large house with no interruptions, phone, or visitors: the sea at the bottom of the street, the hills at the top. *Perfect* mental and physical well-being. Each day we feel stronger and wider awake. . . . Yesterday, while we were marketing . . . a blinding shining street between dark pueblos shone arched over by the most *perfect* complete rainbow I've ever seen, one end rooted in the mountains, the other in the sea . . . (145).

Imagined well-being is all of one piece—not frayed or partial—and the experience of perfection consequently generalizes here from life to husband to house to health, even spilling over onto the landscape. Such perfection, such completeness, has nowhere to go save awry, and the following journal entry records that "wrongness is growing" (146).

The vivid language and the omnipotent perfection Sylvia Plath expresses here affirm Daniel Lagache's depiction of the imaginary ideal ego as "a narcissistic ideal . . . involv[ing] a primary identification with another being invested with omnipotence" (202).[6] Just such mirrored borrowing marks Plath's journal entries recording the couple's perfection. There is little doubt that mirroring applies when Plath writes of herself and Hughes: "it is as if he is the *perfect* male counterpart to my own self: each of us giving the other an extension of the life we believe in living: never becoming slaves to routine, secure jobs, money: but writing constantly, walking the world with every pore open, & living with love & faith. It sounds so paragon" (154). The narcissistic omnipotence reaches a final crescendo: "apart, we rotted in luxury, adored & spoiled by lovers. Cruelly walking over them. Together, we are the most faithful, creative, healthy simple couple imaginable!" (154).

The exuberance and omnipotence of Plath's *Idealich*, the "paragon" of the most faithful, most creative, most healthy imaginary couple, feeds the apparent mastery of the mirror image where fragmented desire becomes whole in the virtual world of the other. The other offers not simply mastery but *ideal* mastery (Sem I 148). That Sylvia's sense of mastery is tied to Ted's success and not her own emerges as Plath ponders the gap between her "desire & ambition and [her] naked abilities" (155) in a journal entry of March 4, 1957 nine months after the marriage. Plath seems cognizant of the dependence: "I get quite appalled when I realize my whole being, in its refusing and refusing after my 3–year struggle to build it flexible and strong again, my whole being has grown and interwound so completely with Ted's that if anything were to happen to him, I do not see how I could live. I would either go mad, or kill myself. I cannot conceive of life without him" (156). The realization of dependence and the acknowledgment of weakness leads immediately to a mirroring compensation: "After twenty-five years of searching in the best places, there is just no one like him. Who fits. Who fits so *perfectly* and is so *perfectly* the male being complement to me" (156). Laplanche and Pontalis point out that the independence of the speaking subject vis-à-vis the ideal ego is a sham, and that expressions that seem to suggest idealization of an other are inevitably recouped by a recursive gesture toward narcissistic omnipotence (201). The other person who seems to be the object of discussion turns out to be only a prop for the mirror that shows the ego what it wishes to see in its self. This motion from subject to mirror to ego is precisely the sequence of Plath's musings.

A July 17 journal entry follows the same pattern. The competitive need to excel through her writing which she defines as the central need of her nature "to be articulate" (163) turns almost immediately to her frustration "all reading mocks me (others wrote it, I didn't)" (164) and to her inability to successfully substitute marriage for work. "The only thing that sustains me, yet is not enjoyed fully, is the endless deep love I live in" (164) she writes, and immediately associates marriage with professional frustration: "Without that [love], I would rush about, seeking solace, never finding it, and not keeping the steady quiet deadly determined center I have even now at the end of one of my greatest droughts: It Will Come. If I Work" (164). This seemingly realistic admission of frustration and dependence concludes with yet another triumph of the ideal ego:

> Oh, to live like this. We will work. And he sets the sea of my life steady, flooding it with the deep rich color of his mind and his love and constant amaze at his *perfect* being: as if I had conjured, at last, a god from

the slack tides, coming up with his spear shining, and the cockleshells and rare fish trailing in his wake, and he trailing the world: for my earth goddess, he the sun, the sea, the black complement power: yang to ying [sic]. (166)

The entire pattern of idealization followed by grandiose reclamation can take as little as one line, as in the May 1, 1958 journal remark "Oh, he is unbelievable and the more so because he is my husband" (220).

In late March of 1958, the journals record a now familiar voice: "I feel, miraculously, I have the impossible, the wonderful—I am *perfectly* at one with Ted, body and soul, as the ridiculous song says—our vocation is writing, our love is each other—and the world is ours to explore" (212). Plath muses over her early dating days and her mother's caution that she was "too critical" and would end up an "old maid." "Well, perhaps I would have been if Ted hadn't been born," Plath concludes (212), and her depiction of the many imperfect others she rejected implies that the mirroring ideal ego turns the superego's criticism away from the ego. The ease with which Plath's superego imperatives give way to her grandiosity suggests a profound connection that is vividly articulated in Plath's own self-depiction: "I am, at bottom, simple, credulous, feminine and loving to be mastered, cared for—but I will kill with my mind, my ice-eye, anyone who is weak, false, sickly in soul—and so I have done" (212).

"my jealous, queen-bitch superego" (322)

Since dependence on a love relationship replicates the dilemma of infantile mirroring, its solution must be socially Oedipal, structurally triangular. For Plath, the Oedipal incident took place when Ted did not arrive to wait for Sylvia on the last day of her teaching year at Smith. She went in search of him and found him walking with a young coed. Plath was outraged, but waited several days to record the incident in her journal, by which point it had taken on an oddly narrative quality in comparison to the journal's many flights of fancy and impressionistic sketches. Of the fancied infidelity, Plath concluded: "Irony: in almost two years [I've been] turned from a crazy *perfectionist* and promiscuous human-being-love, to a misanthrope . . . a nasty, catty and malicious misanthrope. . . . So I put the two of us in our separate, oh, infinitely superior world. . . . I got the final insight: not only am I just as nasty as everybody else, but so is Ted" (228). The symbolic entrance of "everybody else" into the closed, imagined, perfect world of two creates a third element that opens up the symbolic combinatory, changing the perfect Ted-Sylvia/flawed world into a spectrum of possibilities that includes a catty Sylvia, a malicious Sylvia, a nasty Ted. This Oedipal breaking of the imaginary mirror seems to have changed Plath's psychic dynamic in other ways as well. From this point on, while Plath continues to idealize Hughes, she now situates him as her ego ideal rather than her mirroring other.

Now when Plath writes of Hughes, she does not take his bigness upon herself. In June, a month after the Oedipal incident, she writes of him "I have . . . the magic and hourly company of a husband so magnificent . . . big, creative in a giant way, that I imagine I made him up—only he offers so much extra surprise that I know he is real and deep as an iceberg in its element" (239). The alteration from being to having is striking; the grandiose voice that once claimed Huges was excellent "the more so because he is my husband" now accords that husband the distance and the reality acknowledged in the capacity to surprise. Where the ego ideal emerges in the symbolic and is recognized as such, we may be sure that the superego will be recognized as well. Where the grandiose voice once recuperated an ideal power, the superego now spreads a pall: "So I have all this, and my limbs are paralyzed" Plath announces (239).

Post crisis, Plath is able to see the dynamics of her ideal ego—the dependency and the mirroring—as unhealthy and unproductive aspects of her own psyche. Now, her journals suggest a subjectivity that is no mere pretext for the ideal ego. She astutely analyzes the problem of the imaginary as such: "My danger, partly, I think, is becoming too dependent on Ted. He is didactic, fanatic. . . . It is as if I were sucked into a tempting but disastrous whirlpool. Between us there are no barriers—it is rather as if neither of us—or especially myself—had any skin, or one skin between us and we kept bumping into and abrading each other. I enjoy it when Ted is off for a bit" (245). The seductive danger of yielding to the temptation to merge is balanced against the damage, the "abrading" that merger brings—especially for Plath. The pleasure she once located in merger she now feels in distance. All in all, the negotiation of the symbolic seems well in hand and we may wonder where the perfectionism has gone. In fact, it has been released a bit, expressed now as a question: "Will I write here in *perfect* health from our little Boston apartment in a month and more?" (253) and a few days later as a wish "I find myself horrified at voicing the American dream of a home . . . my visions of a home, of course, being an artist's estate, in a *perfect* privacy of wilderness acres, on the coast of Maine" (253). The word "per-fect" seems to have unloaded its psychic charge entirely when Plath's notes on animal possession in Central Africa record a "were-lion . . . employed for years in *perfect* contentment keeping the roads of Chirome in good repair" (258). Perfect, here, is just another word.

The symbolic realignment of husband and wife according to the polar dictates of the ego ideal/superego arrangement seems clear when we contrast the previous grandiose mirroring of the seagod and the earthgoddess with Plath's self-critical restructuring of the couple's roles: "I love too much, too wholly, too simply for any cleverness. Use imagi-nation. Write and work to please. No criticism or nagging. [Omission.] He is a genius. I his wife" (258). Plath now seems convinced that a psy-chic separation is vital and that her dependence on her husband affects her work: "I must be happy first in my own work and struggle to that end, so my life does not hang on Ted's"(258). While she still sees herself as necessarily connected to him ("Who else in the world could I live with and love?"), she also allows a new voice to creep in, a voice expressing the lopsided law of the household and her resentment of it: "must not nag . . . but he nags all the time" (258). Perhaps it is a testament to Plath's newly reconstructed subjectivity that she chooses to reenter analysis with Boston psychiatrist Ruth Beuscher at this time.

A very long and detailed journal entry records the feelings brought up in Plath's analysis, and it is significant that the record is cast as her attempt to "work like hell" through the "sludge & crap" because she's paying for the sessions and feels duty-bound to get her money's worth (265). She records the liberation from oppressive constriction she feels when Beuscher says "I give you permission to hate your mother" (265), and much of the journal entry that follows records her aggressive feel-ings toward Aurelia. Her anger vented, Plath goes on to write of her hus-band in terms we have heard before:

> So he has all I could ask for. I could have had money and men with steady jobs. But they were dull, or sick, or vain, or spoiled. They made me gag in the long run. What I wanted was inside a person that made you *perfectly* happy with them if you were naked on the Sahara: they were strong and loving in soul and body. Simple and tough.
>
> So I knew what I wanted when I saw it. I needed, after thirteen long years of having no man who could take all my love and give me a steady flow of love in return, a man who would make a *perfect* circuit of love and all else with me. I found one. (269)

The change from being to having is striking. Moreover, though the entry speaks of Ted and of an ideal mate, it disjoins the two. The language and pronoun choice throughout show a detachment previously lacking. She wanted "a person." She needed "a man." The indifference of the generic second person "you" further distances the analysis, marking the you as a position assumable by the ego rather than assuming the position of the you unaware. Even the narcissistic objectification is foregrounded as such in the claim that she knew what she wanted when she saw "it," and Lacan would undoubtedly point out the aptness of the emphasis on such imaginary seeing. Freed from the mirroring identification of herself with Ted, Sylvia Plath now connects Ted to her father, writing in terms that collapse the marital into the familial Oedipal situation: "I identify him with my father at certain times, and these times take on great impor-tance: e.g., that one fight at the end of the school year when I found him not-there on the special day and with another woman" (278). "I had a furious access of rage" Plath concludes of the return of her repressed feelings, pointing toward a contact with the aggressivity which the mir-roring relation had frozen until the Oedipal moment.

The Panic Bird

Ted Hughes's essay on Sylvia Plath's journals frequently describes the role of the repressed in Plath's writing and Plath's struggle with it. He writes in humanistic terms of her "hidden workshop, the tangle of roots, the cru-cible [that] controlled everything" (156). He speaks evocatively of her "nightmare sense of claustrophobia and suspended life, her sense of being only the flimsy, brittle husk of what was going heavily and fierily on, some-where out of reach" (156). Lacan makes a similar distinction from an ana-lytic perspective when he writes that the task of censorship in repression is to split the subject's world, to "[cut] it in two, into one accessible part, which is recognized, and one inaccessible, forbidden part" (Sem I 195). This separation between the speaking self and the inaccessible crucible, this split in her symbolic world, did not prevent Plath from confronting the gap itself. In fact, Sylvia Plath speaks directly to the inaccessible parts of her own psyche in her extraordinary "Letter to a Demon" written October 1, 1957, in the early weeks of her first teaching semester at Smith.

Plath begins her "Letter" by recognizing her now-familiar paralysis: "Last night I felt the sensation I have been reading about to no avail in James: the sick, soul-annihilating flux of fear in my blood switching its current to defiant fight." Her alternation from fear to "defiant fight" seems to channelize the aggressivity Lacan attributes to the ideal ego. However, just as the imaginary is disjunct from the symbolic, and just as there are no imaginary solutions to symbolic problems, the fighter is no match for the demon. Instead, Plath continues: "I could not sleep, although tired, and lay feeling my nerves shaved to pain & the groaning inner voice: oh, you can't teach, can't do anything. Can't write, can't think" (176). Here, clearly, is the accusation of the superego written in the intrapsychic extremes that only subjectivity can achieve since any external message delivered with such exaggeration would readily be rejected. "And I lay under the negative icy flood of denial, thinking that voice was all my own, a part of me, and it must somehow conquer me and leave me with my worst visions: having had the chance to battle it & win day by day, and having failed" (176).

The entry on her "murderous self" is notable for its half-dozen mentions of perfectionism, and Plath's extraordinary resistance to owning this self: "I shall not give it my name." The two pages are worth quoting at length because they register the disjunction between insight and feeling; no matter how clearly Plath describes the structure of her perfectionism, she still cannot reach the repression, and settles for a program to "shame it" and to go on "knocking its nose in" :

> Its biggest weapon is and has been the image of myself as a *perfect* success: in writing, teaching and living. As soon as I sniff nonsuccess in the form of rejections, puzzled faces in class when I'm blurring a point, or a cold horror in personal relationships, I accuse myself of being a hypocrite, posing as better than I am, and being, at bottom, lousy.(176)

> I have a good self, that loves skies, hills, ideas, tasty meals, bright colors. My demon would murder this self by demanding that it be a paragon, and saying it should run away if it is anything less. . . . I have this demon who wants me to run away screaming if I am going to be flawed, fallible. It wants me to think I'm so good I must be *perfect*. Or nothing. (177)

> Minute by minute to fight upward. Out from under that black cloud which would annihilate my whole being with its demand for *perfection* and measure, not of what I am, but of what I am not. (178)

No more knuckling under, groaning, moaning: one gets used to pain. This hurts. Not being *perfect* hurts. Having to bother about work in order to eat & have a house hurts. So what. It's about time. This is the month which ends a quarter of a century for me, lived under the shadow of fear: fear that I would fall short of some abstract *perfection*: I have often fought, fought & won, not *perfection*, but an acceptance of myself as having a right to live on my own human, fallible terms.(178–79)

The last line is, of course, a lovely lie.

The overwhelming weight of this symptomatic, paralyzing perfectionism accounts for the extreme grandiosity of the earlier mirroring. Mirroring identification has provided an empowering alternative to the confrontation with the repressed, and it is worth taking a moment here to recall the terms in which Plath's honeymoon oneness was framed in order to clearly understand the failure of mirroring as a psychic counterbalance to repression: "He is the *perfect* male counterpart to my own self: each of us giving the other an extension of the life we believe in living: never becoming slaves to routine, secure jobs, money: but writing constantly" (154). Here, in the all or nothing terms of the imaginary, is the demand for freedom—defined as writing—in a world where the rent magically pays itself. This paragon mirror world offers an "orthopaedic" mastery at the very high price of the assumption of the "armour of an alienating identity" (*Écrits* 4)—Ted's identity. Although she writes that this sounds "so paragon," there is little evidence in Plath's *Journals* to suggest that Ted Hughes's values coincide perfectly with Plath's own youthful ideals. Instead, her facticious agency and her illusion of control are gained via the fantastical assumption of the mirrored perfect writerliness that exacerbates the very paralysis she seeks to avoid.

Once the perfect mirroring was shattered in the Oedipal "infidelity," the reflection was gone but the perfection remained, relocating itself in Ted Hughes's subject position. Now, "Ted is the ideal, the one possible person" (320), and as an ego ideal Ted would also inevitably perform the superego's opposite functions. The halts and inhibitions which make up the superego (Sem I 284), its vigilance and security function (134), its censorship (135) all come to be functions Ted Hughes takes on in his wife's post–Oedipal awareness. The *Journals* increasingly record Plath's need to keep both her work and her feelings to herself. She writes, "Must work and get out of paralysis—write and show him nothing"

(259), "don't share sorrow with Ted of rejection" (289), "will not tell Ted of rejection" (290), "Must try poems. DO NOT SHOW ANY TO TED" (294), "Tell T. nothing" (302). The husband who once offered freedom from the Panic Bird now threatens to induce its fluttering: "I sometimes feel a paralysis come over me: his opinion is so important to me" (294). Here, the Lacanian maxim that the formation of the ego-ideal heightens the demands on the ego and encourages repression to the full seems borne out, though an inverse formulation seems more appropriate since the ego ideals have heightened the repression and encouraged the ego's demands (Sem I 126), Plath's own writerly demand to be "a woman famous among women" (259).

The Colossus and Other Crises

The assumption on which Freud's talking cure rests, and the assumption that informs psychoanalytic practice generally, is that the catch-22 of repression and idealism bound together at the symptom yields to analysis. The first phase of analysis, according to Lacan, is the recognition of the imaginary investments (Sem I 186). The unity or wholeness which Plath frequently associates with perfection suggests that what she had fixed in the mirror of her perfect mate were the fragments of her own vulnerabilities. This orthopedic wholeness bought at the price of fixity recalls what Hughes refers to as Plath's claustrophobic interiority—the self-replicating mirror world in which "everything became another image of itself, another lens into itself" (156). Where the analyst might use free association to encourage the repressed to speak, Hughes and Plath hit upon a creative alternative—the Ouija board. One of the Ouija spirits, named Prince Otto [Otto was Sylvia Plath's father's name] "was said to be a great power in the underworld. When she pressed for a more personal communication," Hughes writes, "she would be told that Prince Otto could not speak to her directly because he was under orders from The Colossus. And when she pressed for an audience with The Colossus, they would say he was inaccessible" (155). The inaccessibility of The Colossus seems particularly apt when we recall its connection to the young Sylvia Plath who once found great satisfaction in writing. It was this young Sylvia who wrote "my happiness streams from having wrenched a piece out of my life, a piece of hurt and beauty, and transformed it to typewritten words on paper" (16); it was this young Sylvia who spoke to herself as the Kid Colossus.

Hughes dates the origin of Plath's real voice from a dream in which The Colossus finally appeared:

> Late in 1959 . . . she had a dream, which at the time made a visionary impact on her, in which she was trying to reassemble a giant, shattered, stone Colossus. In the light of her private mythology, we can see this dream was momentous, and she versified it, addressing the ruins as "Father," in a poem which she regarded, at the time, as a breakthrough. But the real significance of the dream emerges, perhaps, a few days later, when the quarry of anthropomorphic ruins reappears, in a poem titled "The Stones." In this second poem, the ruins are none other than her hospital city, the factory where men are remade, and where, among the fragments, a new self has been put together. Or rather an old shattered self, reduced by violence to its essential core, has been repaired and renovated and born again, and—most significant of all—speaks with a new voice. ("Sylvia" 157)

Plath's dream offers an extraordinary illustration of the discovery of the fragmentation in the imaginary register. Hughes's depiction of Plath as the subject of humanism possessed of an essential inner core suggests that Plath was in touch with an inner, born-again self. Lacan, by contrast, would see the poetic release of full speech as the freedom with which the imagined images can constellate symbolic patterns more reflective of Plath's truth, more adequate to her horrifying history of loss, of electroshock, of psychic struggle.

Hughes's rejection of Plath's first simplistic association between her dead father and the Colossus is astute as is his connection between the shattering of the fixed, stone Colossus and Plath's own newfound freedom to speak. These observations are readily assimilable to Lacan's description of full speech. The Kid Colossus, an entified ideal ego, molded itself from Plath's youthful ideals and then gazed on its image in the mirror Ted Hughes provided. Shattered, it had no power to silence her. But the freeing up of her imagination is only half of the story of Sylvia Plath's full speaking, for the poet who had once written "He is a genius. I his wife" eventually wrote to her mother, "I am a genius of a writer; I have it in me. I am writing the best poems of my life; they will make my name" (*Letters* 468). Here, Plath puts herself in the symbolic position she had previously allocated to Ted. If she was free from the burden of the Colossus, she was also free to share a symbolic space with all those masters to whom she had earlier apprenticed herself. When she freed herself, finally, to speak, Plath freed herself from her symptom, from all the registrations of her perfectionism. The Lacanian analyst would say of such an outcome: when a subject manages to speak the real, it speaks ineffable truth. Ted Hughes agrees, concluding that "when a real self finds language, and manages to speak, it is surely a dazzling event—as *Ariel* was" (Foreword xv).

Page 136 blank.

7

Being and Otherness

As half of a signifying binary, the "Other" is a term with a rich and lengthy philosophical history dating at least from Plato's *Sophist* in which the Stranger participates in a dialogue on the ontological problems of being and nonbeing, of the One and the Other.[1] This Platonic strain of thinking about alterity ontologically continues into the present day in the work of Emmanuel Levinas, who is countered by de Beauvoir, who influences philosophical feminisms, which influence theories of identity more generally.[2] Philosophical explorations of Otherness roughly contemporary with Lacan abound, and Hegel (via Kojève), Heidegger, and Sartre all present important statements on alterity. Lacan's place in the history of alterity is unique, however, since his decentering of subjectivity is paralleled by a decentering of Otherness. Moreover, Lacan explores an intrapsychic otherness that differs profoundly both from interpersonal theories of identity and from the philosophical problem of other minds. Specifically, Lacan's Schema L uses the registers to illustrate a gap between the Subject and the ego that is echoed by a gap between the Other and the other. The registers are definitional to these twin decenterings since the "decentering of the Subject" is just another way of saying that the Subject and the ego inhabit disjunct registers. Likewise, the disjunction between the symbolic linguistic Other and the imaginary mirroring other signifies a decentering of the former from the latter, capturing the dynamic that occasions the linguistic unconscious.

Sometimes Lacan refers to the symbolic Other as the big Other and the imaginary other as the little other, but for the most part Lacan simply uses capitalization to distinguish the Other from the other. Though no reader would misread "subject" for "ego," the much subtler rhetorical distinction between "Other" and "other" can easily be missed by readers unfamiliar with register theory. Since Lacan frequently discusses the Other topically without explicit reference to the other or to register theory, the reader must supply the missing theoretical context. Envision the fate of a first-time reader of Lacan who, interested in British Literature, picks up Seminar VII on ethics to read "Courtly love as anamorphosis." This reader sees: "In many cases, it seems that a function like that of a blessing or salutation is for the courtly lover the supreme gift, the sign of the Other as such, and nothing more" (152). Lacking the implied but unspecified discursive context of the registers, this reader can easily take Lacan's "sign of the Other" to be a token received from an "Other" person. Only familiarity with Lacan's theory of the registers can reveal the point made here about the intrapsychic "sign of the Other" as a decentering connection with the signifier in the unconscious that the courtly lover mis/takes for transcendence. Similarly, when Lacan writes in Seminar II that "the obsessional is always an other" he is talking about the obsessional's *ego*-involvement, not the obsessional's loss of identity. Again, Lacan's point assumes the registers, allying the obsessional with the rhetorically explicit "other" *and* alienating the obsessional from the discursively implicit "Other." Lacking the framework of the theory of the registers, a reader would be hard-pressed to unravel either of these Lacanian invocations of alterity.

The problem of reading Lacanian Otherness is compounded by the currency of the idea of the Other in theory generally. This currency arose with the interest in area studies, was inscribed in the topical dominance of race, class, and gender, and is reinscribed in present postcolonial theories of national identity. Consequently, a plethora of critical discourses use the term "Other" to signify quite differently from Lacan. Though they appear to share terms, Lacan's theory of the registers and contemporary theories of identity construct Otherness in distinct and sometimes incompatible ways. In identity politics, the decentering of the Subject can lead to an equal and opposite reaction: a centering—an entification—of the Other as object, an "it" denied the status of a "Thou." Some theoretical discourses position Otherness in a single (ethnic, sexed, racial, positional) attribute of a specific person or group. Since alterity is crucial to an understanding of the Lacanian registers, and since the Other of contemporary theory means many things to many discourses, it will be useful to review the implications of register theory by distinguishing Lacan's treatment of Otherness from alternative uses of the term.

The Other in Theories of Identity

Many contemporary theories of identity use the Other as half of a Self/Other dichotomy that distinguishes one person from another person. For instance, pointing out an oppositional racial distinction, Terry Goldie's "The Representation of the Indigene" states, "At least since Fanon's *Black Skin, White Masks* (1952) it has been a commonplace to use 'Other' and 'Not-self' for the white view of blacks and for the resulting black view of themselves."[3] Racial selves rather than subjects are at issue here in Goldie's distinction between white people and black people. The same interpersonal dichotomy of race appears in Abdul R. Jan-Mohamed's "The Economy of Manichean Allegory":

> Troubled by the nagging contradiction between the theoretical justification of exploitation and the barbarity of its actual practice, [colonialist fiction] also attempts to mask the contradiction by obsessively portraying the supposed inferiority and barbarity of the racial Other, thereby insisting on the profound moral difference between self and Other. (Ashcroft 23)

Again, an implicit humanism reenters the discourse on race, imported by the idea of the racial self. Goldie discusses the racial distinctions between the Self and the Other in terms of specific attributes, saying that "Presumably the first instance in which one human perceived another as Other in racial terms came when the first recognized the second as different in colour, facial features, language" (235). Here Goldie makes the previously implicit humanism explicit, but not without reason. In critiques like these, which explore inhumanity, humanizing the Other makes a political statement.

A similar distinction appears in feminist discourses which discuss woman as Other, particularly those discourses directed against patriarchy. Where political rights are at issue, discourses refer both to woman as an Other human being and to the subject as a political entity, a theoretical move that unifies the "subject" as a *person* subjected to the law of the land. Thus, adopting the language of oppositional feminism, Raman Selden[4] generalizes about feminist theory: "In many different societies, women, like colonised subjects, have been relegated to the position of 'other', 'colonised' by various forms of patriarchal domination" (249). Simone de Beauvoir's *Second Sex* emphasizes the humanism that is at stake in the Self/Other dichotomy, writing of the Biblical *Genesis*:

"[H]umanity is male and man defines woman not in herself but as relative to him. . . . He is the Subject, he is the Absolute—she is the Other"; this "expression of a duality . . . of the Self and the Other" is socially and historically pervasive, de Beauvoir points out (xxii). Of de Beauvoir's and Virginia Woolf's feminisms, Selden continues: "Being dispersed among men, women have no separate history, no natural solidarity; nor have they combined as other oppressed groups have. Woman is riveted into a lop-sided relationship with man: he is the 'One', she the 'Other' . . . and, à la Virginia Woolf's 'looking glass', the assumption of woman as 'Other' is further internalised by women themselves" (210). Here, Selden's analysis of the woman's internalization of her attributes parallels Goldie's analysis of black identification above, and both invoke a discourse on Otherness that has Platonic rather than psychoanalytic roots.

National identity, too, presents itself in terms of Selves and Others, adopting the plural construction characteristic of discourses about identity. Here, Homi Bhabha discusses the postcolonial condition: "[The Derridean *entre*] makes it possible to begin envisaging national, anti-nationalist, histories of the 'people'. It is in this space that we will find those words with which we can speak of Ourselves and Others."[5] Similarly, Xiaomei Chen concludes a discussion of "Occidentalism as Counterdiscourse" with the following analysis that treats East and West as implicit human agents:

> [I]t seems imperative that we a least try to find a reasonable balance between Self and Other, between East and West, so that no culture is fundamentally privileged over its Others. Perhaps the realities of history cannot allow such a balance to be fully realized. Indeed, it is even necessary to affirm that these master tropes are necessarily veiled by the fictional. What must be stressed here is that even imagining such a balance—surely one of the first requirements of a new order of things—can never be possible without each Self being confronted by an Other, or by the Other being approached from the point of view of the Self in its own specific historical and cultural conditions.6

The idea here, that Otherness is both agentic and a matter of point of view, is taken up by Judith Butler in a discussion of sexual identity when she writes in *Bodies That Matter* that "gay and lesbian identity positions [can] constitute themselves through the production and repudiation of a heterosexual Other" (112). As Butler's analysis shows, Otherness can be relative, making the interpersonal dichotomy of Self and Other endlessly reversible.

Judith Butler's critique of the "exclusionary logic" of the Other as it is signifies in the Self/Other binary of identity points toward the limited usefulness of oppositional constructions. Lacanian logic, moreover, demonstrates the intrapsychic resistance that manifests when just such signifying binaries as white/black, East/West, or heterosexual/homosexual merge with the imaginary, a dynamic explored in Chapter 4. Like intrapsychic resistance, political resistance has a use, particularly where brute survival is at issue. However, resistance denies the epistemological fact that in order to replicate the Self/Other signifying difference— in order to shape a foundational symbolic distinction—both terms necessarily implicate each other. In many of the discussions above, "fundamental privilege" is less the issue than foundational privilege. Civilized, superior Western white male heterosexual colonizers are *foundationally* privileged; we know *in advance* and without appeal to circumstance or situation that this is so. Foundational difference, because it is preidentificatory and preinterpretive, makes a truth claim about the world. In and of itself, such a claim is insufficient for the analysis of process, whether intrapsychic, social, or political. Discourses which align the Other with the marginal or with the subversive do not confront the problem of process, just as JanMohamed's exemplary redistribution of the attribute of "barbarity" from colonizer to colonized above stops short of an inquiry into ego identification as a transitive process. Allied binaries and binary realignments only build a thicker epistemological foundation.

Thick epistemology is vulnerable epistemology. As we saw in detail in Chapter 4, and as JanMohamed's portable barbarity points out above, multiple binaries align and realign, attributes can be assigned and reassigned. Infelicitous combinatories undermine foundational privilege, whether the claim of privilege operates as an entitlement or an accusation. So long as there is an investment in the foundational signifying difference, the emergence of the combinatory's undesirable elements will arouse resistance. For instance, Melville Chater's paean to the new South African Union in a 1931 edition of *The National Geographic* sets up and reinforces a typical colonialist foundational distinction between hard-working, intelligent whites entitled to the prosperity they enjoy and lazy, superstitious blacks (who presumably have what they have "earned" as well).[7] When Chater's foray over the veldt discovers a "forlorn scene" of "dismal shacks, where some frowzy men and women and a plethora of dull-faced children [lounge] in the sunshine" he rescues his foundations: "Yet they [are] whites, or, rather, 'poor white,' representing a South African aspect of that retrogressive type which is found in many lands" (441). When this relativizing of whiteness seems inadequate to explain "so formidable a number as 120,000 to 150,000" poor whites, Chater attributes the deterioration of the poor whites to "that too-easeful existence, based on slave help and game aplenty" (441). Having inadvertently tainted the white superiority he has sought to construct as essentially the outcome of white hard work by the insertion of slavery into the picture, Chater reasserts his foundation: in a stunning attempt to purify white superiority, he redistributes a poor white squatter to the black half of his equation by comparing the squatter's language to that of "the American 'black-face' comedian"(441).

Chater's inadvertent denaturalizing of blackness has stumbled upon a blackness constructed by whites for white entertainment. He has entered the territory of the combinatory of combinatories, the Lacanian unconscious—the Lacanian Other. A more contemporary and purposeful recuperation of race from the stasis of foundational difference is effected by Honduran comedian Carlos Mencia who jokes that Los Angelinos meeting someone from Honduras or El Salvador or Guatemala inevitably ask "Now, what part of Mexico is that?" Mencia exposes the exclusionary work of the foundational binary that identifies race in Black/White terms with a logic that reintroduces the combinatory: If you're white, you're white in L.A. Go to Miami and you're still white. If you're black in L.A., go to New York and you're still black. Referring to himself, Mencia points out that in L.A. he's a Mexican. "If I go to Miami, I'm a Cuban. And if I go to New York, I'm. . . ." He gestures to the audience who respond "Puerto Rican." "See," he concludes, "You know what I'm talking about."[8] Shunted off to the racial unconscious by a foundational Black/White race-ism, Mencia's own race must be articulated by indirection. Thus, the unary signifier "Hispanic" remains in the linguistic Otherness and only enters the joke obliquely, as a signifier for another signifier—[Hispanic]/Mexican, [Hispanic]/Cuban, [Hispanic]/Puerto Rican. Mencia's comedic tactic parallels the strategy Benita Parry praises in Bhabha's postcolonial theory: Bhabha "show[s] the wide range of stereotypes and the shifting subject positions assigned to the colonized in the colonialist text" in order to liberate "an autonomous native 'difference'" from the binary European/Other."[9] Similarly, Judith Butler's *Bodies That Matter* works with the exclusionary logics of both male/female and heterosexual/homosexual to open up the combinatory expressions of sexual orientation these foundational binaries preclude. Since these latter examples of linguistic identity have ventured into the territory of complex Otherness evocative of Lacanians theory of the registers, this is a good point at which to distinguish clearly the doubling of alterity in the symbolic and the imaginary.

There is No Other of the Other:
(But There Is an other of the Other)

The journey that eventually leads Lacan to the aphoristic insistence that "there is no Other of the Other" (there is no metalanguage beyond language) begins with a denaturalization of paranoid psychosis. The ideas Lacan forms during his medical training lead him to counter the prevailing psychiatric view of psychosis as a biologically based personality trait by positing a developmental phenomenology he only later finds in Freud. Interested in *folies à deux*, and especially as such madness manifests in women's "inspired" speech and writings, Lacan is very much a man attuned to the surrealist 1930s.[10] What he writes for medical journals he revises for surrealist journals, but his interest is consistently in the otherness of the other—an interest that culminates in mirror stage theory. The interpersonal here seems undeniable. Lacan writes about the crime of the two Papin sisters. He writes his thesis on Aimée's attack on a famous French actress. Moreover, Lacan's many references to Hegel's struggle for recognition between the Master and the Slave certainly imply an agon between people rather than a contest within. Lacan's mirror stage essay points out that a pigeon matures via an encounter with another of its own kind. Even the mirroring moment can be read as involving the infant and the mother. All in all, early on, Lacan seems deeply involved with the interpersonal, the social, even the cultural.

Read against the retrospect of his later interests, mirror stage theory appears to be Lacan's failed attempt to explain the dynamics of an intrapsychic otherness. In his theory of the registers, he is much more successful. The dominance of a formative phenomenology in the earlier essay slants it in the direction of the interpersonal. In the theory of the registers, by contrast, the phenomenal is folded within the structure of language and intrapsychic structure is irremediably fissured with the gaps between the imaginary, the symbolic, and the real. Since none of the registers is confluent with the others, Lacan avoids the problem of a seamless solipsism. He avoids a tabula rasa subjectivity passively molded from without as well. Hence, it is not experience but its imaginary residue that figures in the imaginary register. It is not the many instances of communication with other people but language as a whole that signifies in the symbolic. Nor is the model without constraint since the real is always there as an unimaginable, unsignifiable limit on what would otherwise constitute a psychic *en abîme* of mirroring or signification without end.

Models of the psyche necessarily inform analytic praxis, and Lacan's theory of the registers is his attempt to come to grips with the gap between the two. While Schema L as the sketch on Lacan's chalkboard is not the model on the analyst's couch, there is an intriguing and ambiguous family relationship between the two. Though the terms may be the same, the contexts differ, and working across the contextual divide can make Lacan's theory appear to contradict itself, rendering straightforward terminology paradoxical. The problem of discussing alterity is made all the more difficult for Lacan because he continually engages the divide between the interpersonal situation of analysis in practice and the intrapsychic dynamics that underwrite whatever interventions analytic practice makes. Praxis motivates the transition from mirror stage theory to register theory as the latter is announced in Lacan's manifesto on the function of speech and language in the Freudian field. His paper takes issue with non-Lacanian forms of analysis that he finds therapeutically inadequate precisely because of their emphases on the interpersonal. Increasingly, Lacan insists that analysis must be a process in which the analyst creates a therapeutic context where the analysand's intrapsychic processes are the only processes in play. The cadaverous, "dead" position of the Lacanian analyst is meant to strip the analytic situation of its interactive attributes. Thus, Lacan's discussion of Otherness must be read with special attention to context for three reasons: because Otherness is a term that bilocates in the theoretical shifts within Lacan's own work, because it is a term that bilocates in the intrapsychic and the interpersonal, and because it is a signifier shared by both the discourse of analysis and everyday language.

Since the idea of otherness is a term whose name—"the other"—remains the same but whose implications change, Lacan provides many interpretations of otherness. Some of the examples contrast the other with the Other and emphasize the distinction between the registers. In his second seminar, for instance, he compares the "radical Other" as one "pole of the subjective relation," with the "other which isn't an other at all, since it is essentially coupled with the ego, in a relation which is always reflexive, interchangeable" (321). Bearing in mind that Lacan is discussing a subjective rather than an intersubjective relation, and that the reflexive coupling of other with ego is an intrapsychic phenomenon for which another person is, at best, a prop or a pretext, consider this elaboration of the analyst's alterity: the analyst "partakes of the radical nature of the Other, in so far as he is what is most inaccessible" to the extent that the analyst's own [ego] is "effaced" and the analyst's resistance is not aroused (324). The analyst's refusal to play along with the game dictated by the ego of the analysand throws the analysand back into a confrontation with the intrapsychic gap between the other and the Other, since expecting to confirm the former the analysand encounters the latter. So, "what leaves the imaginary of the ego of the subject is in accordance not with this other to which he is accustomed, and who is just his partner, the person who is made so as to enter into his game, but precisely with this radical Other which is hidden from him" (324). Without another person to play along with the habitual imaginary game, the subject looks to the intrapsychic Other. If the analysis is successful, the Other will yield to the subject its truth.

Appropriately, one of Lacan's exemplary readings of radical alterity occurs in his Seminar III on psychosis where an analytic case study explores the speech of a paranoid young woman. In this reworking of his analytic roots, Lacan presents a clear decentering of the imaginary other from the symbolic Other. The disjunction is evident in Lacan's redefinition of psychotic projection—which might seem to be classically imaginary—as a mechanism that has been "placed outside the general symbolization structuring the subject" and returns "from without" (47). Lacan's patient is a "girl" who tells him about her "run-in in the hallway with an ill-mannered sort of chap," a married man who was also the illicit lover of her neighbor. While passing her in the hall, the man had devalued her by saying a dirty word to her. But she herself had spoken to him first, saying "I've just been to the butcher's" [the *charcutier*, who specializes in pork]. He had responded: "Sow!" In his analysis, Lacan's own response to the girl is a mistake, he admits. He interprets. He shows his analysand that he understands her comment "I've just been to the butcher's" as a reference to pork, and by doing so he "enter[s] into the patient's game . . . collaborat[ing] in [her] resistance" (48). Though he does not explicitly articulate his failure in terms of the registers, the distinction is clear. Lacan, through his display of "understanding," has reinforced the patient's imaginary at the expense of asking, symbolically, *why* there is something in the patient's speech to be understood. The analytic question is: "Why did she say, *I've just been to the butcher's* and not *Pig*?" (48–49).

Lacan goes on to insist that the interaction between the girl who might have said "Pig!" and the man who calls her "Sow!" is not an instance of his maxim that in speech the subject receives her message in an inverted form. In other words, here, the message should not be constructed as a symbolic exchange since the message at issue "is not identical with speech, far from it" (Sem III 49). The girl herself is enmeshed in the desire of her neighbor and the neighbor's lover, a desire of which she is censorious to the point of wondering whether it is possible "through taking legal action, to get them into hospital" (49). She had been friends with the neighbor until the love affair interrupted the friendship; afterwards she intruded on the couple while they were dining or reading or "at their toilet" until they threw her out. So Lacan rereads the conversation's intrapsychic implications: "*Sow*, what is that? It is effectively her message, but is it not rather her message to herself?" (49). The analysand's ego has met her alter ego in the hallway; the moment is a mirror.

Lacan connects this case study to his schema of subjectivity:

> Is it the reality of objects that is at issue? Who normally speaks in reality, for us? Is it reality, exactly, when someone speaks to us? The point of the remarks I made to you last time on the other and the Other, the other with a small o and the Other with a big O, was to get you to notice that when the Other with a big O speaks it is not purely and simply the reality in front of you, namely the individual who is holding forth. The Other is beyond that reality.
>
> In true speech the Other is that before which you make yourself recognized. But you can make yourself recognized by it only because it is recognized first. (50–51)

Having thus clarified the impersonal nature of the big Other, Lacan notes that in the paranoid insult, the Other is not in question since the patient doesn't recognize the Other "behind him who is speaking. She receives her own speech from him, but not inverted, her own speech is in the other who is herself, the little other, her reflection in the mirror, her counterpart" (51). Though she seems to look at another person, the girl sees only herself.

The distinction Lacan makes here between the Other and the other, between the symbolic and the imaginary, involves the pact of language. Part of the process of recognition for the subject as a subject involves the risky business of addressing the absolute Other beyond all that is known. Addressed to another person, the very Otherness of speech puts that person in a position to be recognized by the speaker and to recognize the speaker in return because both speakers share a symbolic commitment of which neither speaker is the origin. Committed speech is *discourse*, which for Lacan "includes acts, steps, the contortions of puppets, yourselves included, caught up in the game. . . . An utterance commits you to maintaining it through your discourse, or to repudiating it, or to objecting to it, or to conforming to it, to refuting it, but, even more, to complying with many things that are within the rules of the game" (51). With these relationships between the registers, alterity, discourse, and the pact in mind, I want to return to two discourses on identity and Otherness that address Lacan's register theory directly—one by invoking it, another by repudiating it—in order to explore the link between discourse and symptom.

Discourse, Symptom, and Otherness
"The unconscious is the discourse of the Other"

In the previous chapter, the relationship between the symptom and the Lacanian registers was presented in terms of identification. While issues of identification dominate the first-person discourse in Sylvia Plath's *Journals*, issues of interpretation arise in these discourses about identity. The following two examples—Abdul R. JanMohamed's "The Economy of Manichean Allegory" and Judith Butler's "The Lesbian Phallus and the Morphological Imaginary"—offer critiques, and as critiques they are discourses about discourses, metadiscourses in which identity signifies. Because these are discourses of a different level of complexity, what is at issue here is the deflection of the discursive flow as such. In the first instance, JanMohamed uses the Lacanian registers to make a distinction between forms of colonial discourse. A useful error— possibly a symptom—occurs in JanMohamed's essay at the point where the discourse of postcolonialism disrupts the discourse on the registers forcing an either/or choice between irreconcilable constructions of Otherness. This error provides a helpful comparison to a similar error in Butler's chapter, an error productive of a symptom at every level of Butler's discourse, from the literal, to the paradigmatic, to the interpretive. Since from the analytic point of view both the error and the symptom locate discursive truth, both JanMohamed and Butler tell the truth about the encounter between theories of identity and the Lacanian registers.

The registers appear as unified and unifying descriptive categories when Abdul R. JanMohamed writes, "I would argue that colonialist literature is divisible into two broad categories: the 'imaginary' and the 'symbolic'" (Ashcroft 19). Next, JanMohamed goes on to transcend the categorical in a sophisticated contrast between the work that aggressivity does in the "imaginary" text and the work that mediation and problematization do in the "symbolic" text. Having employed a *Lacanian* discourse to frame his discussion of the colonialist novel, however, Jan-Mohamed writes that some "symbolic" novels are "conceived in the 'symbolic' realm of intersubjectivity, heterogeneity, and particularity but are seduced by the specularity of 'imaginary' Otherness" (20). This sudden collapsing of the distinction between the registers in the error "'imaginary' Otherness" is jarring to any reader familiar with Lacan. Abdul R. JanMohamed has broken the law.

Since JanMohamed's essay provides exemplary instances both of discursive creativity and of discursive failure as they impact the relation between the writer and his reader, I want to review the sequence above in two ways. First, I will look at the interpersonal symbolic law of discourse that, once invoked, binds writer to reader in an intrasubjective and impersonal pact. The writer's thesis invokes Lacan's discourse of the registers and asks the reader to be bound by the pact that this discourse constitutes. This is a symbolic pact *par excellence* since neither the writer nor the reader originate the discourse but both agree to be bound by its rules in order to allow the possibility of a meaningful exchange, in order to agree on the terms by which they will produce meanings together. Since the writer has selected a Lacanian discourse, "imaginary" and "symbolic" cease to be overdetermined signifiers in the linguistic unconscious. "Imaginary" and "symbolic" now invoke a set of relations defined by Lacan's discourse, a discourse in which these terms signify in quite specific ways. Because and only because he has involved his reader in this pact of the registers, JanMohamed is free to explore the implications of the encounter between Lacanian theory and the colonialist novel. As the writer elaborates the particulars of the work of the imaginary in the colonialist novel, the reader can appreciate JanMohamed's insight because the reader sees the colonialist novel in fresh and interesting ways and because the fruitful encounter between the Lacanian imaginary and colonialist fiction reveals new and unforeseen implications of the imaginary register itself. Creativity thus requires the law; creativity is paradoxically both bound to the law and unbound by it.

The moment JanMohamed writes "'imaginary' Otherness," he breaks the law of Lacanian discourse and cancels his pact with the reader. Until the violation occurs, the reader is bound by the pact called "Lacanian discourse"; "imaginary," "symbolic," and "Otherness" hold out the possibility of meaning-making (though they do not guarantee it). At the breaking of the pact, the terms cease to be terms within a discourse; released from the pact they are signifiers only. Lacking their discursive support, "imaginary" and "Otherness" thus signify randomly. Because he has broken his Lacanian pact with the reader, the reader has no possible way to grasp what JanMohamed might be trying to signify by "'imaginary' Otherness." No context can stabilize what fractured discursive syntax has set free. Since signification outside the pact is idiosyncratic, the effect of the broken pact is to change "imaginary" and "Otherness" into random markers that preclude creativity in both the writing and the reading. The markers come and go—in and out of the linguistic unconscious—for reasons that may or may not be related to the colonialist novel, the stated project at hand. Once the pact has been broken by the writer, the reader can always declare the discursive failure an accident and continue as if the pact were still in place—but the reader is now on alert and any additional error will render the text indecipherable in terms of its stated project.[11]

Besides the rupture of interpersonal give and take between writer and reader, the collapse of this fruitful contact between the discourse of the colonial novel and Lacan's discourse of the registers in JanMohamed's essay signifies intrapsychically as the deformation of one discourse by another. If repeated, "'imaginary' Otherness" becomes a symptom rather than an error, and the essay manifests a subjective encounter with Otherness far beyond its postcolonial critique. Consequently, the discursive symptom provides a profitable alternative to the sterile fusion Rachel Bowlby cautioned against in Chapter 1. Because Lacan's distinction between the registers implies a decentering of Otherness that JanMohamed cannot maintain while simultaneously committed to a postcolonial construction of Self and Other, the reader is moved to ask why there is a symptom in the discourse at this point. It seems that the entified Other appears here as the symptom of a postcolonial commitment that runs deeper than the Lacanian discourse to which the writer is ostensibly committed. Since the Other of humanism cannot signify save by suturing the gap between the imaginary other and the symbolic Other, this is precisely what JanMohamed does. The repressed postcolonial humanism returns in the symptomatic fusion of "'imaginary' Otherness."

The discursive symptom manifest in Abdul R. JanMohamed's essay signifies psychoanalytically because he intends to use the Lacanian registers to frame his exploration of the colonial novel. A very different discursive symptom arises in Judith Butler's influential critique of Lacanian analysis, *Bodies That Matter*, a critique in which she doubts that the registers signify at all. Here, a fusion of Lacanian registers pervades Butler's discussion of "The Lesbian Phallus and the Morphological Imaginary." While both Butler and JanMohamed effect symptomatic erasures of the Lacanian other, the symptomatic erasure in Butler manifests distinctively—as an inability to accurately quote Lacan's own text in spite of her extraordinary scholarly rigor.[12] The misquotations pervade her discussion from the very moment when Butler denies the distinction between the registers, but the symptom is prefigured by her insertion of Lacan's structural theory of the registers into his essay on the mirror stage.

Butler's chapter conflates psychoanalytic models that are theoretically and historically distinct—both Freudian models and Lacanian ones, and this conflation lays the theoretical groundwork from which the symptomatic misquotations arise. Thus, Butler reads "On Narcissism" against *The Ego and the Id* though the former belongs to a mid-Freudian model that differs significantly from the last "entified" model of a psyche composed of Id-Ego-Superego. Similarly, Butler uses Lacan's mirror stage essay to argue for the imaginary nature of the phallus in "The Signification of the Phallus"—even though the former essay provides a coda to Lacan's early phenomenal and developmental model of the psyche while the latter condenses a portion of the seminar on desire, a seminar reflecting Lacan's structural theorizing at its strongest. As we have earlier seen, though mirror stage theory and register theory do share signifiers, their variant theoretical models constellate variant signifieds; if the terms remain the same, their meanings have structurally altered. However, the alteration fails to make its way into Butler's critical assimilation of the latter model to its predecessor.

Butler's most overtly symptomatic collapsing of the Lacanian registers reveals itself in her persistent error in directly quoting the text of

Lacan's early seminars. Like JanMohamed, Butler substitutes the symbolic Other for the mirroring other. It is as if, having merged mirror stage theory with register theory, Butler is literally unable to see a significatory difference between the two. As a result, Butler does not distinguish the imaginary other from the symbolic Other, a collapse of terminological distinction equivalent to suggesting there is no difference between the subject and the ego. Since the distinction within alterity is so central to Lacanian theory generally and to his model of the subject of the unconscious specifically, other and Other are definitional. Moreover, the other and the Other draw a precise and consistent distinction between the mirroring imaginary and the symbolic treasury of signifiers. By continually effacing the imaginary other with the symbolic Other, Butler indeed does what she explicitly states as her essay's goal: she "rewrit[es] the morphological imaginary" (72) though the rewriting is far more literal than her subheading implies.

Where Lacan speaks of the body finding its unity "in the image of the other" with a small *o* (Sem II 54), Butler rewrites "in the image of the Other" with a capital (75), and where Lacan writes "the imaginary structuration of the ego forms around the specular image of the body itself, of the image of the other" small *o*, imaginary other (Sem II 94), Butler again revises to "the image of the Other" with a capital *O* (76) collapsing Lacan's straightforward structural distinction and begging the issue of structural difference. Butler perpetuates the error in her own discussion, commenting that "the specular image of the body itself is in some sense the image of the Other" (76) and that the "extrapolating function" of narcissism is the "principle by which any other object or Other is known" (77). There is no small irony in Butler's symptomatic misquotation of Lacan given her rigorous inclusion of parallel phrases from both French and English texts, and carefully documented citations from both the French and English seminars.[13] But as Lacan points out, the unconscious is always visible, right there, literally spelled out in the symptom in the text—and Butler's text proves no exception to this Lacanian rule.

The symptomatic disappearance of the imaginary other in Butler's thoroughgoing critique of the mirror stage essay parallels the conflation of the registers in JanMohamed's essay. In the latter, the symptom arises at the moment of discursive incompatibility between the postcolonial paradigm of Self and Other and the Lacanian distinction between an other and the Other as the unconscious locus of language. Is there a similar discursive rupture in Butler's argument? Looking more closely at Butler's actual text may be helpful here. The substitutions begin in citations in which Lacan specifically mentions the body in connection with the registers—so Butler's central concern in *Bodies That Matter* and her theory of performativity are both at stake when the misquotations begin. Her page-long explication of Lacan's mirror stage theory in which five symptomatic substitutions of the symbolic Other for the imaginary other occur also addresses the body, specifically the "organs [that] are caught up in the narcissistic relation" (76–77). The following page of text, on which the symptomatic substitution occurs three more times, argues that the previously generic "organs" may be "the male genitals" (77), and if so, Lacan's mirror stage theory grounds itself on a specifically masculine narcissism. Butler concludes that the narcissistically engaged masculine organs now condition and structure every object and Other and as a result, the "extrapolating function" of narcissism raised to an epistemological principle becomes phallogocentric. In short, a phallic imaginary is masculine and any explanatory function such an imaginary might serve is inherently phallogocentric. Therefore, it is from Lacan's phallogocentrism that Butler's lesbian phallus liberates us, providing a subversive substitute for the hetero/sexist Phallic Signifier that she herself has taken great pains to introduce into the Lacanian imaginary.

Here, more explicitly, is the problem. Lacan theorizes that there is a privileged signifier in the symbolic register and that this privileged symbolic signifier is the phallus. Butler wants to argue against the real of the body, wants to argue that the body is "a process whereby regulatory norms materialize 'sex' and achieve this materialization through a forcible reiteration of those norms" (2). Thus, Butler's theory of materialization stops short of the radical constructionist claim that the body is only a symbolic construct. She finds an appealing alternative to constructionism in Lacan's early theory where the imagined, alienated body appears in the mirror. This Lacanian mirroring replication supports Butler's theory of materialization. But Lacan did not stop with his mirror stage theory, and though he once situated the body helpfully in the imaginary, he later positioned the phallus in the symbolic register—where Butler very much needs it *not* to be if her argument for a projective materialization of a phantasmatic phallus is to succeed. Consequently, a collapsing of Lacanian paradigms and issues ensues.

After arguing for the imaginary nature of the penis, Butler goes on to suggest that Lacan has simply renamed the penis the phallus (80); further, that the penis is the "privileged referent" to be symbolized by the phallus (84); and finally, that the relationship between penis and phallus (and by implication between imaginary and symbolic) is the relationship of signified to signifier (90). But issues of significatory slippage are not issues of reference, nor are they issues of meaning, and this series of conflations simply reiterates the earlier fusion of psychoanalytic models, creating a theoretical pastiche against which Butler then argues with great sophistication and subtlety.[14] Given the persistent insertion of the symbolic into the imaginary, and the assimilation of the symbolic construct phallus to the image of the penis, it is not surprising to hear Butler conclude that "if the phallus is an imaginary effect, a wishful transfiguration, then it is not merely the *symbolic* status of the phallus that is called into question, but the very distinction between the symbolic and the imaginary" (79). But just whose wishful transfiguration does Butler's text demonstrate we may want to ask since the symptom, Freud tells us, marks the location of the wish and it has clearly been Butler's wish to do away with the distinction between the registers all along. Since Butler's critique merges Lacan's phallic discourse of desire with his theory of the registers, I want here to return to this most controversial essay in order to distinguish the former discourse from the latter and to return the phallic signifier to the symbolic register.

Man's [sic] Desire Is the Desire of the Other

While the unconscious locates power in Otherness, the phallic signifier, by contrast, locates power in subjectivity. Unlike the unity of the imaginary imago, which provides a simple referential marker, the symbolic phallic signifier constrains Otherness by buttoning a signification, an identification, and a discourse together into one neat package. In the wildly overdetermined signifying multiplicity of the symbolic register, the phallus provides a determined and determining force. It is precisely the phallic propensity for self-replication that inseminates the reproduction—the reiteration as Butler calls it—of the Subject. What is at issue in Lacan's polemic "The Signification of the Phallus" is the predominant role of this phallic signifier as the *Aufhebung* of signifying difference per se. Since this is a far more complex idea than either the decentering of the subject or the reduplication of alterity, we will proceed slowly. Lacan insists that seven years of Seminars have brought him to the conclusion that he must "promulgate as necessary to any articulation of analytic

phenomena the notion of the signifier, as opposed to that of the signified" (284); he must insist on the priority of the marker over its meanings. Freud's discovery, which predates Saussure's retroactive linguistic
explication of it, "gives to the signifier/signified opposition the full
extent of its implications: namely that the signifier has an active function
in determining certain effects in which the signifiable appears as sub-
mitting to its mark" (284). Thus, the active, agentic function of language
resides in mark-making, and signifying is an active rather than a reflective process.

That the subject is the product of a linguistic unconscious should
not be taken as evidence of the subject's "cultural" construction (284),
nor should the subject be seen as product of an "ideological psycho-
genesis" (285). Lacan sees Horney's feminist social-psychological
analysis as the latter and dismisses all such "question-begging appeal to
the concrete" (285). Appeal to the concrete is beside the Freudian
point. The only laws that interest Lacan are the laws that govern the
other scene of the unconscious, the laws of combination and substitution—of metaphor and metonymy—by which signifiers generate the
"determining effects for the institution of the subject" (285). Lacan
goes on to define the Other as that by which he "designate[s] . . . the
very locus evoked by the recourse to speech in any relation in which the
Other intervenes" (285). The logic of the signifier is thus anterior to the
production of meaning, the "awakening of the signified" (285)—suggesting that meaning is discovered rather than made wherever the
unconscious is in play.

Lacan next invokes his theory of the registers to reiterate his argument for the symbolic character of the phallus as a privileged signifier.
The phallus of Freudian doctrine cannot be assigned to the imaginary
register because it "is not a phantasy" (285). Nor is it constrained by the
biological real of "the organ, penis or clitoris, that it symbolizes" (285).
"For the phallus is a signifier," Lacan concludes, having made his case
for the location of the signifying phallus in the symbolic register. But it
is a signifier with a difference from other signifiers. The phallus is a signifier that can "designate as a whole the effects of the signified" (285).
We can tell that a phallic signifier is present by its effects. And what are
these effects? The linguistic fate of the speaking being is to be unable to
articulate need save as a demand that empowers the Other as a reposi-
tory of love. The residue of inarticulable need returns from this Otherness as desire.

Need/demand/desire. Lacan reiterates the relationship between the three: "desire is neither the appetite for satisfaction, nor the demand for love, but the difference that results from the subtraction of the first from the second" (287). Thus, while real needs can be satisfied, imaginary demands may persist—opening a gap generative of desire. This intrapsychic formula for desire leads Lacan to think relationally, and so he goes on to rework the role of the Other in terms of the sexual relation. Now, the sexual relation is rendered enigmatic because it is "doubly 'signifying'" and ambiguous because of "the Other in question." The ambiguity arises here from the fact that the Other has a place in both the discourse of the registers and the discourse of desire. Here, moreover, the intrapsychic and the interpersonal seem utterly and ambiguously mixed. Thus, "for both partners in the relation, both the subject and the Other, it is not enough to be subjects of need, or objects of love, . . . they must stand for the cause of desire" (287). Subject/object/Other meet Subject/object/Other Lacan appears to be saying—weaving a double discourse of the intrapsychic with the interactive.

Since the sexual relation seems to involve the signifying phallus irretrievably in the interpersonal beyond of signification, I want to review the intrapsychic dynamics of this crucial Lacanian concept. First, Lacan has repeatedly told us that the signifier is binary—and he has exemplified this binary signifier in paired relations such as day/night, and red cards/black cards. The sexed (reproductive) relation is binary as well, feminine/masculine. Next, however, Lacan tells us that the phallus is a "privileged signifier," a signifier of the sexual relation that we are to take in the "literal (typographical) sense of the term" (287). And how is this literal phallic pictogram of "the sexual relation" written? ϕ Thus, Lacan concludes, the phallus is "equivalent . . . to the (logical) copula" (287). In the larger context of Lacan's discussion of the binary symbolic signifier, the phallus is the foundation *signifying as such*. The phallic signifier, the foundational difference in and of itself, is rendered latent by the emergence of the signifying binary terms. "The phallus is the signifier of this *Aufhebung* itself, which it inaugurates (initiates) by its disappearance" (288); thus "reproduction" disappears leaving behind the signifying difference "female"/"male" or "race" disappears from the foundational distinction "black"/"white." Where has the phallus gone now that the paired terms appear? It is retained as the bar separating the terms, a signifier rendered inarticulable by the terms it leaves behind, yet simultaneously a signifier imperative to their signifying difference.

To those who feel this reading of "The Signification of the Phallus" constitutes a recuperation of an irreparably phallogocentric discourse, I can only say that Lacan's logic of the phallus captures the foundation in foundational thinking vividly. As a result, this phal*log*-*i*centrism provides an extraordinarily valuable analytic tool. For me, the phallogicentrism of the essay is a discourse separable from the essay's 1950s-style cultural discourse on the role of the man and the role of the woman in the comedy of intercourse. Whether sexed reproductive difference is itself foundational for psychoanalysis or whether sexed reproductive difference is exemplary is an issue beyond the scope of this project, though one's position on this issue will obviously determine one's reading of "The Signification of the Phallus." When Lacan begins to read the cultural "relation between the sexes" (289) in the essay's concluding polemic against Melanie Klein, he lapses into a heteronormative construction of sexed love that ends with an apparent affirmation of Freud's intuition that there is "only one libido" and it is masculine. On first reading, years ago now, this section of the essay struck me as irrecuparably sexist and heterosexist—though it is imperative here to point out that the Freudian libido has nothing (no thing?) in common with the Lacanian imaginary. I can only note with some amusement that I found penciled in my margin of this concluding section "time for a lesbian deconstruction." On this account, Judith Butler has read my desire. Now, since Butler has returned, I want to bring back theories of identity for one last encounter with Lacan.

> "The unconscious is the *discourse*
> [emphasis mine] of the Other"

The widespread insistence that Lacan's brief écrit on the phallus is about dominance (and only dominance) *rather than* difference exemplifies the kind of foundationalism Lacan indicates by the phrase "*having* the phallus." Moreover, folding this foundation back into an imaginary identification—presuming that one is oneself the "Other" of a Self/Other binary—is an instance of "*being* the phallus." Gayatri Spivak notes just such a phallic politics of identification in "the fierce turf battles in radical cultural studies in multiracial cultures as well as on the geo-graphed globe, where the only possible politics seems sometimes to be the politics of identity in the name of *being* the Other."[15] Preferring the symbolic to the imaginary (as Lacan himself does), Spivak applauds those who stand up for the rights of groups with whom they are not primarily identified. Playing the φ card (whether the phallic investment is in sex, race, class, nation) may well be the solution to putting one's own identity concerns on the table—both for Lacan and for his critics—but in terms of the registers, this solution refuses the encounter with the unconscious as the *discourse* of the Other. Instead, the primarily identified analyst understands rather than listens; knows in advance rather than finds out. Consequently, phallic foundationalism is a tactic with which Lacan does not agree, though it is a tactic to which he is not himself perpetually immune, especially when he is caught up in polemics over the practice of psychoanalysis.

In matters of politics more generally, Lacan remains skeptical, feeling that those who oppose oppression today will, once empowered, commit the very oppression they accuse. He compares the idealistic reformer to Hegel's *belle âme*. The beautiful soul lives "(in every sense, even the economic sense of making a living) precisely on the disorder that it denounces" (EE 126), enabling us to "understand how the constitution of the object is subordinated to the realization of the subject" (80). More briefly and cynically put, the entified "Other" may be no more than a pretext for the subject's speech—or tenure. By contrast, analysis shows the way in which "identity is realized as disjunctive of the subject" (80). It is precisely because the subject is not one with the ego identity that interpersonal misapprehension can trigger the anxiety of intrapsychic Otherness. Since the gesture of disowning Otherness is so very protective of identity, it seems counterintuitive to own alienation when it appears. At the moment of alienation the subject has not merely reached its boundaries, it has exceeded them. Grasping onto fixed identity as an anchor with which to master the impending decentering is only logical—yet mastery is ineffectual, and "analysts have to deal with slaves who think they are masters, and who find in a language whose mission is universal the support of their servitude, and the bonds of its ambiguity" (EE 81).

Since Lacanian analysis supports neither the discourse of categorical identity nor the rhetoric of blame that so frequently accompanies it, it might appear that Lacan has little to offer political analysis, especially where issues of identity are foremost. However, I believe that neither the otherness of hostile objectification nor the Otherness productive of alienation alone offers nearly the resource for political critique that examining the disjunction *between* the two affords. Carlos Mencia's joke points to the alternative, to the location of politicized difference in another scene that addresses the phallic investment itself rather than the terms by which that investment is veiled. Analysis can indeed locate the political in another scene that is both a decentering of the subject and an exposé of the epistemology of a fixed or fixable Otherness. If ego identity is the certainty from which the subject is decentered, then "the art of the analyst must be to suspend the subject's certainties until their last mirages have been consumed" (EE 43). If "psychoanalysis . . . reveals both the one and the other [the individual and the collective] to be no more than mirages" (80) then analysis seems at odds with the Platonic emphasis on a Self/Other binary though not with identity politics as a whole. Where identity is at issue, Lacan insists that "it is not a question of knowing whether I speak of myself in a way that conforms to what I am, but rather of knowing whether I am the same as that of which I speak" (165). Regarding alterity, Lacan's register theory would have us withhold our demands and acknowledge our desires as our own so that we can better listen for the discourse of the Other—if the Other's Truth is what we genuinely desire to hear. And what is Truth? "Truth is nothing other than that which knowledge can apprehend as knowledge only by setting ignorance to work A real crisis in which the imaginary is resolved, thus engendering a new symbolic form" (296).

In the idea of Truth, the discourse of desire once again encounters the discourse of the registers, and this study of register theory as desire's other side is nearly complete. What I have postulated as the otherness of the two Lacanian discourses—that one is invariably the flip side of the other—now seems to suggest that the two discourses are joined at the Other as well. Thus the Other has become an intrapsychic nexus in which the discourse of the registers passes over into the discourse of desire and vice versa. Before I conclude, I want to add one more Lacanian Other to the Other of the registers and the Other of desire. It is the Other as an authentic subject of interpersonal exchange, the Other of whom the subject is innocent. Lacan speaks of this "authentic Other" as another subject to be appreciated for its alterity, its capacity to surprise. This authentic Other is available to any subject who is willing, like the analyst, to annul the resistance of its intrapsychic other and to accept the anxiety aroused within its intrapsychic Otherness. Then the vital encounter between two authentic subjects can aim "at the passage of true speech, joining the subject to an other subject, on the other side of the wall of language. That is the final relation of the subject to a genuine Other, to the Other who gives the answer one doesn't expect, which defines the terminal point in analysis" (Sem II 246).

And the terminal point in this discussion . . .

Page 160 blank.

Notes

Introduction

1. See *The Seminar of Jacques Lacan, Book I, Freud's Papers on Technique, 1953–1954*, trans. John Forrester, ed. Jacques-Alain Miller (New York: W.W. Norton & Company, 1988) 73. Hereafter, Seminar I will be cited in the text as Sem I.

2. For a thorough analysis of Freud's archaeological metaphor, see Bowie, *Freud, Proust and Lacan: Theory as Fiction*, chapter 1, "Freud's Dreams of Knowledge," especially 18–26. Lis Moller, *The Freudian Reading* (Philadelphia: U of Pennsylvania P, 1991) explores the same theme. See chapter 2, "*Gradiva*: Psychoanalysis as Archaeology."

3. The metaphor of the musical register effectively emphasizes both the qualitative nature of the distinctions Lacan makes between the imaginary, the symbolic, and the real and the fact that each register incorporates a range of phenomena. For instance, imaginary processes tend toward unity while symbolic processes involve differentiation. Within the imaginary register alone, however, Lacan might talk about identification, or about the relation with the imaginary mother, or about the imago, and so on.

4. My thanks to vocalist Kathleen Lane, Department of Music, Idaho State University for her helpful insights on the registers of the singing voice and the texture of music.

5. The idea of linguistic registers applies in Lacan more loosely, as when linguists talk about the "register of law" or the "register of medicine" or the "register of linguistics" to designate each professional vocabulary and the context in which that vocabulary signifies. This use of the term "register" overlaps what Lacan (and much of contemporary theory) refers to as a "discourse" spoken by a specific discourse community. The former term emphasizes semantics, while the latter term emphasizes speech as a practice.

6. Secondary works about theory generally fall into one of three approaches: the explication or "guide to" whose purpose is to clarify a theorist's

work, the argument whose purpose is to critique or challenge the theory it discusses, and the application whose purpose is to demonstrate a theory's encounter with another text. Combining these approaches makes a heavier demand on the reader. At issue for me (as a theorist who teaches theory to both undergraduates and graduate students) is *when* secondary works have value—not *whether*. My position here is that Lacanian analysis is best learned by reading Lacan's own texts first, with a companion explication as a reference if necessary. Only then can a critique or an application be meaningful. Read before primary texts (or in lieu of them!), critiques and applications tend either to confuse their readers or, worse, to give readers a false sense of mastery. Even an important introductory work like Elizabeth Grosz's *Jacques Lacan: A Feminist Introduction* (London: Routledge, 1990) accommodates two distinct paradigms, requiring the reader to keep the feminist paradigm in play while acquiring the Lacan. Interdisciplinary critiques do position Lacan in the larger intellectual community, and one very helpful example of this approach is David S. Caudill's *Lacan and the Subject of Law* (Atlantic Highlands, NJ: Humanities Press, 1997). However, I return to Lacan's main texts and issues in this work because I feel that Lacan best clarifies Lacan.

7. First published as "Freud et Lacan," *La nouvelle critique* 161/162 (1964/65): 88–108 and reprinted in *Positions, 1964–1975* (Paris: Editions Sociales, 1976) 9–34. The article first appeared in English in *The New Left Review* in 1969 but has been most widely disseminated in *Lenin and Philosophy* (New York: Monthly Review Press, 1971) 189–219. Perry Anderson, *In the Tracks of Historical Materialism*, details the theoretical problems involved in Althusserian Marxism itself (London: Verso, 1983). Anderson argues for a "local defeat" of Marxist theoretical ideas by the French structuralists whose ideas amounted to an 'epistemic' shift, which Marxisms like that of Althusser sought to counter through appropriation. Interestingly, Sherry Turkle makes the parallel suggestion that "psychoanalysis, a theory with two faces, was the Trojan Horse for French structuralism." See Turkle, "The New Philosophy and the Agony of Structuralism: Enter the Trojan Horse," *Chicago Review* 32.3 (1981): 24. Also, see Jameson, *The Political Unconscious, Narrative as a Socially Symbolic Act* (New York: Cornell UP, 1981). For a thorough discussion of Jameson's use of Lacan, see Michael Clark, "Imagining the Real: Jameson's Use of Lacan," *New Orleans Review* 11.1 (1984): 67–72.

8. See *The Subject of Semiotics* (New York: Oxford University Press, 1983): 130.

9. Compare *Écrits: A Selection,* trans. Alan Sheridan, ed. Jacques-Alain Miller (New York: Norton, 1977)—hereafter cited as EE—and *The Four Fundamental Concepts of Psycho-Analysis*, Seminar 11, trans. Alan Sheridan, ed. Jacques-Alain Miller (New York: W.W. Norton & Company, 1977) to *The Sem-*

inar of Jacques Lacan, Book I, Freud's Papers on Technique, 1953–1954, trans. John Forrester, ed. Jacques-Alain Miller (New York: W.W. Norton & Company, 1988), *The Seminar of Jacques Lacan, Book II, The Ego in Freud's Theory and in the Technique of Psychoanalysis 1954–1955,* trans. Sylvana Tomaselli, ed. Jacques-Alain Miller (New York: W.W. Norton & Company, 1988)—hereafter cited as Sem II—and *The Seminar of Jacques Lacan, Book III, The Psychoses, 1955–1956,* trans. Russell Grigg, ed. Jacques-Alain Miller (New York: W.W. Norton & Company, 1993)—hereafter cited as Sem III. The paradigm was available in the extremely useful thesaurus of Lacanian terms and critical concepts appearing in the back of both the French and the English versions of *Écrits,* and in Lacan's many drawings. The schema of subjectivity, Schema L, and a detailed commentary on this "schema of the intersubjective dialectic" can be found in Sheridan's English *Écrits* 332–33. I suspect that readers who began their Lacan studies with these indices and illustrations grasped Lacan's paradigm in a way readers of his brief essays did not.

10. See Michael Clark's *Jacques Lacan, An Annotated Bibliography,* (New York: Garland, 1988) 2 vols.

11. See Rachel Bowlby, "Two by Three," *Paragraph: A Journal of Modern Critical Theory* 13.1 (1990): 89–96.

Chapter 1
A Funny Thing Happened on the Way to the *Symposium*

1. "An Introduction to Seminars I and II, Lacan's Orientation Prior to 1953 (II)," in *Reading Seminars I and II, Lacan's Return to Freud,* ed. Richard Feldstein, Bruce Fink, and Maire Jaanus (Albany: SUNY Press, 1996).

2. See the "Classified Index of the major concepts" in the English *Écrits,* 326–31. Miller provides a thesaurus of Lacan's project as a whole and the work done by specific terms within the larger Lacanian discourse.

3. *Jacques Lacan,* trans. David Macey (London: Routledge, 1977).

4. Plato, *The Dialogues of Plato,* trans. B. Jowett (Oxford: Clarendon Press, 1892) 559–562.

5. Freud, SE 7, 136. (SE stands for *The Standard Edition of the Complete Psychological Works of Sigmund Freud.* Trans. and ed. James Strachey. New York: W.W. Norton & Company, 1953–73.) I am indebted to Rachel Bowlby for this reference and for her insightful analysis of the opposed readings of Freud and Bowie as detailed in "Two by Three," *Paragraph: A Journal of Modern Critical Theory* 13.1 (1990): 89–96.

6. *Beyond the Pleasure Principle,* SE 18, 57–58. Freud's source is Jowett's translation.

7. Note 20, *Beyond the Pleasure Principle* 70.

8. *Vested Interests* (New York: HarperCollins, 1993).

9. Garber cites Pauline Kael's review of *Tootsie*, which suggests that though the male disguiser's strength might be deemed condescending, Hoffman's portrayal was indeed in "good faith," *New Yorker* 27 December 1982: 71.

10. Garber here cites Elaine Showalter as exemplary: "Critical Cross-Dressing: Male Feminists and the Woman of the Year," *Raritan* 3.2 (Fall 1983): 138.

11. Here, Garber follows Lacan explicitly; Lacan frequently describes the symbolic as a "third term," usually in conjunction with discussion of the Oedipus complex and the family triangle.

12. *S/Z,* trans. Richard Miller (New York: The Noonday Press, 1974).

13. "The Tutor-Code of Classical Cinema," *Film Quarterly* 28.1 (1974): 22–31.

14. Jean-Pierre Oudart, "La Suture," *Cahiers du Cinéma* (1969), trans. Kari Hanet, "Cinema and Suture." *Screen* 18.4 (1977–78): 35–47.

15. Schema L appears on page 243 (Sem II) as an illustration of subjectivity within a larger discussion of the register of language which Tomaselli translates "Introduction of the big Other."

16. John Brenkman, "The Other and the One: Psychoanalysis, Reading, the *Symposium*," in *Literature and Psychoanalysis*, ed. Shoshana Felman (Baltimore: Johns Hopkins UP, 1989) 396–456.

17. Translated by Bruce Fink, in *Reading Seminar XI, Lacan's Four Fundamental Concepts of Psychoanalysis*, eds. Richard Feldstein, Bruce Fink, and Maire Jaanus (Albany: SUNY Press, 1995) 259–282.

Chapter 2
The Master in the Mirror

1. Translated by Sheridan in *Écrits: A Selection* 1–7. First published in the *Revue française de psychanalyse* 4 (October–December, 1949): 449–55.

2. "L'aggressivité en psychanalyse," a theoretical report read at the eleventh Congrès des psychanalystes de langue française in Brussels, May, 1948 was first published in the *Revue française de psychanalyse* 3 (July–September, 1948): 367–88. Translated by Sheridan in *Écrits: A Selection* 8–29.

3. Catherine David, "Psychanalyse: Faut-il brûler Lacan?" *Le nouvel observateur* 15 September 1993: 4–14.

4. See Gallop, *Reading Lacan* 75.

5. Palmier, *Lacan* (Paris: Editions Universitaires, 1972).

6. Palmier's error is described in detail by Jane Gallop, and I am indebted to her both for the anecdote and for the translation. Gallop reads with a translator's eye to detail, and with her own characteristic humor. Remarking on the absent abstract and the void where Palmier's alleged reading takes place, Gallop remarks, "Quite imprecise, at certain points, indeed!" See *Reading Lacan*, 76.

7. See Clark's bibliography, 124.

8. I am indebted to Jane Gallop, *Reading Lacan* for this reference. See her relevant discussion, 75–76. Gallop cites Lacan's 1946 essay "Remarks on Mental Causality," French *Écrits* 195.

9. An astute discussion of Lacan's continual reference to Augustine can be found in Shuli Barzilai, "Augustine in Contexts: Lacan's Repetition of a Scene from the Confessions," Literature and Theology, 11.2 (June 1997): 200–221.

10. "Le complexe, facteur concret de la psychologie familiale," *Encyclopédie française* VIII: *La vie mentale.* Ed. Henri Wallon (Paris: Larousse, Société de gestion de l'Encyclopédié française, 1938): 8.40.5–8.40.16. Also, "Les complexes familiaux en pathologie," same source, 8.42.1–8.42.8. The articles were published in book form as *Les complexes familiaux dans la formation de l'individu: essai d'analyse d'une fonction en psychologie* (Paris: Navarin, 1984). Summary and analysis of Lacan's early encyclopedia articles on the family appear both in Clark and in Jonathan Scott Lee's *Jacques Lacan* (Amherst: U of Massachusetts P, 1990) 13–17.

11. Clark, 127, cites Lacan, 8.40.10.

12. Kojève's lectures were preserved and edited by the French writer Raymond Quesneau and published in French under the title *Introduction à la Lecture de Hegel* (Paris: Gallimard, 1947). The English translation by James H. Nichols, Jr. offers a selection of the French text "made with two goals in mind: to present the outlines of Kojève's interpretation of the *Phenomenology of Spirit*, and to present the most characteristic aspects of his own thought," Translator's Note, *Introduction to the Reading of Hegel*, ed. Allan Bloom (Ithaca: Cornell UP, 1969) xiii.

13. Aimé Patri, "Dialectique du Maître et de l'Esclave," *Le Contrat Social* 5.4 (July–August 1961): 234, cited by Allan Bloom in his Editor's Introduction to Kojève, vii.

14. See, particularly, Mikkel Borch-Jacobsen's critique of Kojève and of Lacan's use of Hegel in *Lacan: The Absolute Master* (Stanford: Stanford UP, 1991) especially the third chapter's sections on desire and mastery, 84–96. I have chosen to treat the idea of desire at length in Chapter 5, though Jacobsen rightly addresses the incommensurability of the desire of Kojève with the desire of Lacan.

15. Ver Eecke, "Hegel as Lacan's Source for Necessity in Psychoanalytic Theory," in *Interpreting Lacan*, ed. Joseph H. Smith and William Kerrigan (New Haven: Yale U P, 1983) 113–38.

16. G.W.F. Hegel, *Phenomenology of Spirit*, trans. A. V. Miller (Oxford: Oxford U P, 1977).

17. H.B. Acton, "Hegel," in *Hegel Selections*, ed. M. J. Inwood (New York: Macmillan, 1989): 8–9.

18. See Seminar II, chapter 6, 64–76. Lacan here uses the idea of the machine to depict a symbolic that is the dialectical beyond of the imaginary struggle.

19. With Henri Claude and P. Migault, "Folies simultanées," Société médico-psychologique, 21 May 1931. Published in *Annales médico-psychologique* 1 (1931): 483–90.

20. With H. Claude and G. Heuyer, "Un cas de démence précocissisme," Société médico-psychologique, 5 September 1933. Published in *Annales médico-psychologique* 1 (1933): 620–24. See also, "Motifs du crime paranoïaque: le crime des soeurs Papin," *Le minotaure* 3/4 (1933): 25–28.

21. Discussion of M. Bonaparte, "Vues paléobiologiques et biopsychiques," Société psychanalytique de Paris, 19 January 1937. Published in *Revue française de psychanalyse* 3 (1938): 551.

22. Lacan's thesis asserts that the paranoid's disturbance springs from events in her life rather than from biological origins, an assertion expressly psychoanalytic rather than psychiatric. See Clark xxxvi and 3–6.

23. Michael Clark provides a supporting etymological detail on the origin of the idea of the 'other' which supports the concept of its plurality: "Lacan uses the term '*l'autrui*' here [in the encyclopedia article "Le complexe, facteur concret de la psychologie familiale"], which literally means 'the others,' but it takes on the specialized sense of '*l'autre*,' 'the other,' that he later develops at length. This special usage is signaled by Lacan's use of the article with the noun, which is used familiarly by itself as '*autrui*'" (127).

24. Tallis, "Some Reflections on the Mirror Stage," *Trivium* 21 (Summer 1986): 5–44.

25. See Tallis, and see Roustang, *The Lacanian Delusion*. One exception to the generally positive perception of Lacan's use of Hegel in works such as Jonathan Scott Lee's *Jacques Lacan*, is Mikkel Borch-Jacobsen's *Lacan: the Absolute Master* (Stanford: Stanford UP, 1991). See particularly chapter 1, "Crime and Punishment," which addresses the dialectic and chapter 3, "Through the Looking Glass," which critiques the uses of philosophy in mirror stage theory.

26. For a line by line explication of this paragraph, see Gallop, *Reading Lacan*, Chapter 3, especially pages 80–82.

27. Lacan here refers to Anna Freud's 1936 classic work *The Ego and the Mechanisms of Defence* (London: The Hogarth Press and the Institute of Psycho-analysis, 1968).

28. Maria Ines Rotmiler de Zentner, "The Identification and the Ideal," *Papers of the Freudian School of Melbourne* (1981): 103–18.

29. See "On Narcissism: An Introduction," SE 14, 73–102.

30. Suzanne Ginestet-Delbreil, "L'identification par incorporation," *Psychanalyse et apocalypse*, ed. René Major (Paris: Confrontations, 1982) 75–86.

Chapter 3
The Poe-etics of Register Theory

1. See particularly Catherine Clément, *The Lives and Legends of Jacques Lacan*, and Philippe Julien, *Le retour à Freud de Jacques Lacan: l'application au miroir*. Julien's subtitle clearly indicates his assumption that Lacan's later theory derives from his mirror stage theory in psychoanalytic application. Clement, by contrast, presents the elements of Lacan's theory within a narrative structured on Lacan's career and his biography. Both approaches foreground the continuities within Lacanian theory; both stress the imaginary as the dominant Lacanian construct.

2. Though Bowie notes that the symbolic, the imaginary, and the real, are not personifiable as are Freud's id, ego, and superego, Bowie himself elevates the registers into a categorical epic in which the imaginary, symbolic, and real inflate themselves to "become warring principles in a grandiose cosmological allegory" (*Lacan* 91), "an unholy trinity whose members could as easily be called Fraud, Absence and Impossibility" (112).

3. The gulf between psychoanalysis and psychoanalytic literary analysis is cleverly detailed by Jane Gallop, *Reading Lacan*, 31–36. Gallop describes her brief foray out of Lacan's text and into a training analysis that she quickly abandoned, following the pattern of Catherine Clément. The latter declared that the experience of analysis—which would inevitably include the real of analysis— made Lacan's texts into resistant "opaque blocks" instead of clarifying them. Clément's conclusion actually reinforces Lacan's notion of the real as a set of constraints upon and barriers to the free operation of interpretation. A very different vision of the connections of theory, of practice, and of the real of psychoanalysis emerges from Stuart Schneiderman whose *Jacques Lacan: The Death of an Intellectual Hero* (Cambridge: Harvard UP, 1983) details Schneiderman's

abandonment of his career as a literary critic for his subsequent analysis by and analytic training with Lacan himself.

4. See Laplanche and Pontalis, *The Language of Psychoanalysis*, trans. Donald Nicholson-Smith (New York: W.W. Norton & Company, 1973), especially the entries on internalization, introjection, and incorporation.

5. Ellie Ragland's chapter "The Relationship of Sense and Sign," *Jacques Lacan and the Philosophy of Psychoanalysis*, especially pages 208–33, discusses the image as a "unary signifier." Ragland argues that the signifying chain of speech itself is "reducible to the ordered pair of an Imaginary unary and Symbolic binary signifier" (226).

6. See Seminar III, chapter 21 "The quilting point," especially 268–70, in which Lacan discusses the function of the name of the father as one such point at which the signifier and signified are "knotted" together.

7. Lacan cites Freud's early work on dreams and representation to show the implication of image with memory. See Seminar I, 75.

8. Though Saussure's terms, signifier and signified, suggest "things," it is crucial to bear in mind that there are no "atoms" of language. While a phonemic transcription of speech or a text of words appears to be composed of just such foundational atoms, "the unary signifier" here should be conceptualized as a *fusional signifying*. In French, signifier and signified seem more clearly to be "the signifying" and "consequences of the signifying."

9. Ragland draws heavily on Lacan's later seminars, particularly Seminar XI on the fundamental concepts of psychoanalysis, and Seminar XX on the abstruse and difficult Lacanian notations of the signifier and the barred subject of the unconscious. Though they do not use the term "unary signifier," the Seminar I discussions of the specular ego presented with numerous illustrations of the unifying illusions of the imaginary and the Seminar III discussion of psychosis explicate the unifying power of the image.

10. "The Symbolic Order (I)," in *Reading Seminars I and II: Lacan's Return to Freud*, 39–46. See also the companion essays "The Symbolic Order (II)" and "Transference."

11. With Wladimir Granoff, "Fetishism: the Symbolic, the Imaginary and the Real," 274.

12. Identification as a process differs from the notion of identity as something fixed "in" the person. One concept of fixed identity based on the theory of Heinz Lichtenstein is articulated by Norman Holland, "Unity Identity Text Self" in *Reader-Response Criticism*, ed. Jane P. Tompkins (Baltimore: Johns Hopkins, 1988) 118–33. "Out of the newborn child's inheritance of potentialities, its mother-person actuates a specific way of being, namely, being the child

that fits this particular mother. The mother thus imprints on the infant, not a specific identity or even a sense of its own identity, but a 'primary identity,' itself irreversible but capable of infinite variation. This primary identity stands as an invariant which provides all the later transformations of the individual, as he develops with an unchanging inner form or core of continuity" (120–21). This inner core manifests itself as the individual's sense of personal continuity, the awareness of others' sense of one's own existence, a continuity of style, and of others' sense of that style's significance (120). Though Lacan's mirror stage certainly involves the mother as a mirroring other, his work clearly rejects all notion of a fixed identity stamped on the child by the mother. The human process of identifying oneself through the mirroring of an other indicates a fluid rather than a fixed identity.

13. Poe's text is quoted in *The Seminar of Jacques Lacan: Book II*, 179–80. The summary here is my own.

14. *Arguing with Lacan: Ego Psychology and Language* (New Haven: Yale UP, 1991). Smith, taking the position of Ego Psychology, argues that the ego has nondefensive functions and is thus capable of nondefensive identifications. Lacan, Smith points out, would not agree with this position and would see the primary *moi* identifications as purely defensive and exclusionary.

15. "Seminar on 'The Purloined Letter,'" in John P. Muller and William J. Richardson's *The Purloined Poe*, 30. Muller and Richardson discuss some of Lacan's additional material in "Lacan's Seminar on 'The Purloined Letter': Overview," *The Purloined Poe*, 55–76 and include many of Lacan's diagrams of sequences of three. The addenda to "Le Séminaire sur 'La Lettre Volée'" in the French *Écrits* present various approaches to triplicity. "Présentation de la Suite," 41–44, recalls Lacan's Seminar II use of Greek letters to label sequences of three in order to tie such complex sequences to the function of the unconscious. "Introduction," 44–53, employs various diagrams based on threefold sequences of plus and minus to describe, again, the interaction between subjectivity and sequence. Here, sequences are tied to Lacan's Schema L, to intersubjectivity, and to the registers. Finally, "Parenthèse des Parenthèses" uses a zero and one binary sequence organized in patterns and parentheses to return the discussion to chance, the subject of the odd/even game with which Lacan's first explorations of "The Purloined Letter" begins in Seminar II.

16. See "On Reading Poetry," in *The Purloined Poe*, ed. John P. Muller and William J. Richardson (Baltimore: Johns Hopkins, 1988) 144–47.

17. See Lacan, "Seminar on 'The Purloined Letter,'" 40, and Felman, "On Reading Poetry," 144–46.

18. Lacan, French *Écrits* 90, translated by Muller and Richardson, *Lacan and Language* 28.

Chapter 4
Lacanian Epistemology

1. Jean Paul Sartre, *Orphée Noir* (Paris: Presses Universitaires de France, 1948) xlff. Quoted in Franz Fanon, *Black Skin/White Masks* (New York: Grove, 1967) 132–33.

2. Toni Morrison, *Beloved* (New York: Plume-Penguin, 1988).

3. Roy Harris, *Reading Saussure* (LaSalle, IL: Open Court, 1987) 53.

4. Greenblatt borrows heavily on Lacan's theory of subjectivity and on the relations between the subject and the Other in his book *Renaissance Self-Fashioning: From More to Shakespeare* (University of Chicago Press, 1980).

5. I cite from a table entitled "Distinctive Feature Composition of English Consonants" in *Linguistics*, 2d. Ed., by Adrian Akmajian, Richard A. Demers, and Robert M. Harnish (Cambridge: MIT Press, 1984) 144–45. Binary tables such as the one the authors offer here show the work of the combinatory distinctions that are concealed in the popular illustrations that superimpose the phonemes on a drawing of the human vocal tract. The former illustrates the phonemes as constructs, the latter illustrates the phonemes as essences.

6. See Jean Paul Sartre, *Being and Nothingness*, trans. Hazel E. Barnes (New York: Philosophical Library, 1956), especially part 3, chapter 1, section 4 "The Look" for a similar discussion of the construction via a third perspective.

7. Lacan's Schema 1, Schema 2, and Schema 3 are illustrated in "Le désir et son interprétation," ed. J.-B. Pontalis, *Bulletin de psychologie* 13.5 (1960): 263–72.

8. *Tootsie*, dir. Sydney Pollack, Columbia Pictures, 1982.

Chapter 5
The Discourse of Desire and the Registers in *Hamlet*

1. Seminar IV, *La relation d'object et les structures freudiennes*, is untranslated to date. It is available in French through Les Editions du Seuil (Paris, 1996). Abstracts of the seminar are summarized in Michael Clark's *Jacques Lacan*, an annotated bibliography 1: 50–53. Seminar V, *Les formations de l'inconscient*, remains unpublished as of 1998. It is abstracted in the *Bulletin de psychologie* 11, 4/5 (1958): 293–96; 12, 2/3 (1958): 182–92; and 12, 4 (1958): 250–56, and the abstracts are summarized in Clark, 53–55. The best access to the material in these two seminars is Joël Dor's *Introduction à la lecture de Lacan, L'inconscient structuré comme un langage* (Paris: Denoël, 1985).

2. Seminar VI, *Le désir et son interprétation*, is only partially translated to date. The earliest sessions are summarized in the *Bulletin de psychologie* 13.5

(1960): 263–72 and 13.6 (1960): 329–35, and are abstracted by Clark, 56–57. The complete *Hamlet* seminars edited by Jacques-Alain Miller are published in French in *Ornicar?* 24 (1981): 7–31; 25 (1982): 13–36; and 26/27 (1983): 7–44. Of these, the final three sessions discussing Lacan's detailed reading of Hamlet's delay, the object Ophelia, and the dynamics of castration are published as "Desire and the Interpretation of Desire in Hamlet," trans. James Hulbert, ed. Jacques-Alain Miller, in *Literature and Psychoanalysis*, ed. Shoshana Felman (Baltimore: Johns Hopkins, 1982) 11–52.

3. "Psychoanalysis Unbound," *New Literary History* 12.1 (1980): 199–206.

4. See *The Interpretation of Dreams*, trans. and ed. James Strachey (New York: Avon, 1965): 298–300.

5. "The Oedipus Complex as an Explanation of Hamlet's Mystery," *The American Journal of Psychology* (January 1910): 72–113, later appears in an extended version as "A Psycho-Analytic Study of Hamlet," the first chapter of *Essays in Applied Psycho-Analysis* (London: The International Psycho-Analytical Press, 1923) 1–98. In 1949, still further elaborated, the essay appears in book form as *Hamlet and Oedipus* (New York: Norton, 1976). It is the 1910 essay Lacan recommends to his seminar participants.

6. See "Le Canevas (fin)," Lacan's seminar for 11 March 1959, 20.

7. Freud's *Leonardo da Vinci and a Memory of his Childhood* presents a psychohistorical study of Leonardo's childhood memory of being attacked by a vulture and that memory's impact on his family history and his rise from obscurity to fame.

8. Jones's 1923 essay, particularly, draws heavily on the literary speculations of Frank Harris in *The Man Shakespeare and his Tragic Life-Story*, 1909 (see Jones's note, 10) and *Shakespeare and his Love*, 1910 (see Jones, 60–61 and notes, 60).

9. See "Le désir de la mère," 19, in Lacan's *Hamlet* seminars.

10. "The Importance of Symbol-formation in the Development of the Ego," *The Writings of Melanie Klein*, vol. 1 (London: Hogarth Press, 1975) 219–32.

11. Lacanian analysis suggests that socialized male dominance constitutes a suture within androcentric culture. If the signifying difference penis/clitoris is considered in light of the image of the phallus, positions of naturalizable power and disempowerment evolve. The logic of suture supports low-level, resistant claims about gender difference, claims explicitly supporting the Hegelian master/servant positions to which Lacan so frequently refers. Where biological difference and homosocial privilege conspire, the male occupies the position of the

master since phallic images and the penis as signifier of sexed difference collude. The male position inevitably stitches the imaginary to the symbolic in andro-centric culture; the male, consequently, signifies unproblematically. In patri-archy, those born with the clitoral marker do not have the luxury of suturing the registers. No culturally endorsed image fuses woman with her symbolic signifier. She is the servant; it is her "nature" to register difference—not only symbolically (where the differences are differences of content) but structurally (where differ-ence connotes being and not-being). Retrospectively, primary identifications with the positions of fusion (male/master) and disjunction (female/servant) invite valorizing experiences. Having the phallus in patriarchy means perceiving that one has the power to define a reality in which men signify in a way that women do not. It is important to note that this reading takes the Oedipus literally in a way that Lacan does not.

12. In Lemaire, 83, who cites "Les formations de l'inconscient," *Bulletin de Psychologie*, 1956–57.

13. See especially pages 1–10 of the Translators' Introduction to Daniel Paul Schreber's *Memoirs of My Nervous Illness* (Cambridge: Harvard U P, 1988) by Ida Macalpine and Richard A. Hunter. Samuel M. Weber's introduction (vii–liv) outlines the interest of both Freud and Lacan in the Schreber case.

14. See Weber, particularly xxxix–xl.

15. Lacan commits a good deal of print to the Schreber material, writing about Schreber throughout much of his third Seminar on the psychoses, and devoting a lengthy essay to the case. *Écrits's* "On the possible treatment of psy-chosis" even accords Schreber his own schema (EE 212).

16. Ce n'est pas son désir pour sa mère, c'est le désir de sa mère. See "Ham-let, le désir de la mère," 20.

17. See Bruce Fink, "The Subject and the Other's Desire," in Feldstein, Fink, and Jaanus, *Reading Seminars I and II*, 81. This essay offers a lucid step-by-step explanation of the process by which the child becomes a subject. Fink differentiates the child's alienation in the imaginary from the child's separation and consequent splitting.

Chapter 6
Symptomatic Perfectionism in *The Journals of Sylvia Plath*

1. "Edge" appears in *The Collected Poems* of Sylvia Plath (New York: Harper & Row, Publishers, 1981) 272–73. Journal citations are from *The Jour-nals of Sylvia Plath* (New York: Ballantine, 1982).

2. Ted Hughes wrote two introductions to Sylvia Plath's *Journals*. The briefer foreword appears in the Ballantine edition to *The Journals of Sylvia*

Plath, xiii–xv. An essay-length introduction, "Sylvia Plath and her *Journals*," is in *Ariel Ascending*, ed. Paul Alexander (New York: Harper & Row, 1985) 152–64. See Janet Malcolm's "The Silent Woman—I" in *The New Yorker* LXIX 27 (Aug 23 & 30, 1993) 84–86 for a provocative discussion of Hughes's two pieces.

3. *Enjoy Your Symptom!* (New York: Routledge, 1992). Žižek discusses what he feels is a reversal in the direction of the Lacanian symptom between the early Lacan and the Lacan of the last Seminars on the position of man's relationship to woman.

4. The emphasis in this and the following citations which include the words "perfect" or "perfection" are mine. I emphasize the word so that readers can more easily see the work the symptom "perfect" does in Plath's text.

5. See Aurelia Plath, ed., *Letters Home, by Sylvia Plath, Correspondence 1950–1963* (New York: HarperPerrenial, 1992).

6. In J. Laplanche and J.-B. Pontalis, *The Language of Psycho-Analysis*, trans. Donald Nicholson-Smith (New York: W.W. Norton & Company, 1973).

Chapter 7
Being and Otherness

1. Plato, *Sophist*, in *Plato: Collected Dialogues*, trans. F.M. Cornford, ed. Edith Hamilton and Huntington Cairns (Princeton: Princeton UP, 1961). For a discussion of otherness in Plato's *Sophist* see "Non-Being" in Stanley Rosen's *Plato's "Sophist"* (New Haven: Yale UP, 1993) 269–90.

2. See de Beauvoir's note on Levinas in the introduction to *The Second Sex* (New York: Vintage, 1989) xxii. The note is interesting because de Beauvoir contains Levinas's discussion of radical alterity as absolute contrariety by insisting it is written from a masculine point of view that disregards "the reciprocity of subject and object." However, for Levinas, as for Lacan, subject and object are decidedly nonreciprocal—the point Lacan expresses by distinguishing the imaginary register of the image from the symbolic register of the radical Other. Levinas reconsiders the idea of alterity in *Outside the Subject,* trans. Michael B. Smith (Stanford: Stanford UP, 1994). See, particularly, the concluding essay by that name.

3. In Ashcroft, Griffiths, and Tiffin, *The Post–colonial Studies Reader* (New York: Routledge, 1995) 233. Fanon himself appropriates the term "Other" in *Black Skin, White Masks* (New York: Grove, 1967) from a number of analysts and philosophers who use it, including Jean Veneuse, Sartre, and Lacan.

4. Raman Selden, *A Reader's Guide to Contemporary Literary Theory*, 3d ed. (Lexington: UP of Kentucky, 1993).

5. Homi K. Bhabha "Cultural Diversity and Cultural Differences" in *The Post-colonial Studies Reader* (209).

6. In Appiah and Gates, Jr., *Identities* (Chicago: U of Chicago P, 1995) 89.

7. "Under the South African Union," *The National Geographic Magazine* 59.4 (April 1931): 391–512.

8. *The Tonight Show*, NBC, August 8, 1997.

9. "Current Theories of Colonial Discourse," in *The Post-colonial Studies Reader*, 41. See also Homi K. Bhabha's detailed study of postcolonialism and alterity in "The Other Question: Stereotype, Discrimination and the Discourse of Colonialism," chapter three in his collection *The Location of Culture* (London: Routledge, 1994).

10. An entertaining account of Lacan's early interests and of his overwhelming reliance on case studies involving women can be found in Catherine Clément's "The Ladies' Way" in *The Lives and Legends of Jacques Lacan*, trans. Arthur Goldhammer (New York: Columbia UP, 1983) 53–101.

11. It might seem that a reader innocent of Lacanian discourse might be a "better" reader of JanMohamed's essay, since the naïve reader would not discern the discursive impossibility of the "'imaginary' Otherness." But in discourse as elsewhere, ignorance of the law is no excuse. Since the naïve reader has no discursive pact with the writer, what passes for reading is an extra-symbolic exercise in idiosyncrasy. Lacking the pact, "reading" would be a species of parasitic narcissism held together—if it is held together at all—by the reader's imaginary identification with the writer, a mirroring instance of "reading" as "writing."

12. Butler is an astute critic of psychoanalysis and has, throughout her career, raised significant issues about psychoanalytic theory. Her article "Gender Trouble, Feminist Theory, and Psychoanalytic Discourse" offers Butler's characteristically precise analysis of psychoanalysis's and feminist theory's implications for each other. See *Feminism/ Postmodernism*, ed. Linda Nicholson (New York: Routledge, 1990): 324–40.

13. The irony of Butler's reading and its notable omission of the imaginary other is emphasized by her apt focus on Lacan's most emphatically structural of the early seminars, *The Seminar of Jacques Lacan: Book II: The Ego in Freud's Theory and in the Technique of Psychoanalysis*, trans. Sylvana Tomaselli, ed. Jacques-Alain Miller (New York: W.W. Norton & Company, 1988).

14. Reducing Lacanian theory to a unified field as Judith Butler does supports binary notions of subject and symbolic Other, turning Lacan's intrapsychic model into an interpersonal model and rewriting Lacan in the terms of theories of identity more discursively assimilable to a paradigm of performativity. This interpersonal model is clearly politicizable and compatible with the kinds of

Foucauldian and deconstructive political impulses that characterize Butler's own theory of "performance as citation and gender as iteration" (Whitford, cover). Politically, then, Butler needs to situate the point of infinite substitution within a dualistic imaginary to accomplish her own theoretical goals. Thus, the imaginary, in Butler's analysis, is regarded as a field that functions in a structurally unproblematic way.

15. "Acting Bits/Identity Talk," in Appiah and Gates, Jr., 159.

Page 176 blank.

Bibliography

Acton, H. B. "Hegel." *Hegel Selections*. Ed. M. J. Inwood. New York: Macmillan, 1989. 8–9.

Althusser, Louis. *Lenin and Philosophy and Other Essays*. Trans. Ben Brewster. New York: New Left Books, 1971.

———. "La découverte du docteur Freud." *Dialogue franco-soviétique sur la psychanalyse*. Private publication, 1984. 81–97.

Anderson, Perry. *In the Tracks of Historical Materialism*. London: Verso, 1983.

Ashcroft, Bill, Gareth Griffiths, and Helen Tiffin, eds. *The Post-colonial Studies Reader*. London: Routledge, 1995.

St. Augustine. "De locutionis significatione." *De Magistro* [*The Teacher*]. Trans. Robert P. Russell. Washington: Catholic U of America P, 1968. 7–61.

Barthes, Roland. "The Death of the Author." *Image-Music-Text*. Trans. and ed. Stephen Heath. London: Fontana, 1977.

———. *S/Z*. Trans. Richard Miller. New York: The Noonday Press, 1974.

———. *Elements of Semiology*. Trans. Annette Lavers and Colin Smith. New York: Hill and Wang, 1991.

Barzilai, Shuli. "Borders of Language: Kristeva's Critique of Lacan." *PMLA* 106 2 (1991): 294–305.

———. "Augustine in Contexts: Lacan's Repetition of a Scene from the Confessions." *Literature and Theology* 11.2 (June 1997): 200–221.

Beauvoir, Simone de. *The Second Sex*. New York: Vintage, 1989.

Belsey, Catherine. *The Subject of Tragedy*. London: Methuen, 1985.

Bhabha, Homi K. "The Other Question: Stereotype, Discrimination and the Discourse of Colonialism." *The Location of Culture*. London: Routledge, 1994.

———. "Cultural Diversity and Cultural Differences" in *The Post-colonial Studies Reader*.

Bloom, Allan. Editor's Introduction. *Introduction to the Reading of Hegel*. By Alexandre Kojève. Ithaca: Cornell UP, 1969. vii–xii.

Borch-Jacobsen, Mikkel. *Lacan: the Absolute Master*. Stanford: Stanford UP, 1991.

Bowie, Malcolm. "Jacques Lacan." *Structuralism and Since: From Lévi-Strauss to Derrida*. Ed. John Sturrock. Oxford: Oxford UP, 1979. 116–63.

———. *Freud, Proust and Lacan: Theory as Fiction*. London: Cambridge UP, 1988.

———. *Lacan*. Cambridge: Harvard UP, 1991.

Bowlby, Rachel. "Two by Three." *Paragraph: A Journal of Modern Critical Theory* 13 1 (1990): 89–96.

Brenkman, John. "The Other and the One: Psychoanalysis, Reading, the *Symposium*." *Literature and Psychoanalysis*. Ed. Shoshana Felman. Baltimore: Johns Hopkins UP, 1982. 396–456.

Britton, Andrew. "The Ideology of *Screen*," *Movie* 26 (1978/79): 2–28.

Brockbank, Philip J. "Hamlet the Bonesetter." *Shakespeare Survey*. London: Cambridge UP, 1977. 103–15.

Butler, Judith. *Bodies That Matter*. New York: Routledge, 1993.

———. *Subjects of Desire*. New York: Columbia UP, 1987.

———. "Gender Trouble, Feminist Theory, and Psychoanalytic Discourse." In *Feminism/Postmodernism*. Ed. Linda Nicholson. New York: Routledge, 1990. 324–40.

Caudill, David S. *Lacan and the Subject of Law*. Atlantic Highlands, N.J.: Humanities Press, 1997.

Chater, Melville. "Under the South African Union." *The National Geographic Magazine* 59.4 (April 1931): 391–512.

Chen, Xiaomei. "Occidentalism as Counterdiscourse." *Identities*. Ed. Kwame Anthony Appiah and Henry Louis Gates, Jr. Chicago: U of Chicago P, 1995. 63–89.

Chessick, Richard D. "Critique: Some Unusual Books Published in 1978." *American Journal of Psychotherapy* 33 (1979): 312–15.

Clare, Anthony. "French Guru." *New Society* 1 December 1977, 535–36.

Clark, Michael. *Jacques Lacan: An Annotated Bibliography*. 2 Vol. New York: Garland, 1988.

———. "Imagining the Real: Jameson's Use of Lacan," *New Orleans Review* 11.1 (1984): 67–72.

Clément, Catherine. *The Lives and Legends of Jacques Lacan*. Trans. Arthur Goldhammer. New York: Columbia UP, 1983.

———. "Louis Althusser à l'assaut de la forteresse Lacan." *Le matin* 17 March 1980: 35.

Copjec, Joan. "Apparatus and Umbra: A Feminist Critique of Film Theory." *DAI* 47 (1987): 4212A.

David, Catherine. "Psychanalyse: Faut-il brûler Lacan?" *Le nouvel observateur* 15 September 1993: 4–14.

Dayan, Daniel. "The Tutor-Code of Classical Cinema." *Film Quarterly* 28.1 (1974): 22–31.

Delacampagne, Christian. "Le moi selon Lacan et Freud." *Le monde* 7 April 1978: 17.

Dor, Joël. *Introduction à la lecture de Lacan, L'inconscient structuré comme un langage*. Paris: Denoël, 1985.

Dowling, William C. *Jameson, Althusser, Marx, An Introduction to "The Political Unconscious."* New York: Cornell UP, 1984.

Eastman, Arthur M. *A Short History of Shakespearean Criticism*. New York: Norton, 1968.

Elliott, Anthony. *Social Theory and Psychoanalysis in Transition*. Oxford: Blackwell, 1992.

Erlich, Avi. *Hamlet's Absent Father*. Princeton: Princeton UP, 1977.

Fanon, Franz. *Black Skin, White Masks*. New York: Grove, 1967.

Feldstein, Richard, Bruce Fink, and Maire Jaanus, eds. *Reading Seminars I and II: Lacan's Return to Freud*. Albany: SUNY Press, 1996.

Felman, Shoshana. "On Reading Poetry." *The Purloined Poe*. Eds. John P. Muller and William J. Richardson. Baltimore: Johns Hopkins UP, 1988. 144–47.

———. "To Open the Question." *Literature and Psychoanalysis*. Baltimore: Johns Hopkins UP, 1982. 5–10.

Ferguson, Francis. *The Idea of a Theatre*. Garden City, New York: Doubleday, 1954.

Fink, Bruce. "The Subject and the Other's Desire." *Reading Seminars I and II: Lacan's Return to Freud*. 76–97.

Fleming, Keith. "*Hamlet and Oedipus* Today: Jones and Lacan," *Hamlet Studies* 4 1/2 (Summer and Winter 1982): 54–71.

Freud, Anna. *The Ego and the Mechanisms of Defence* (1936). London: Hogarth Press and the Institute of Psycho-analysis, 1968.

Freud, Sigmund. *The Standard Edition of the Complete Psychological Works of Sigmund Freud.* Trans. and ed. James Strachey. London: Hogarth Press and the Institute of Psycho-Analysis; New York: Norton, 1953–73.

———. *The Interpretation of Dreams.* Trans. and ed. James Strachey. New York: Avon, 1965.

———. "On Narcissism: An Introduction." SE XIV.

———. *Three Essays on the Theory of Sexuality.* SE VII.

———. *Beyond the Pleasure Principle.* SE XVIII.

Gaillard, Françoise. "Au nom de la Loi: Lacan, Althusser et l'idéologie." *Socio-critique* Paris: Fernand Nathan, 1979. 11–24.

Gallop, Jane. *Reading Lacan* Ithaca: Cornell UP, 1985.

Garber, Marjorie. *Vested Interests: Cross-Dressing and Cultural Anxiety.* New York: HarperCollins, 1993.

Ginestet-Delbreil, Suzanne. "L'identification par incorporation." *Psychanalyse et apocalypse.* Ed. René Major. Paris: Confrontations, 1982. 75–86.

Goldie, Terry. "The Representation of the Indigene." *The Post-colonial Studies Reader.* Ed. Bill Ashcroft, Gareth Griffiths, and Helen Tiffin. London: Routledge, 1995. 232–36.

Green, André. "The Unbinding Process." *New Literary History* 12 1 (1980): 11–39.

Greimas, A. J. *On Meaning.* Trans. Paul J. Perron and Frank H.Collins. Minneapolis: U of Minnesota P, 1987.

Grosz, Elizabeth. *Jacques Lacan: A Feminist Introduction.* London: Routledge, 1990.

Harris, Frank. *The Man Shakespeare and his Tragic Life-Story.* London: Frank Palmer, 1909.

———. *The Women of Shakespeare.* New York: Mitchell Kennerly, 1912.

Harris, Roy. *Reading Saussure.* La Salle, Ill.: Open Court, 1987.

Hawkes, Terrence. *Structuralism and Semiotics.* Berkeley: U of California P, 1977.

Hegel, G. W. F. *Hegel Selections.* Ed. M. J. Inwood. New York: Macmillan, 1989.

———. *The Phenomenology of Mind* (or *Spirit*). Trans. J. B. Baillie. London: Allen & Unwin, 1967.

Heidegger, Martin. *Being and Time.* Trans. John Macquarrie and Edward Robinson. New York: Harper & Row, 1962.

Holland, Norman. "Unity Identity Text Self." *Reader-Response Criticism*. Ed. Jane P. Tompkins. Baltimore: Johns Hopkins UP, 1988. 118–33.

Hughes, Ted. Foreword. *The Journals of Sylvia Plath*. By Plath. Ed. Ted Hughes. New York: Ballantine, 1982. xiii–xv.

———. "Sylvia Plath and her *Journals*." *Ariel Ascending*. Ed. Paul Alexander. New York: Harper & Row, 1985. 152–64.

Hulbert, James. "Desire and the Interpretation of Desire in *Hamlet*." *Yale French Studies* 55/56 (1977): 11–52.

Jameson, Fredric. "Imaginary and Symbolic in Lacan: Marxism, Psychoanalytic Criticism, and the Problem of the Subject." *Literature and Psychoanalysis*. Ed. Shoshana Felman. Baltimore: Johns Hopkins UP, 1989. 338–96.

———. Foreword. *On Meaning*. By A. J. Greimas.

———. *The Political Unconscious: Narrative as a Socially Symbolic Act*. Ithaca Cornell UP, 1981.

JanMohamed, Abdul R. "The Economy of Manichean Allegory." *The Post-colonial Studies Reader*. Ed. Bill Ashcroft, Gareth Griffiths, and Helen Tiffin. London: Routledge, 1995. 18–23.

Jones, Ernest. "The Oedipus Complex as an Explanation of Hamlet's Mystery." *The American Journal of Psychology* (January 1910): 72–113.

———. "A Psycho-Analytic Study of Hamlet." *Essays in Applied Psycho-Analysis*. London: International Psycho-Analytical Press, 1923. 1–98.

———. *Hamlet and Oedipus*. New York: Norton, 1976.

———. "Rationalization in Every Day Life." *Journal of Abnormal Psychology* 3 (Aug.–Sept. 1908): 161–69.

Kael, Pauline. Rev. of *Tootsie*. *New Yorker* December 27, 1982. 71.

Kerrigan, William. "Psychoanalysis Unbound." *New Literary History* 12 1 (1980): 199–206.

King, Richard. Rev. of *Écrits, A Selection* by Jacques Lacan. *Georgia Review* 32 (1978): 926–30.

Klein, Melanie. "The Importance of Symbol-Formation in the Development of the Ego." *The Writings of Melanie Klein*. Vol. 1. London: Hogarth Press, 1975. 219–32.

Kojève, Alexandre. *Introduction to the Reading of Hegel*. Trans. James H. Nichols, Jr. Ed. Allan Bloom. Ithaca: Cornell UP, 1969.

———. *Introduction à la Lecture de Hegel*. Ed. Raymond Quesneau. Paris: Gallimard, 1947.

Kolodny, Annette. "Dancing Through the Minefield." *Falling into Theory*. Ed. David H. Richter. Boston: Bedford, 1994. 278–85.

Kris, Anton. Rev. of *Ecrits: A Selection* by Jacques Lacan. *Journal of the American Psychoanalytic Association* 28 (1980): 223–24.

Kristeva, Julia. *Revolution in Poetic Language*. Trans. Margaret Waller. New York: Columbia UP, 1984.

———. *Tales of Love*. Trans. Leon S. Roudiez. New York: Columbia UP, 1987.

———. *The Kristeva Reader*. Ed. Toril Moi. New York: Columbia UP, 1986.

Kuczkowski, Richard. Rev. of *Écrits: A Selection* by Jacques Lacan. *Library Journal* 15 October 1977, 2168.

Lacan, Jacques. "L'aggressivité en psychanalyse." *Revue française de psychanalyse* 3 (July–September, 1948): 367–88.

———. "Aggressivity in psychoanalysis." *Ecrits: A Selection*. 8–29.

———. "Le canevas." *Ornicar?* 24 (1981): 7–17.

———. "Le canevas (fin)." *Ornicar?* 24 (1981): 18–31.

———, with H. Claude and G. Heuyer. "Un cas de démence précocissisme." *Annales médico-psychologique* 1 (1933): 620–24.

———. "Le complexe, facteur concret de la psychologie familiale." *Encyclopédie française VIII: La vie mentale*. Ed. Henri Wallon. Paris: Larousse, Société de gestion de l'Encyclopédié française, 1938. 8.40.5–8.40.16.

———. *Les complexes familiaux dans la formation de l'individu: essai d'analyse d'une fonction en psychologie*. Paris: Navarin, 1984.

———. "Les complexes familiaux en pathologie." *Encyclopédie française* VIII. 8.42.1–8.42.8.

———. *De la psychose paranoïaque dans ses rapports avec la personnalité*. Thèse de Doctorat en Médecine de Paris. Paris: Le François, 1932.

———. "Le désir de la mère." *Ornicar?* 25 (1982): 13–25.

———. "Desire and the Interpretation of Desire in *Hamlet*." Trans. James Hulbert. Ed. Jacques-Alain Miller. *Literature and Psychoanalysis*. Ed. Shoshana Felman. Baltimore: Johns Hopkins UP, 1982. 11–52.

———. "Discourse of Rome" or, more formally, "The Function and Field of Speech and Language in Psychoanalysis." *Écrits: A Selection*. 30–113.

———. *Écrits*. Paris: Éditions du Seuil, 1966.

———. *Écrits: A Selection*. Trans. Alan Sheridan. Ed. Jacques-Alain Miller. New York: Norton, 1977.

———, with Wladimir Granoff, "Fetishism: The Symbolic, the Imaginary, and the Real." *Perversion: Psychodynamics and Therapy.* Ed. Sandor Lorand. Associate ed. Michael Balint. New York: Gramercy Books, 1956.

———, with Henri Claude and P. Migault. "Folies simultanées." *Société médico-psychologique,* 21 May 1931. *Annales médico-psychologique* 1 (1931): 483–90.

———. *The Four Fundamental Concepts of Psycho-Analysis.* Seminar 11. Trans. Alan Sheridan. Ed. Jacques-Alain Miller. New York: Norton, 1977.

———. "Il n'y a pas d'Autre de l'Autre." *Ornicar?* 26/27 (1983): 26–36.

———, trans. "Logos" by Martin Heidegger. *La psychanalyse* 1 (1956): 59–79.

———. "The Mirror stage as formative of the function of the I as revealed in psychoanalytic experience." *Écrits: A Selection.* 1–7.

———. "Motifs du crime paranoïaque: le crime des soeurs Papin." *Le minotaure* 3/4 (1933): 25–28.

———. "Parenthèse des Parenthèses." *Écrits.* 54–57.

———. "Présentation de la Suite." *Écrits.* 41–44.

———. *The Seminar of Jacques Lacan: Book I: Freud's Papers on Technique, 1953–1954.* Trans. John Forrester. Ed. Jacques-Alain Miller. New York: Norton, 1991.

———. *The Seminar of Jacques Lacan: Book II: The Ego in Freud's Theory and in the Technique of Psychoanalysis.* Trans. Sylvana Tomaselli. Ed. Jacques-Alain Miller. New York: Norton, 1988.

———. *The Seminar of Jacques Lacan: Book III: The Psychoses, 1955–1956.* Trans. Russell Grigg. Ed. Jacques-Alain Miller. New York: Norton, 1993.

———. "Seminar on 'The Purloined Letter.'" *The Purloined Poe.* Ed. John P. Muller and William J. Richardson. Baltimore: Johns Hopkins UP, 1988. 28–54.

———. Seminar IV: *La relation d'objet et les structures freudiennes.* Abstracts in *Bulletin de psychologie* 10 (1957): 426–30, 602–05, 742–43, 851–54, and 11 (1957): 31–34.

———. Seminar V: *Les formations de l'inconscient,* unpublished. Abstracts in *Bulletin de psychologie* 11, 4/5 (1958): 293–96; 12, 2/3 (1958): 182–92; and 12, 4 (1958): 250–56.

———. Seminar VI: *Le désir et son interprétation* (1958–59). Ed. Jacques-Alain Miller. *Ornicar?* 24 (1981): 7–31; 25 (1982): 13–36; and 26/27 (1983): 7–44.

———. Seminar VII: *The Ethics of Psychoanalysis* (1959–1960). Ed. Jacques-Alain Miller. Trans. Dennis Porter. New York: Norton, 1992.

———. Seminar XXII: *RSI. Ornicar?* 2 (1975): 87–105; 3 (1975): 95 110; 4 (1975): 91–106; and 5 (1975): 15–66.

———. "Le Séminaire sur 'La Lettre Volée.'" *Écrits.* 11–41.

———. "The signification of the phallus." *Écrits: A Selection.* 281–91.

———. "Some Reflections on the Ego." Trans. Nancy Elisabeth Beaufils. *International Journal of Psycho-Analysis* 34 (1953): 11–17.

———. *Speech and Language in Psychoanalysis.* Trans. Anthony Wilden. Baltimore: Johns Hopkins UP, 1989.

———. "Le stade du miroir comme formateur de la fonction du Je." *Revue française de psychanalyse* 4 (October–December, 1949): 449–55.

———. "Le stade de miroir: théorie d'un moment structurant et génetique de la constitution de la réalité, conçu en relation avec l'expérience et la doctrine psychanalytique." Cited as "The Looking Glass Phase." *The International Journal of Psycho-Analysis* 18 (January, 1937): 78.

———. Rev. of *Le temps vécu: études phénoménologiques et psychopathologiques* by E. Minkowski. *Recherches philosophique* 5 (1935/36): 424–31.

———. Discussion of M. Bonaparte, "Vues paléobiologiques et biopsychiques." *Revue française de psychanalyse* 3 (1938): 551.

Laplanche, J. and J.-B. Pontalis. *The Language of Psycho-Analysis.* Trans. Donald Nicholson-Smith. New York: Norton, 1973.

Leavy, Stanley. Rev. of *Écrits: A Selection* by Jacques Lacan. Trans. Alan Sheridan. Ed. Jacques-Alain Miller. *New York Times Book Review* 2 October 1977: 38–39.

———. Rev. of *Écrits: A Selection* by Jacques Lacan. *Psychoanalytic Quarterly* 46 (1977): 311–17.

Lechte, John. *Julia Kristeva.* London: Routledge, 1990.

Leclaire, Serge. "L'analyste à sa place?" *Cahiers pour l'analyse* 1 (1966): 51–54.

Lecourt, Dominique. "Lacan psylosophe ou philoanalyste." *Franc-Tireur* (Nov.–Dec. 1981).

Lee, Jonathan Scott. *Jacques Lacan.* Amherst: U of Massachusetts P, 1990.

Lemaire, Anika. *Jacques Lacan.* Trans. David Macey. London: Routledge, 1977.

Leupin, Alexandre. "Introduction: Voids and Knots in Knowledge and Truth." *Lacan and the Human Sciences.* Ed. Alexandre Leupin. Lincoln: U of Nebraska P, 1991. 1–23.

Levinas, Emmanuel. *Outside the Subject*. Trans. Michael B. Smith. Stanford: Stanford UP, 1994.

Lévi-Strauss, Claude. *The Savage Mind*. London: Weidenfeld and Nicholson, 1966.

———. *Structural Anthropology*. Trans. C. Jacobson and B. Grundfest Schoepf. Harmondsworth: Penguin, 1968.

Livingston, Howard. "*Hamlet*, Ernest Jones, and the Critics." *Hamlet Studies* 2 1 (Summer 1980): 25–33.

Macalpine, Ida and Richard A. Hunter, trans. Translator's Introduction. *Memoirs of My Nervous Illness*. Cambridge: Harvard UP, 1988. 1–28.

Mencia, Carlos. *The Tonight Show*, NBC, August 8, 1997.

Miller, Jacques-Alain. Editor's Note. *The Four Fundamental Concepts of Psycho-Analysis*. New York: Norton, 1978.

———. Classified Index of the Major Concepts. *Écrits: A Selection*. 326.

———. "An Introduction to Seminars I and II, Lacan's Orientation Prior to 1953," in three sections. *Reading Seminars I and II, Lacan's Return to Freud*. Ed. Richard Feldstein, Bruce Fink, and Maire Jaanus. Albany: SUNY Press, 1996. 3–35.

Mitchell, Juliet and Jacqueline Rose, eds. *Feminine Sexuality, Jacques Lacan and the école freudienne*. Trans. Jacqueline Rose. New York: Norton, 1985.

Moller, Lis. *The Freudian Reading*. Philadelphia: U of Pennsylvania P, 1991.

Montag, Warren. "Marxism and Psychoanalysis: The Impossible Encounter," *The Minnesota Review* 23 (1984): 70–85.

Morton, John. Rev. of *Écrits: A Selection* by Jacques Lacan. *Mankind* 13 3 (1982): 264–65.

Muller, John P. and William J. Richardson. "Lacan's Seminar on 'The Purloined Letter': Overview." *The Purloined Poe*. Baltimore: Johns Hopkins UP, 1988. 55–76.

———. *Lacan and Language: A Reader's Guide to "Écrits."* New York: International Universities Press, 1982.

Nichols, James H., Jr. Translator's Note. *Introduction to the Reading of Hegel*. By Alexandre Kojève. Ithaca: Cornell UP, 1969.

Orgel, Stephen. "Prospero's Wife." *Representing the English Renaissance*. Ed. Stephen Greenblatt. Berkeley: U of California P, 1988. 217–30.

Oudart, Jean-Pierre. "La Suture." *Cahiers du Cinéma* (1969). Trans. Kari Hanet. "Cinema and Suture." *Screen* 18.4 (1977–78): 35–47.

Palmier, Jean-Michel. *Lacan*. Paris: Editions Universitaires, 1972.

Parry, Benita. "Problems in Current Theories of Colonial Discourse." In *The Post-colonial Studies Reader*. Ed. Bill Ashcroft, Gareth Griffiths, and Helen Tiffin. London: Routledge, 1995. 36–44.

Patri, Amié. "Dialectique du Maître et de l'Esclave." *Le Contrat Social* V 4 (July–August 1961): 231–35.

Plath, Aurelia, Ed. *Letters Home, by Sylvia Plath, Correspondence 1950–1963*. New York: HarperPerrenial, 1992.

Plath, Sylvia. *The Collected Poems*. New York: Harper & Row, 1981.

———. *The Journals of Sylvia Plath*. Ed. Ted Hughes. New York: Ballantine, 1982.

Plato. *The Dialogues of Plato*. Trans. B. Jowett. Oxford: Clarendon Press, 1892.

———. *The Sophist. Plato: Collected Dialogues*. Trans. F. M. Cornford. Ed. Edith Hamilton and Huntington Cairns. Princeton: Princeton UP, 1961.

Pollock, George H. Rev. of *Écrits: A Selection* by Jacques Lacan. *American Journal of Psychiatry* 135 (1978): 517.

Pontalis, J.-B. Summary of Seminar VI. *Bulletin de psychologie* 13.5 (1960): 263–72; and 13.6 (1960): 329–35.

Ragland (-Sullivan), Ellie. "Jacques Lacan: *Ecrits*." *Sub-stance* 21 (1978): 166–73.

———. *Jacques Lacan and the Philosophy of Psychoanalysis*. Urbana: U of Illinois P, 1987.

———. Review of *Écrits: A Selection* by Jacques Lacan. *Choice* 14 (1978): 1711.

Rose, Jacqueline. "Paranoia and the Film System." *Screen* 17 4 (1976/77): 85–104.

Rosen, Stanley. *Plato's Sophist*. New Haven: Yale UP, 1993.

Rotmiler de Zentner, Maria Ines. "The Identification and the Ideal." *Papers of the Freudian School of Melbourne* (1981): 103–18.

Roudinesco, Elisabeth. *La bataille de cent ans*. Paris: Éditions du Seuil, 1982.

———. "Madame Soleil entre Althusser et Lacan." *Franc-Tireur* (January 1982).

Roustang, François. *The Lacanian Delusion*. Trans. Greg Sims. New York: Oxford UP, 1990.

Sartre, Jean-Paul. *Being and Nothingness*. Trans. Hazel E. Barnes. New York: Philosophical Library, 1956.

Saussure, Ferdinand de. *Course in General Linguistics.* Trans. Roy Harris. La Salle: Open Court, 1986.

Schneiderman, Stuart. Rev. of *Écrits: A Selection* by Jacques Lacan. *New Republic* 12 November 1977: 34.

———. *Jacques Lacan: The Death of an Intellectual Hero.* Cambridge: Harvard UP, 1983.

Scholes, Robert, Nancy R. Comley, and Gregory L. Ulmer, eds. *Text Book: An Introduction to Literary Language.* New York: St. Martin's, 1988.

Schleifer, Ronald. *A. J. Greimas and the Nature of Meaningfulness.* London: Croom Helm, 1987.

Schreber, Daniel Paul. *Memoirs of My Nervous Illness.* Trans. and ed. Ida Macalpine and Richard A. Hunter. Cambridge: Harvard UP, 1988.

Selden, Raman. *A Reader's Guide to Contemporary Literary Theory*, 3d ed. Lexington: UP of Kentucky, 1993.

Showalter, Elaine. "Critical Cross-Dressing: Male Feminists and the Woman of the Year." *Raritan* 3.2 (Fall 1983): 138.

Smith, Joseph H. *Arguing with Lacan, Ego Psychology and Language.* New Haven: Yale UP, 1991.

Spivak, Gayatri Chakravorty. "Acting Bits/Identity Talk." *Identities.* Ed. Kwame Anthony Appiah and Henry Louis Gates, Jr. Chicago: U of Chicago P, 1995. 147–80.

Tallis, Raymond. "The Mirror Stage: A Critical Reflection." *Trivium* 21 (Summer 1986): 5–44.

Turkle, Sherry. "The New Philosophy and the Agony of Structuralism: Enter the Trojan Horse." *Chicago Review* 32.3 (1981): 24.

Ver Eecke, Wilfried. "Hegel as Lacan's Source for Necessity in Psychoanalytic Theory." *Interpreting Lacan.* Ed. Joseph H. Smith and William Kerrigan. New Haven: Yale UP, 1983. 113–38.

Weber, Samuel M. Introduction to the 1988 Edition. *Memoirs of My Nervous Illness.* Trans. Benjamin Gregg. Cambridge: Harvard UP, 1988.

Wilden, Anthony. Translator's Introduction. *Speech and Language in Psychoanalysis.* Baltimore: Johns Hopkins UP, 1981.

Žižek, Slavoj. *Enjoy Your Symptom!* New York: Routledge, 1992.

Page 188 blank.

Index

www.ingramcontent.com/pod-product-compliance
Lightning Source LLC
Chambersburg PA
CBHW020350270326
41926CB00007B/374